Camels, Tigers & Unicorns

Rethinking Science & Technology-enabled Innovation

Camels, Tigers & Unicorns

Rethinking Science & Technology-enabled Innovation

Uday Phadke
Cartezia, UK

Shailendra Vyakarnam
Cranfield University, UK

World Scientific

NEW JERSEY · LONDON · SINGAPORE · BEIJING · SHANGHAI · HONG KONG · TAIPEI · CHENNAI · TOKYO

Published by

World Scientific Publishing Europe Ltd.

57 Shelton Street, Covent Garden, London WC2H 9HE

Head office: 5 Toh Tuck Link, Singapore 596224

USA office: 27 Warren Street, Suite 401-402, Hackensack, NJ 07601

Library of Congress Cataloging-in-Publication Data
Names: Phadke, Uday, author.
Title: Camels, tigers & unicorns : rethinking science and technology-enabled innovation /
    by Uday Phadke (Cartezia, United Kingdom),
    Shailendra Vyakarnam (Cranfield University, United Kingdom).
Other titles: Camels, tigers and unicorns
Description: New Jersey : World Scientific, [2017] |
    Includes bibliographical references and index.
Identifiers: LCCN 2016055437| ISBN 9781786343215 (hc : alk. paper) |
    ISBN 9781786343222 (pbk : alk. paper)
Subjects: LCSH: Business enterprises--Technological innovations. |
    Information technology--Management. | Marketing.
Classification: LCC HD45 .P497 2017 | DDC 338/.064--dc23
LC record available at https://lccn.loc.gov/2016055437

British Library Cataloguing-in-Publication Data
A catalogue record for this book is available from the British Library.

Desk Editors: Kalpana Bharanikumar/Philly Lim

Typeset by Stallion Press
Email: enquiries@stallionpress.com

Printed in Singapore

Reviews of the Book

This book is different because its insights and recommendations are based on data driven research. That research confirms the realities of multi-year timescales to achieve commercial success, and how venture capital funding is limited to later-stage companies. One of the authors' most important contributions — and their passion to improve how technology is commercialised is manifest in these pages — is their clarification of the 'chasms' that early-stage technology-enabled companies have to cross. This clarity is the bedrock for offering tools that maximise the probability of crossing those chasms — a huge advance on the vague references to the 'valley of death' that are the limit of so much of the existing literature.

The book should command the attention of technology-enabled entrepreneurs, at whatever stage on their journey, and also of those in universities responsible for or associated with spinning out companies, because it is so useful. The authors clearly understand the dynamics of 'early stage', and offer approaches tailored to those dynamics. For example, every entrepreneur is familiar with the inadequacy of conventional approaches to market segmentation, because technology often creates new categories of activity. The authors signpost how to define market spaces that group firms by common structures, processes and dynamics — an approach they demonstrate to work across a dozen industries.

Their 'Commercialisation Canvas' is particularly powerful: it provides a systematic framework to assess the maturity of the product or service, the drivers affecting progress, and the interventions needed to cross the next chasm.

I wish I'd had this guide when building engineering technology businesses myself — as one of the 'Camels' that constitute 98% of technology-enabled businesses, so often outshone by the Tigers and Unicorns...

Dr Peter Collins
Previously with Sulzer Chemtech, Technical Director at PII, Operations Director at Sondex Plc (now part of GE Energy); serial Entrepreneur, now CEO at Permasense.

Camels, Tigers & Unicorns is a welcome addition to the literature on the challenges of taking technology innovation to market. Phadke and Vyakarnam bring some much needed common sense to the description of the innovation commercialisation process. They also reclaim the word 'technology' to cover all technologies rather than be solely focused on digital and software technologies, something I support wholeheartedly.

The authors have conducted a detailed, rigorous analysis of how technology innovations progress, and have built a well-structured model to underpin their thinking. In particular, they stress the need to match technology innovation with customer requirements, together with the need for all other elements of business to be aligned to achieve success.

To my mind, the core of this book is the concept of the three chasm model, identifying the chasms that businesses must cross when commercialising new technology. Most literature covering technology commercialisation addresses the two key challenges of moving technology out of the lab into a prototype product — Chasm I, and then building business volume — Chasm III. Phadke and Vyakarnam have identified an intermediate challenge — Chasm II, which is the transition from a prototype into a viable, commercially sustainable product or service. I have spent most of my working life helping large corporations adapt and use technology innovations, and I recognise Chasm II only too well. Inventors and innovators, often together with those providing the investment money, tend to assume that once a prototype product has been produced, then the hard work is over. The reality is very different. Start-up companies often get stuck at this early stage, failing to fine tune their product offering to meet customer needs and so get traction in the market place. Larger corporations tend to be more adept at this when working in their core areas, but again can come unstuck when trying to diversify into new areas, where the challenges of precisely matching technologies and market needs, together with aligning other business functions, are often underestimated. This book is therefore, very helpful in highlighting this issue and giving guidance on how to address it.

This is not a lightweight airport business book, but will provide valuable insights to anyone involved in the world of science and technology innovation.

Dr Chris Floyd
Previously European Director, Arthur D Little, Business Development Director, Rolls Royce Plc, and Policy Fellow of the Centre for Science and Policy at Cambridge University; now Non-Executive Director of British Engines and ComAp and Advisor to high growth technology companies. Author of 'Managing Technology for Corporate Success' (Gower, 1997).

At last we have an analytical approach to the challenge facing entrepreneurs on their journey from technology enabled concepts to products and market success.

In a career managing technology exploitation in Corporate and early stage companies I know how difficult is the challenge. Phadke and Vyakarnam have created a set of generic foundations that transcend the historic anecdotes of personal experiences, judgements and one off personal biographical success stories.

This book is a *Tour de Force* based upon facts of multiple case studies reduced to a practical set of principles which are relevant to everyone independent of the technology and market opportunity.

The journey of commercial exploitation of technology has many risks and cannot just be reduced to the metrics successfully practiced in ecommerce and market places of customer acquisition costs and life time value. The scope of the book is initially daunting since the authors are meticulous in presenting evidence that support their conclusions and advice. Fortunately it is constructed in such a way as to be both a reference manual and an implementation guide of best practice.

Mandatory reading for all entrepreneurs are the concepts of the Triple Chasm Model and the twelve Commercialisation Vectors. I am sure the latter will capture the interest of the reader and encourage them to study and take note of the comprehensive wisdom within this book.

The book is relevant for all those involved in the creation of technology enabled opportunities be they Corporations, Private Investors, Public Policy creation and of course entrepreneurs themselves.

My only regret is that this book did not exist when I started my career in technology.

Dr John Baits
Previously IBM Laboratory Director USA/UK/Japan, MD for IT & Research Telstra/Australia, and C&W Corporate Director IT &Networks; now CTO DN Capital, VP Engineering intellisense.io.

Camels, Tigers & Unicorns is a refreshing and practical addition to our under-standing of how science and technology (here rightly not limited to the digital space) can be converted into innovation — broadly defined by the authors as 'the creation of new value'. It is refreshing because of the unusually rigorous extent to which its insights are driven by long-run data analysis, and because of the wealth of hands-on experience the authors bring to reframing many common concepts (such as the 'valley of death', here critically unpacked into three distinct chasms faced by growth firms), which until Phadke and Vyakarnam's work, were supported by little more than often misleading anecdotes.

Practitioner focus is accompanied by an acute understanding of the broader policy context, including timely observations on the limitations of venture capital as part of the funding mix at early stages. Deftly summarising much recent literature on entrepreneurship and innovation, *Camels, Tigers & Unicorns* nevertheless tran-scends received wisdom with clarity and originality. The tools carefully deployed chapter-by-chapter are synthesised in the concluding 'workbench', which is likely to become the foundation of much-needed new approaches to advising high-potential technology firms. Notable at a time when industrial strategy is once again being taken seriously in the UK is an emphasis on the importance of the meso-economic environment between the macro and the firm-level, which demands not only re-thinking the relative balance of the public and private sectors, but also confronting many of our implicit economic and political assumptions.

The short, concluding Commercialisation Manifesto — beginning with the need for evidence-based understanding of commercialization and ending with a call for an equally evidence-based discussion of the role of innovation in the global economy — provides a rare and inclusive platform to bring innovators, policy-makers, investors and intermediaries together for an informed and overdue debate on the creation of sustainable value, vital for our collective future.

David Gill
Previously Sloan Fellow at Stanford; background in corporate finance and start-up funding at HSBC and ET Capital; now MD of St John's Innovation Centre, Cambridge and Director of Greater Cambridge Peterborough Enterprise Partnership.

This remarkable book provides a blueprint for developing an effective Industrial Strategy. Based on extensive research over many years, it uncovers barriers to how firms grow and signposts how both governments and businesses can develop strategies to accelerate growth. It challenges the traditional view that economic growth is primarily a matter of improving collaboration between industry and universities. Instead, it presents a view of how companies grow and identifies twelve factors which need to be addressed by companies aspiring to accelerate growth. The text is packed with new concepts and guidance on areas such as how to take a customer-focused view of new products/services, importance of business models and how to develop an overall commercialisation strategy. The findings have significant relevance for business managers, investors, intermediaries (such as government agencies and accountants) and policy makers. I commend this book to both business leaders and government ministers in the hope that by using these findings, they will come together to articulate policies which will accelerate economic growth.

Prof David Hughes
Previously DG, Innovation Group and Chief Scientific Advisor at the UK Govt DTI. Produced the DTI Innovation Report which created the Technology Strategy Board, now re-badged as Innovate UK. Now Managing Director of the Business Innovation Group and visiting Professor of Engineering Management at City University, London.

For Wendy
&
For Annapurna

Foreword

My early career as a scientist strongly shaped my view about the important role that scientists and technologists play in the creation and development of new innovations. My subsequent role as a founder and investor in many companies based on deep science, for example in personal computing and mobile communications in the Cambridge technology cluster, convinced me that building successful companies requires a deeper understanding of a broader set of issues including customers, markets, leadership and management.

Most of us in the investor community, however, have been forced to rely on anecdotes, opinions and rather dated case studies and ideas from management text books, often lacking the methodological rigour familiar to most scientists. The challenge facing all those involved in commercialising science and technology is to understand the drivers, processes and mechanisms involved in this transformation, to increase the probability of successful outcomes.

Phadke and Vyakarnam have tackled this challenge head-on in this very timely book, using a large body of data from their work with hundreds of firms over the last two decades, covering different geographies, market spaces and technologies, not just a limited number of case studies focused on 'outlier' firms. In particular, they have generalised their findings to reframe the whole debate, creating a rational evidence-based conceptual framework for analysis, understanding and intervention.

The authors have articulated several important new concepts in this reframing. They have defined the idea of modified Technology Readiness Levels to assess the relative maturity of the commercialisation process. Based on the primacy of actual customer data, they have identified generic discontinuities in the diffusion of innovation and developed the Triple Chasm Model: this enables any firm to map its journey and to understand the importance of different factors along this trajectory. In doing this, Phadke and Vyakarnam have identified the critical importance of Chasm II when it comes to scaling science and technology firms.

Building on the legacy of Schumpeter, the authors have developed a meso-economic approach which defines 12 commercialisation vectors that drive the process of turning ideas into value. They have created a new concept of market spaces and marketspace-centric value chains which overcome the limitations of conventional market segmentation and the rather static value chains developed in the 1980s. The challenge of deciding how to take new technologies to market, especially those with large disruptive potential, has been a major concern for me over the last two decades. Phadke and Vyakarnam have created a new model for contingent technology development which can provide a powerful basis for tackling this challenge in a rational manner. They have also created a new dynamic approach to strategy formulation and development, based on understanding the changing priorities for firms as they grow.

The authors have integrated the different concepts to create the commercialisation canvas, which provides tools and examples which can be used to: understand the maturity of a firm; to explore and compare different intervention models and approaches; design new forms of intervention; and to increase the effectiveness of interventions. The work described in this book not only addresses the challenge of starting and growing a firm; it also provides guidance for established firms tackling the corporate innovation challenge and the problems of commercialising science and technology across borders.

This book has significant implications for four main audiences.

Practitioners: All those involved in creating new value from science and technology-enabled innovations.

Intervention 'Agencies': All those trying to make this happen better, faster or more effectively, for example, the many national innovation agencies and their intervention facilities, such as the Catapults in the UK.

Investors: Public agencies and the different types of private investors, including business angels, venture capital and private equity.

Policy Makers: This work has significant implications for all those involved in creating the right environment for success, especially in understanding and applying the different meso-economic vectors, not just emphasising the power of markets and the totemic value of innovation.

I believe this is a book that should be read by all those involved in the creation, development and exploitation of science and technology-enabled innovation. I hope it forms the basis for a more rational evidence-based approach to tackling this critical challenge.

Dr Hermann Hauser, KBE, FRS, FREng

Serial Inventor, Entrepreneur and Investor in science and technology-enabled innovation

Author of major report for the UK Government in 2010: **The Current and Future Role of Technology and Innovation Centres**

Founding Partner of Amadeus Capital Partners which invests in science and technology firms in Europe, North America and Asia

Cambridge
December 2016

About the Authors

Uday Phadke

 Dr Uday Phadke studied Engineering at Trinity College, Cambridge and then went on to do a PhD in aerothermodynamics at the University of Sussex. He has worked in a wide range of academic, technical, commercial and strategic roles in Europe, North America and Asia over the last three decades.

He has a deep technology background in a number of areas, including aerospace engineering, digital signal processing, remote sensing, electronics, computing and software, medical diagnostics, engineering design, media and telecommunications, financial technologies and digital media.

He has been actively involved in the building of over 100 technology firms over the last two decades as an advisor, mentor and investor, working closely with technology transfer offices, innovation agencies, incubators and accelerators. He has also been part of the founding team at a number of technology advisory and consulting companies since the early 1980s; since 1997, he has been Chief Executive of Cartezia, the technology business builder based in Cambridge, UK.

He was Entrepreneur-in-Residence at the Judge Business School at the University of Cambridge from 2011 to 2016 and is now actively involved in several innovation policy development initiatives in Europe and Asia.

Shailendra Vyakarnam

 Dr Vyakarnam did his MBA and PhD at Cranfield. He has since combined academic, practitioner and policy interests to provide advice to governments on the development of entrepreneurial ecosystems, technology commercialisation and entrepreneurship education. He has mentored entrepreneurs and held non-executive directorships of small firms in addition to developing growth programmes for SMEs over several years.

From 2003 to 2015, he focused on the development of practitioner-led education for entrepreneurship at the University of Cambridge Judge Business School, where he led The Centre for Entrepreneurial Learning.

Dr Vyakarnam was awarded 'Best Entrepreneurship Professor' at the 2nd Asian Business Schools Awards in 2011. In 2012, he was elected to the prestigious European Academy of Science and Arts. He has held visiting professorships at University of Reading and University of Aarhus, the Indian Institute of Science and the American University of Cairo.

He has taught and mentored hundreds of entrepreneurs in over 20 countries and continues to live his passion for entrepreneurship as founder, director and advisor to several firms. He is now Director of the Bettany Centre for Entrepreneurship at Cranfield University.

Acknowledgements

This book would not have been possible without the founders, leaders and CEOs of over 300 science and technology-enabled firms across Europe, North America, and Asia, who have shared their experiences, data and insights with us over the last three decades, on a confidential basis. While many of these people will recognise some or all parts of their journeys in this book, we have been careful to preserve their confidentiality, without which such a book would not have been possible — we thank them all for making this kind of analysis and insight possible.

This book would also not have been possible without the experiences we have shared with a wide range of people over the last three decades, in academia, start-ups, consulting firms, technology firms covering a wide range of technologies, and investors. We have learned much from these interactions but of course take responsibility for the views and conclusions expressed in this book.

Several hundred people have contributed to this journey and it is impossible to acknowledge them all, but we need to recognise the key influences that have shaped our thinking in many ways, including academic interactions, involvement in start-ups, advisory, business-building and investment interactions, and working with many corporates in Europe, North America, and Asia.

The key techno-commercial clusters which have shaped our thinking are as follows:

In Europe: Cambridge, Oxford, Southampton, York, Edinburgh, Cranfield, Bristol, Bath, Sussex, London, Munich, Toulouse, Stockholm, Arhus, Copenhagen, Paris, Munich, Milan, Madrid, Lisbon, and Frankfurt.

In The Americas: Montreal, Toronto, Vancouver, Boston, San Francisco, San Diego, New York, Seattle, Austin, Cupertino, Chicago, Mexico City, and Havana.

In Asia: Bangalore, Delhi, Mumbai, Hyderabad, Pune, Chennai, Vizag, Ahmedabad, Beijing, Shanghai, Shenzhen, Tokyo, Kuala Lumpur, and Singapore.

In Africa: Nairobi, Kampala, Kigali, and Cairo.

The following people (arranged in alphabetical order) have been involved with us on this journey in a number of different ways (not always wittingly!):

Seth Alpert, Robert Ashcroft, Gerald Avison, John Baits, Max Bautin, Charles Brown, Richard Cawdell, Michael Chamberlain, Victor Christou, Daping Chu, David Cleevely, David Coates, Peter Collins, Simon Cox, Gordon Edge, Nick Evans-Lombe, John Fairclough, Chris Floyd, Helmut Fluhrer, Kaushik Gala, Steve Garnett, Gerry George, Mark Getty, Greg Glass, Richard Green, Tony Hart, Hermann Hauser, Peter Hiscocks, David Hughes, Peter Hyde, Andrew Jackson, Hemant Jalan, Peter Johnson, Andy Keane, Jonathan Klein, Jay Krishnan, Sunil Kumar, Lars Holmgaard Mersh, Tony Milbourne, Mark Mortimer, Charlie Muirhead, Arun Muthirulan, David Naylor, Phil O'Donovan, James van Oosterom, Mike Owen, Mohandas Pai, Keith Pavitt, Adar Pelah, Bob Pettigrew, Martin Phillips, David Pollock, Tony Raven, Taslimarif Saiyed, John Sanderson, Mario Secca, Gillian Secrett, Nigel Shadbolt, Jay Srinivas, Saurabh Srivastava, Ian Stewart, G Sunderaman, Michael Biscoe-Taylor, Jamie Urquhart, Premnath and Manisha Venugopalan, Mike Vieyra, and Bill Weston.

In particular, we would like to thank our close collaborator over the last eight years **Arun Muthirulan** — this book would not have been possible without his active support in analysing the large data set which underpins this book.

We would also like to thank **Dr Peter Johnson** and **Prof David Hughes** who reviewed several drafts of this book, providing a detailed critique of the content coupled with useful guidance and suggestions for improvement.

The analysis and writing of this book was undertaken largely during the period from 2011 to 2016 when the first author (UP) was Entrepreneur-in-Residence at the Judge Business School at the University of Cambridge. The second author (SV) was Director of the Centre for Entrepreneurial Learning at the Judge Business School from 2003 to 2015; he has since moved to lead the Bettany Centre for Entrepreneurship at Cranfield University, School of Management.

Uday Phadke
Shailendra Vyakarnam

Cambridge, UK
November 2016

Contents

Reviews of the Book   v

Foreword   xiii

About the Authors   xvii

Acknowledgements   xix

List of Figures   xxix

List of Tables   xxxiii

Introduction   xxxv

Part I   Models, Chasms, and Vectors   1

Chapter 1   Science and Technology-enabled Innovation   3
            1.1 Defining Science, Technology, and Innovation   3
            1.2 Science and Technology-enabled Innovation   6
            1.3 Base vs Application Technologies   7
            1.4 Measuring Technology Maturity: Modified
                Technology Readiness Levels (mTRLs)   8

Chapter 2   Economic Paradigms and the Meso-economic
            Environment   11
            2.1 Why Economic Paradigms Matter   11
            2.2 The Evolution of Economic Paradigms   13
            2.3 Unpacking the Meso-economic Environment   17

2.4 Dominant Paradigms   21
2.5 Translating Meso-economic Components into Vectors   22

Chapter 3   The Triple Chasm Model   25
3.1 Theories of the Firm and Growth Metrics   25
3.2 Putting the Customer at the Heart of Our
     Analysis   26
3.3 The Three Chasms   27
3.4 Empirical Generalisations and Diffusion Theory   30
3.5 Our Approach to Data Modelling   31
3.6 The Triple Chasm Model   34
3.7 The Triple Chasm Model vs Rogers and Bass   37

Chapter 4   Chasm-crossing and Commercialisation Vectors   41
4.1 Defining Vectors   41
4.2 Relative Importance of Vectors when Crossing
     Chasms   46
4.3 Diffusion Modelling and Vectors   48
4.4 Crossing Chasm I   50
4.5 Crossing Chasm II   51
4.6 Crossing Chasm III   52

Part II   Customers, Propositions, and Synthesis   53

Chapter 5   Market Spaces   55
5.1 Limitations of Conventional Market
     Segmentation   55
5.2 Defining Market Spaces   56
5.3 Market Space-centric Value Chains   57
5.4 Key Market Spaces   60
5.5 Chasm Behaviour Across Market Spaces   64
5.6 Comparing Timescales for Different Market
     Spaces   65

Chapter 6   Proposition Framing and the Competitive
             Environment   67
6.1 Proposition Framing   67

6.2 The Competitive Landscape   69
6.3 Sources of Competitive Differentiation   71
6.4 Partners, Suppliers, and Collaboration   73

Chapter 7   Customer Definition   77
7.1 Typology-based Customer Targeting   77
7.2 Consumers   80
7.3 Business Customers   82
7.4 Affinity and Knowledge-centric Groups   86
7.5 Estimating Market Potential   87

Chapter 8   Technology Development and Deployment   89
8.1 Characterising Technologies   89
8.2 Base vs Application Technologies   92
8.3 Technology Platforms   92
8.4 Applications and Tools   95
8.5 Products and Services   95
8.6 Technology Deployment Strategies   97

Chapter 9   Synthesising New Products and Services 101
9.1 The Synthesis Challenge   101
9.2 Ideation: Approaches to Concept
     Generation   102
9.3 Approaches Based on Technology Mapping   105
9.4 Creative Synthesis   105
9.5 The Proposition Framework   109

Chapter 10   Manufacturing and Assembly   113
10.1 Generic Challenges   113
10.2 Manufacturing Unpacked   113
10.3 Scaling for Manufacture   115
10.4 Manufacturing Process Innovation   116
10.5 Integrated Design, Simulation, and
      Manufacturing   117

Part III   Strategy, Funding, and Go-to-Market   **119**

Chapter 11   Distribution, Marketing, and Sales   121
             11.1 Generic Go-to-Market Challenges   121
             11.2 Channels-to-Market   122
             11.3 Positioning, Branding, and Promotion   125
             11.4 Key Issues for Science and Technology-enabled
                   Firms   127
             11.5 Integrated Service Delivery   129

Chapter 12   Commercialisation Strategy   131
             12.1 Strategic Ecology and Drivers   131
             12.2 Approaches to Strategy Formulation
                   and Development   133
             12.3 Dynamic Vector-based Approach
                   to Commercialisation Strategy   135
             12.4 Changing Strategic Priorities as Firms Grow   138
             12.5 Strategic Responses to the Competitive
                   Environment   140

Chapter 13   Business Models   141
             13.1 Why Business Models Matter   141
             13.2 Defining Business Models   141
             13.3 Business Model Components   143
             13.4 Business Model Narratives and Revenue
                   Generation   147
             13.5 Business Models and Market Spaces   150
             13.6 Business Model Metrics   152

Chapter 14   Intellectual Property Management   155
             14.1 Generic IP Challenges   155
             14.2 IP Typology for Science and
                   Technology-enabled Innovation   157
             14.3 Changing IP Priorities along
                   Commercialisation Journey   161
             14.4 Market Spaces and IP Priorities   163

Chapter 15 Funding and Investment   167
            15.1 Sources of Funding   167
            15.2 Investment in Science and Technology-enabled
                  Innovation   170
            15.3 Private Equity and Venture Capital
                  in Perspective   173
            15.4 Customer Revenues as a Source of Funding   176
            15.5 Equity Funding and Valuation   179

Chapter 16 Human Capital: Talent, Leadership, and Culture   183
            16.1 The Challenge for Technology Firms   183
            16.2 Talent   185
            16.3 Teams   187
            16.4 Organisational Structure and Management   188
            16.5 Leadership   190
            16.6 Culture in Technology Firms   195

**Part IV   The Commercialisation Canvas, Actors,
            and Interventions   199**

Chapter 17 The Commercialisation Canvas for Single-product
            Firms   201
            17.1 The Commercialisation Canvas   201
            17.2 Commercialisation Trajectories   205
            17.3 Maturity Assessment based on the Triple
                  Chasm Framework   208
            17.4 Camels, Tigers, and Unicorns   209
            17.5 Using the Commercialisation Canvas   211

Chapter 18 Commercialising Across Borders   215
            18.1 Why Does This Matter?   215
            18.2 Characterising the Different Types
                  of Interaction   217
            18.3 Managing IP Across Borders   219
            18.4 Managing Business Model Discontinuities   221

Chapter 19   Actors, Roles, and Interventions   225
                   19.1 Interventions in Context   225
                   19.2 Mentors, 'Burst' Interventions and Seed-camps   229
                   19.3 Tech Transfer Offices and Innovation Agencies   231
                   19.4 Makerspaces, Incubators, and Accelerators   233
                   19.5 Addressing the Chasm II Challenge:
                          The Reactor   239

Chapter 20   Innovation in Mature Firms: The Corporate
                Challenge   241
                   20.1 The Corporate Challenge   241
                   20.2 Multi-product Firms and the Commercialisation
                          Framework   243
                   20.3 Organisational Structures and
                          Commercialisation   246
                   20.4 Corporate Research and Development   248
                   20.5 Product Portfolio Management   251
                   20.6 Build, Buy, or Partner?   253

Chapter 21   Orchestrating the Journey: The Workbench   259
                   21.1 Our Approach   259
                   21.2 Overview of the Workbench   260
                   21.3 Core Data and Metadata Underpinning
                          the Workbench   263
                   21.4 Case Studies   263
                   21.5 Using the Workbench   265

Chapter 22   The Commercialisation Manifesto   267

Notes   271

Index   287

List of Figures

Figure 1:   The Meso-economic Environment.   18

Figure 2:   Characterising Chasms.   29

Figure 3:   Customer Growth for Media and Entertainment Market Space.   32

Figure 4:   Normalised Customer Growth for Media and Entertainment Market Space.   34

Figure 5:   The Triple Chasm Model (Linear-Linear Axes).   36

Figure 6:   The Triple Chasm Model (Log-Linear Axes).   37

Figure 7:   Rogers, Bass, and the Triple Chasm Model.   39

Figure 8:   The 12 Vectors and Sub-vectors.   42

Figure 9:   Relative Importance of Vectors Across the Chasms.   47

Figure 10:   Value Chain for Media and Entertainment Market Space.   59

Figure 11:   Characteristic Times for Different Market Spaces.   66

Figure 12:   Proposition Framing in the Media and Entertainment Market Space.   68

Figure 13:   Market, Technology and Regulatory Drivers — *Composite* View for the Media and Entertainment Market Space.   70

Figure 14:   Partners, Suppliers, and Collaboration in the Media and Entertainment Market Space.   74

Figure 15:   Customer Typology-based Targeting.   79

Figure 16:   Business Segmentation by Size.   84

Figure 17:   Usage of Technology by Businesses.   85
Figure 18:   Platform for Multi-Channel Loyalty Programmes.   94
Figure 19:   Comparing Technology Deployment Strategies.   98
Figure 20:   Synthesising New Products and Services — Generic
             Approaches.   102
Figure 21:   Technology Mapping Applied to Media
             and Entertainment Market Space.   106
Figure 22:   Creative Synthesis.   108
Figure 23:   The Proposition Framework.   109
Figure 24:   Technology Scaling Challenge — Example from the
             'White' Biotechnology Market Space.   115
Figure 25:   Comparing Channels-to-Market.   123
Figure 26:   Relative Importance of the m7Ps — An Example.   126
Figure 27:   Relative Importance of Go-to-Market Vectors on the
             Commercialisation Journey.   128
Figure 28:   Vector-based Commercialisation Strategy
             Formulation.   137
Figure 29:   Typical Commercialisation Strategy
             for a Post-Chasm II Firm.   138
Figure 30:   Changes in Strategic Priorities with Firm
             Maturity — An Example.   139
Figure 31:   Business Model Components.   144
Figure 32:   IP Potential Sources of Commercial Value.   158
Figure 33:   Relative Importance of IP Components Along
             the Commercialisation Journey.   162
Figure 34:   IP Priorities for Digital-intensive Market Spaces.   163
Figure 35:   IP Priorities for Engineering-intensive Market Spaces. 164
Figure 36:   Funding Sources vs the Triple Chasm Model.   172
Figure 37:   Detailed View of Funding Sources Across the Chasms. 173
Figure 38:   Venture Funding Rhetoric vs Reality.   177
Figure 39:   Variation in Human Capital Metrics Across the
             Commercialisation Journey.   186
Figure 40:   Teams and Organisational Structures vs
             Commercialisation Journey.   192
Figure 41:   Approaches to Leadership in Different Market Spaces. 194
Figure 42:   The Culture Web Framework.   197

Figure 43: The Commercialisation Canvas. 202
Figure 44: Typical Trajectory for Science and Technology
Commercialisation. 207
Figure 45: Chasm-based Assessment of Maturity
in an Ecosystem. 208
Figure 46: Commercialisation Across Borders. 220
Figure 47: Actors, Roles, and Interventions vs Triple Chasm
Model. 226
Figure 48: Burst Interventions and Seed-camps. 230
Figure 49: TTOs and Innovation Agencies. 232
Figure 50: Typical Incubator Contributions. 235
Figure 51: Typical Accelerator Contributions. 237
Figure 52: Profile of a New Intervention — The Reactor. 238
Figure 53: Firm Size vs Organisational Structure. 247
Figure 54: Mapping Corporate R&D vs the Commercialisation
Journey. 249
Figure 55: Typical Product Portfolio Map. 252
Figure 56: Corporate Innovation — The Buy Option. 255
Figure 57: The Workbench. 262
Figure 58: Case Studies Used in the Workbench. 264

List of Tables

Table 1:	Science and Technology Classification Based on *Frascati*.	5
Table 2:	Modified Technology Readiness Levels.	9
Table 3:	Typical Duration of Chasms.	35
Table 4:	Variation in Diffusion Coefficients Across Chasms.	36
Table 5:	Variation in v_e and v_i Across the Three Chasms.	49
Table 6:	Integrated Approach to Consumer Profiling.	81
Table 7:	Technology Deployment Model.	90
Table 8:	Mapping Base vs Application Technologies for Media and Entertainment Market Space.	93
Table 9:	Health-related Applications and Tools.	96
Table 10:	Overview of Approaches to Concept Generation.	104
Table 11:	Deconstructing Manufacturing Challenges.	114
Table 12:	Go-to-Market Challenges.	122
Table 13:	Strategic Ecology.	133
Table 14:	Approaches to Strategy Formulation and Development.	136
Table 15:	Business Model — Potential Revenue Sources.	145
Table 16:	Overview of Funding Sources.	169
Table 17:	Valuation Components.	180
Table 18:	Human Capital Management — The Key Variables.	184
Table 19:	Organisation and Management vs Teams.	191
Table 20:	Comparing Camels, Tigers, and Unicorns.	212

Introduction

The Origins of this Book

The idea for this book originated from a heated round table discussion in Cambridge, England in 2011 between proponents of the idea that Cambridge and other technology clusters around the world could become more successful by emulating the Silicon Valley experience and those who argued that these lessons, based mainly on digital technologies and access to prodigious amounts of risk capital, were limited in their scope. These proponents suggested that the Cambridge experience based on taking 'deeper' science and technology ideas to market in conditions with more resource constraints in fact provided more meaningful insights with wider global relevance. This admittedly small group believed that rebadging the Cambridge experience as Silicon Fen was dangerous because it coupled a small number of anecdotal insights with a simplistic narrative of how ideas combine with investment to create significant new firms. In particular, they argued that interest in entrepreneurship, technology-enabled innovation and the creation of new commercial value was not matched by a clear and systematic understanding of how this actually happens.

We shared some of this scepticism, based on our experience of working in many market spaces across the world, including Silicon Valley and Cambridge. We realised, however, that we needed to provide a more realistic account of how science and technology-enabled innovation is commercialised, based on a significant body of global data coupled with detailed analysis, not just insights from a few well-chosen case studies. We also recognised that this task would probably require us to create new conceptual approaches, models and tools with far greater granularity than those deployed in most academic and business narratives and literature. In particular, we realised that some of our conclusions were likely to challenge conventional wisdom, so we needed a robust and defensible approach to data collection, analysis, interpretation, and presentation.

So why does this matter?

This debate is of much wider interest than any conflicting narratives between Silicon Valley and Cambridge. The commercialisation of science and technology-enabled innovation is a serious topic of interest, debate and discussion for a wide range of global audiences: scientists and technologists, entrepreneurs, educators, start-up firms, larger established firms, investors, economists and those responsible for developing and executing industrial polices. These audiences are interested in different aspects of commercialisation but share one common objective: to understand how science and technology-based ideas can be turned into commercial value more effectively. This interest is global, irrespective of prevailing ideologies, which may favour lesser or greater state intervention in long-term industrial strategies.

As we discovered when we embarked on our programme of research, analysis, and interpretation, this interest is unfortunately not matched by rigorous analysis and insights supported by detailed data, integrated into a coherent picture which supports practical decision making. Despite the vast number of publications addressing entrepreneurship, innovation and the business strategies required to build new organisations and firms, there is relatively little in the literature which systematically addresses the challenges of turning ideas into commercially valuable propositions: this book is intended to directly address this gap.

Why this Book is Needed

We have spent the last three decades in various commercial firms and academic institutions working on the different steps involved in transforming scientific and technological ideas into commercial products and services. During this time, we have collaborated with many colleagues from all over the world: turning ideas into valuable outputs is a team sport which does not recognise geographic boundaries. On this journey, we have come to appreciate that popular enthusiasm for commercialising science and technology is not generally reflected in a clear understanding of the structures, processes and mechanisms involved in actually achieving this. In particular, there are many gaps between 'popular folklore' and a real understanding of how this transformation actually works.

This gap is serious because it affects not just the population at large but particularly those involved in generating ideas, transforming them into viable products and services, and funding the process. And inevitably, given the enormous potential impact of commercial value creation, it is also subject to political and social bias where ideological narratives often hold sway in the absence of real evidence.

When contemplating the idea for this book, we embarked on a serious research exercise in the hope of finding a solid body of literature we could draw on. We found a great deal has been written about entrepreneurship and innovation in general, for example, see the books by Martin, Timmons, and Bhide,[1-3] but we discovered that surprisingly little *systematic* work has been done on the *commercialisation* of science and technology-based ideas and the associated intellectual property. To compound this problem, much of what has been written is based on analysing a few well-chosen case studies, which tend to focus on 'outlier' firms not necessarily representative of the majority of firms: in the absence of a robust data set based on a solid body of evidence, the objective in most cases appears to have been to create simple grid-based generalisations which can be used to offer 'strategic' advice to senior executives, mostly in large firms.

Only some of this can be explained by the cultural divide between those actively involved in science and technology and those concerned with trade and commerce, similar to the divide identified in C P Snow's classic text on *The Two Cultures and Scientific Revolutions*.[4] In our view, there are two other possible explanations for this gap: the difficulty in understanding an inherently nonlinear and complex process with many variables affecting the outcome, and ideological narratives based on economic orthodoxy which have encouraged the supposed ability to separate the generation of ideas from their exploitation in markets. We will be exploring this later in the context of how ideological motivation can affect how commercialisation activity is funded and how the results are exploited.

At a more prosaic level, this debate is reflected in a number of quite different ways, including the technology transfer industry which has grown dramatically over the last 20 years and 'reality television' shows where entrepreneurs compete for commercial backing from a small number of successful (and presumably 'sagacious') business people.

There has been little rigorous research and analysis following Schumpeter's seminal work[5] on new value creation: instead, this gap has been largely filled by Business School-inspired Case studies on specific successes and failures. There are some exceptions to this, in particular, the attempts to explore the key drivers for change in geographic innovation clusters on the East and West Coasts of the US, and several European clusters.[6-9] While they provide useful insights based on empirical data, they do not provide a generalised body of knowledge and insights based on an explicit methodology underpinned by a rigorous data set.

This gap needs to be addressed urgently now, especially given the global debate on how ideas are generated, funded, and turned into useful outputs, and how the benefits of this are distributed in societal and global terms.

Who This Book is Aimed at

The contents of this book are likely to be of interest to a wide range of audiences, but this book is aimed firmly at **Practitioners** who are actively engaged in turning science and technology-enabled ideas into commercially valuable products and services. These include the following:

Entrepreneurs focused on technology and technology-enabled business ideas, often working in start-up teams.

Leaders and Managers in Technology Firms: This includes executives and employees, who are tasked with creating new products and services, marketing and selling them, getting them into the hands of customers and often supporting their use.

Scientists and Technologists Engaged in Innovation: This includes research scientists in academic institutions and corporate environments, 'single' inventors and groups of scientific entrepreneurs operating outside recognised structures.

In addition, this book should be of interest to the following groups:

Researchers and Students: This includes science and commerce students doing PhDs and MBA students, who are interested in how ideas are commercialised.

Business and Strategy Consultants: Those who work with and advise science and technology firms.

Leaders and **Managers** of publicly and privately funded 'intervention agencies' which provide a wide range of services to support innovation, acceleration, and commercialisation of science and technology-based concepts and ideas. This includes incubators, accelerators, and technology-transfer agencies.

Policy Makers: This includes politicians, economists and civil servants who can fundamentally affect decisions about allocation of resources, investment regimes, capacity-building, regulation, national and cross-border incentives, and various incentives including tax structures.

Investors: This includes governments, corporates, private–public funding bodies and private financial investors (angels, venture funds, banks, and private equity).

Our Terminology

As we embarked on writing this book, we realised that we needed an explicit terminology to frame and explain the findings of our research. We use the following terms which are discussed in detail in the appropriate chapters:

We use the idea of the **Journey** to describe the development over time of an idea into a distinct product or service by a firm, which is then used by customers.

We use the word **Firm** to describe the commercial vehicle which undertakes this journey, rather than the more common word business, because we want to explicitly link it to previous work on the theory of the firm, as used by most economists.

We describe the maturity of the idea and the firm along the commercialisation journey based on whether the firm has crossed Chasms I, II, and III. We use the idea of **Chasms** in a very specific sense based on the Triple Chasm Model we have developed using primary customer adoption data.

We use a **modified Technology Readiness Level (mTRL)**, which we discuss early in the book, coupled with the Triple Chasm Model, to provide greater granularity in describing the maturity of the firm.

We use the concept of **Commercialisation Vectors** to describe the key variables which affect the progress of this journey.

We use the concept of **Market Spaces** to describe new and emerging market environments which addresses the limitations of conventional approaches to market segmentation. We also use these to define '**market space-centric value chains**', which overcome the limitations of conventional 'static' firm-centric value chains.

We then combine the vectors and maturity of the firm to create the **Commercialisation Canvas**, which effectively couples these two key dimensions into a single canvas or picture onto which we can project the position and trajectory of any firm.

We can then paint the typical roles of the key **Actors** involved in the commercialisation journey onto this canvas: These actors include entrepreneurs, different sizes of firms, investors, and others working actively to change the pace and trajectory of firms on the canvas.

We define different types of **Interventions** provided by some of these actors which can facilitate progress on the commercialisation journey.

We identify and discuss 12 key vectors in the book, which in aggregate can shape the commercialisation trajectory of a firm: each **Vector** is a key variable with multiple **Sub-vectors**, which impact on a particular aspect of a firm's performance. While the terminology associated with vectors may be familiar to the average reader, we define these terms more explicitly when we describe each vector because we ascribe quite specific meanings to some of these terms.

We then present a **Commercialisation Workbench**, which provides tools and examples of their application, which can be used by firms to accelerate their commercialisation journeys.

Finally, we present our **Commercialisation Manifesto**, which we hope will serve as a call to action for all those involved in commercialising science and technology-enabled innovation.

Our Approach

This book is based on research we conducted over the period 1995–2015 based on data from a number of sources.

The starting point for our analysis was primary customer adoption data we obtained from the 300 science and technology-enabled firms in our data set. For each of these firms, we were interested in how the actual numbers of customers of the firm changed over time. Our data covered a very wide range of market spaces spanning different technologies, geographies, and customer types.

In addition to this customer data, we also collected quantitative and qualitative data on other aspects of the firm, covering all 12 vectors which affected its performance and trajectory, including technology deployment, funding, and business models.

We also collected additional commercial data on a wide range of firms, including firms not in our data set, from a wide range of private and public investors, including angels, venture capitalists, private equity, banks, and state funding agencies.

A range of intervention agencies, including incubators, accelerators, and technology-transfer offices also provided techno-commercial data on the firms in their portfolios, and also their views on what they perceived as the biggest challenges.

We augmented these different sources of data in two ways: we ran a number of private surveys and 'round tables' where technology firms and other key stakeholders such as national intervention agencies, provided additional qualitative insights, and we used data from published sources, including academics, national agencies and regional organisations, to corroborate and 'sense-check' our primary data.

Much of the data on customers and other vectors was provided under strict conditions of anonymity, which is why the book does not make specific references to named firms or organisations. The use of this large primary data set differentiates our work from typical Case Study-type approaches which look at a specific firm or a relatively small number of firms; these can often provide detailed insights but tend to focus on 'outlier' firms which have been outstanding successes or failures.

Our overall approach naturally reflects the different traditions and perspectives of the two authors of this book: we see this as a source of strength in our analysis and interpretation because it enables us to appreciate the many different perspectives on the broad commercialisation challenge.

The first author (UP) is focused on the scaling of innovation and how mature firms can innovate based on: detailed understanding and insight into a wide range of technologies, expertise in the creation of new products and services, in-depth practical experience with entrepreneurs and start-ups, extended experience of working with larger established firms, experience in scaling technology-enabled firms, and experience as an investor in early-stage technology firms. The second author (SV) is more strongly focused on early stages of the innovation process, in particular: detailed understanding of the research and university communities, practical experience and insights working with entrepreneurs and early-stage start-ups, and understanding the motivation and behaviour of entrepreneurs, especially at the earlier stages of growth.

In this book, we adopt a **systematic** 4-part approach to explaining our view on how science and technology is commercialised, as described below.

Part I

We start by defining science, technology and innovation and explaining the differences between them. We discuss technology-enabled innovation, provide a framework for classifying different types of science and technology, and present a revised system for defining mTRLs: this consolidates ideas developed initially by NASA and the aerospace industry.

We then discuss why prevailing economic thinking can have a significant impact on the direction and progress of science and technology-enabled innovation. We explore the evolution of economic paradigms before discussing the importance of the meso-economic environment from a practical perspective. We then discuss the current dominance of pseudo-neo-liberal thinking and how this affects the translation of meso-economic drivers into commercialisation vectors.

We draw on the wide range of empirical data we have been collecting over the last 20 years to present some general observations about the commercialisation journey: the principal conclusion of this research is the identification of three discontinuities or chasms faced by virtually all firms on their commercialisation journeys. In particular, we describe and discuss how these conclusions apply to a wide range of technologies, markets and market spaces. We then apply diffusion theory to draw out empirical generalisations which shed fresh light on the commercialisation process and provide new structural insights based on the Triple Chasm Model.

We discuss the key vectors which drive the interventions required to cross each of the chasms based on our quantitative data combined with the experience and insights gained from building new firms over the last 20 years. The 12 vectors cover the following: market spaces; proposition framing and competition; customer definition; distribution, marketing, and sales; commercialisation strategy; business model development; intellectual property management; manufacturing and assembly; product and service definition and synthesis; technology development and deployment; talent, leadership, and culture; and funding and investment. We discuss the relative importance of these different vectors when crossing each of the three chasms.

Part II

We start by taking a fresh approach to defining market spaces which deals with the limitations of conventional market segmentation. We define new market space-centric value chains which help us to overcome the limitations of traditional firm-centric value chains before discussing differences in chasm structure across these market spaces. We also compare typical maturity timescales, reflecting the time required to reach the maximum number of cumulative customers, for firms in different market spaces.

We then explore how market space value chains can be used to frame new propositions in the context of the competitive environment and regulatory constraints. We look at the roles of partners and suppliers and the potential for collaboration before suggesting a new approach to developing competitive strategies which integrates previous thinking based on positioning, resources, and capabilities.

This leads us to a more systematic way of looking at different types of customers and the key factors which shape their behaviour. In particular, we distinguish between four different types of customers: consumers, businesses, governments, and affinity and knowledge-centric groups.

We then present a Technology Deployment Framework which allows us to understand and profile the different ways in which science and technology-enabled innovation can be taken to market: the framework starts with base technologies as the basic building block with several levels of integration eventually culminating in the deployment of integrated products and services.

We explore in detail the synthesis of new products and services, 'deconstructing' propositions based on a new model we have developed, and looking at the wider provision of services underpinned by products.

Finally, in Part II, we look at manufacturing and assembly challenges involved in taking new technologies to market, including scaling new processes for high-volume manufacturing. We also provide an overview of innovations in manufacturing methods and processes.

Part III

In Part III, we start by discussing go-to-market challenges, including channels to market, positioning, branding and promotion, and service-centric delivery.

We then explore the key issues in the development of a dynamic commercial strategy for the firm which goes beyond the conventional 'static' approaches based on positioning or resources and capabilities.

We explore business models which are the key to successful deployment of new products and services. We also look at how intellectual property is characterised and how it can support sustainable business models.

We discuss the challenges of funding new technology-enabled products and services, exploring the gap between the rhetoric and the reality of how commercialisation is funded. In particular, we look at how venture capital actually works and the importance of customer funding.

Finally, in Part III, we look at the Human Talent required to progress and how it is organised and motivated. In particular, we discuss the importance of talent, including entrepreneurial talent, how teams function, organisational structure and management, leadership styles and the overall importance of the firm's culture.

Part IV

We start by framing the overall commercialisation journey for single product firms in the context of the Triple Chasm Model, mTRLs, and the key vectors to create the commercialisation canvas. We look at a new way of assessing the maturity of science and technology firms, based on the Triple Chasm Model. The commercialisation canvas provides the fundamental framework for understanding the *scaling* challenges for all firms: it also provides the basis for assessing the progress of any firm and the effectiveness of 'external' interventions.

We then look at the specific challenges of commercialising across borders using the detailed Canvas. We characterise different types of cross-border commercialisation, looking in particular at managing intellectual property across borders, the need for different business models and differences in distribution systems.

Using the commercialisation canvas, we explore the roles of the key actors involved in the commercialisation journey including: innovators and entrepreneurs; start-up teams; IP-generating organisations and agencies; incubators, makerspaces and accelerators; angel investors, venture capital and private equity; and mature established firms or Corporates. This analysis highlights a critical gap in the provision of intervention support around Chasm II, which is a major contributor to the failure of many science and technology firms.

We apply the learnings developed in previous chapters to multi-product firms, which includes most large established firms in order to explore the big corporate innovation challenge: Build, Buy, or Partner?

Finally, we summarise the new commercialisation Workbench we have developed and refined with the firms in our data set to support the commercialisation process. The Workbench consists of the canvas, tools, and case studies to facilitate and support the commercialisation journey.

We conclude by presenting our commercialisation manifesto, which sets out how the various actors in the science and technology commercialisation journey can utilise the insights from our research and analysis to improve the chances of success.

Camels, Tigers, and Unicorns

The title of this book needs an introductory explanation: borrowing from popular practice, we define some simple archetypes based on animal metaphors in order to reinforce our primary findings about the scaling challenges facing firms enabled by science and technology innovation.

In the context of the Triple Chasm Model, 'camels' describes firms which adopt an organised and patient approach to commercialisation. This reflects an understanding that this is a long and difficult journey which needs to be broken down into discrete steps based on access to internal resources with a clear focus on the key challenges involved in crossing each of the three chasms. The analogy with how camels cross the desert, based on patient progress from one oasis to another, is what we wish to convey, as well as the adaptations enjoyed by camels to cope in the harsh environments they occupy. When we refer to camels, we mean, for example, engineering firms which ensure they are suitably equipped at each stage of the journey and make patient planned progress, unlike the popular perception, rarely borne out in reality, of a firm which can develop a new software product in days and reach market maturity in months!

The term 'tigers' has a number of antecedents and we use the metaphor here to describe those firms which are very agile and able to adapt quickly to change. Tigers inhabit volatile market spaces where conditions can change very quickly, such as, for example, in media and entertainment. We are also referring to firms which adapt themselves well to a number of difficult environments where the competition is less predictable and agility is therefore an important attribute. What this means is that the challenges of crossing chasms may be qualitatively different than for camels: the key feature of tigers is that they typically need significant external funding to navigate these environments, which is why they turn to investment from angels and venture capital.

Unicorns are mythical creatures and we use the term to describe those firms which do not adhere to conventional commercial logic but use 'magical' notions to address the challenge of crossing chasms, especially

Chasm II. For example, unicorns typically address the Chasm II challenge by denying the need to have a sustainable business model at this point: instead, their approach assumes that with sufficient capital available, they can acquire a large number of 'customers', who are not paying for services but can be claimed as customers because they are users. In this mindset, the approach is to create sufficient momentum and market dominance so that some kind of sustainable business model will appear in the future. This rarely happens of course, which is why so much is written about the failure rates of unicorns! This kind of betting strategy may of course suit some types of investors where there is a surplus of capital. One way of dealing with these failures is to move the goal posts: which is why the media definition of unicorns has morphed recently, mainly at the instigation of investors, based on some arbitrary threshold of the firm's value, where this valuation is also based on the dynamics of an investment bubble.

Part I

Models, Chasms, and Vectors

Chapter 1

Science and Technology-enabled Innovation

1.1 Defining Science, Technology, and Innovation

We start by defining what we mean by science and technology. Science and technology are often conflated in popular colloquial use, especially when technology products are being discussed. The two words are often used interchangeably in commentary and discussions about products which consumers interact with on a daily basis, for example, mobile phones, computers, and digital display devices.

Over the past decade, there has been a tendency to use the term 'technology' to refer almost exclusively to digital technologies and the use of these technologies in media-related products and services. Journalists, commentators, and investors, in particular, frequently use the word 'technology' to refer almost exclusively to digital technologies and associated products and services. From this perspective, other technologies associated with, for example, life sciences or engineering, are relegated to 'other technologies' of lesser relevance or interest. This ignores the fact that digital technologies constitute a small part of the overall technology space, and many different technologies often need to be integrated to create new products and services. New material technologies, for example, can impact bioscience, aerospace, and digital markets.

We want to reclaim the way in which science and technology is perceived: our view is based on the broader definition of science and technology which **encompasses all science and technology**.

Within this broad definition, we recognise that there has been serious philosophical debate between academics about the relationship between science and technology and precisely what the terms mean. The word 'Science' derives from the Latin *scientia* (knowledge) which is a system of acquiring knowledge based on the scientific method as well as the organised body of knowledge gained through such research. Science as defined in this way is sometimes termed pure science to differentiate it from applied science,[10] which is the application of scientific research to specific human needs. Technology is a broad concept that deals with the usage and knowledge of scientific tools and crafts, and how it affects our ability to control and adapt to our environment. It is generally regarded as a consequence of science, although several technological advances actually predate the two concepts.

The definition of science and technology we use here is based on a practical *operational* view based on the first four categories of the *Frascati* classification scheme[11] originally developed for global Research & Development mapping by the OECD. We use this as the basis for our science and technology coverage, ignoring categories 5 and 6 which cover Social Sciences and the Humanities. The *Frascati* classification was developed following a suggestion from Freeman[12] that we needed a practical category model which allowed us to understand and measure the impact of political, social, economic and technical interventions in modern economies. The *Frascati* classification scheme sidesteps philosophical distinctions between science and technology and importantly uses definitions based on recognisable industry segments, for example, in medicine and agriculture. The *Frascati* classification has been extensively used by researchers over the last three decades to measure a range of inputs and outputs in the commercialisation process, for example, patents, products, industries, investment and national policies, which enables comparative measurements across markets, regions, and territories.

The *Frascati* classification is reviewed every few years and in detail operates at the 4-digit classification level, but we use the simplified version based on coverage at the 2-digit level. Table 1 shows our operational

Table 1:   Science and Technology Classification Based on *Frascati*.

1. Natural sciences	1.1 Mathematics
	1.2 Computer and information sciences
	1.3 Physical sciences
	1.4 Chemical sciences
	1.5 Earth and related environmental sciences
	1.6 Biological sciences
	1.7 Other natural sciences
2. Engineering and technology	2.1 Civil engineering
	2.2 Electrical engineering, electronic engineering, information engineering
	2.3 Mechanical engineering
	2.4 Chemical engineering
	2.5 Materials engineering
	2.6 Medical engineering
	2.7 Environmental engineering
	2.8 Environmental biotechnology
	2.9 Industrial biotechnology
	2.10 Nanotechnology
	2.11 Other engineering and technologies
3. Medical and health sciences	3.1 Basic medicine
	3.2 Clinical medicine
	3.3 Health sciences
	3.4 Health biotechnology
	3.5 Other medical sciences
4. Agricultural sciences	4.1 Agriculture, forestry, and fisheries
	4.2 Animal and dairy science
	4.3 Veterinary science
	4.4 Agricultural biotechnology
	4.5 Other agricultural sciences

definition of science and technology categories. Our use of this classification has been driven largely by the need to maintain continuity with previous data collection and analysis efforts in spite of our recognition that this schema has some weaknesses. When we examine the behaviour of firms later in Chapters 5 and 6, we use market spaces as the basis for our segmentation, not the technology categories derived from *Frascati*.

The word **innovation** is used in many ways and contexts, so we need to be clear what we mean when we use the word: put very simply *innovation is about the creation of new value*. In more practical terms, innovation is the implementation of a new or significantly improved product, process, marketing method, or organisational approach. This includes scientific, technological, organisational, financial and commercial activities which lead to the implementation of innovations.

1.2 Science and Technology-enabled Innovation

Science and technology-enabled innovation can be commercialised in a number of different ways. As Akio Morita, the driving force behind a new generation of consumer electronics products has noted succinctly 'science does not equal technology and technology does not equal innovation'.[13] Science and technology-enabled innovations can be commercialised in a variety of ways.

Science and technology can be used to create **innovative products and services** with different functions, forms, and benefits. For example, technology innovation has enabled the creation of a whole family of mobile computing and communications devices such as smartphones, new ways of generating power from solar energy and new digital printing machines.

They can enable **process innovations** in a wide number of areas including manufacturing supply chains, genome sequencing and delivery of mobile-health solutions. These innovations can deliver better integration of functionality, faster processing speeds and more sophisticated functionality.

Innovations can change the **nature of markets** in a number of ways: by creating new market spaces, enabling the creation of new types of players, transforming the roles of existing players, and delivering entirely new classes of products and services to customers. Examples of this include the creation of new publishing market spaces, new energy markets, and new distribution systems, all enabled by digital technology. These innovations in markets can be incremental, or create new 'adjacent' markets, or enable entirely new marketplaces.

The inn   the
creation of n   way
in which cus   ces.
For example,   ibu-
tion have cr   ally
enabled by te

Science   luct
and service **distribution** systems and networks. Examples of this include e-commerce networks, online retail, and extended supply chains in the automotive and aerospace industries.

Linking all these together, science and technology is enabling significant **innovations in business models**, for example, the creation of software as a service (SaaS) and platform as a service (PaaS) models in the media and entertainment and telecommunication industries.

1.3 Base vs Application Technologies

When looking at science and technology commercialisation, the challenge is to understand how to characterise technologies from an application or use perspective. Understanding this process in detail is critical, as Nelson[14] has pointed out, because it can affect the impact and size of the commercial outcome. Most research and development perspectives have focused on the intrinsic and potential value of a technology on the one hand and the creation of formal definitions, for example, patents, on the other. Pavitt's extensive work[15] based on the volume of patents illustrated the inherent complexity and the difficulty of using patents as a proxy for detailed understanding of this process.

Saviotti[16,17] and Dosi[18] discussed this complexity and the challenge of handling co-occurrences and linkages where technology interactions could produce different outcomes, sometimes in quite different markets. For example, patents in computing architectures could impact the creation of new products and services in many different areas, ranging from navigation systems to synthetic biology. Clearly, we need a systematic and consistent approach when looking at science and technology exploitation.

The approach we have adopted here is to differentiate between base and application technologies. Following Saviotti, we define *base technologies* as artefacts or technology building blocks with wide applicability. We define *application technologies* as integrated systems or subsystems which can be directly mapped to market space value chains, which we discuss in more detail in Chapter 5.

The relationship between base and application technologies can determine the potential and range of a technology, but this relationship depends on the market space, so that the ways in which base and application technologies go to market is influenced by the specific characteristics of a market space. This relationship may be significantly different for different market spaces.

We explore the relationship between application technologies and market spaces in more detail in Chapter 8.

1.4 Measuring Technology Maturity: Modified Technology Readiness Levels (mTRLs)

As we look in detail at how science and technology is commercialised we need a way of characterising the level of maturity of the technology along the development pathway. In particular, we need a generic view of maturity which is independent of the specific characteristics of a technology, but one which maps onto the overall process.

NASA first developed and published a model which addresses this question in 1995: while it is rooted in the concept of space missions, the NASA Technology Readiness Model[19] provides the basis for the approach we adopt here.

Our modified Technology Readiness Model, shown in Table 2, rests strongly on linking technologies to products and services and to the way in which they link to customers. While some descriptions of the NASA Technology Readiness Level (TRL) model cover in detail the status of hardware, software and systems at each level, our definition is more generic and indeed applies where the usual definitions of hardware, software and systems do not apply.

Table 2: **Modified Technology Readiness Levels.**

mTRL	mTRL from Exploitation Perspective
0	Research in progress
1	Validated research: start concept definition (early impedance matching)
2	Initial concept defined
3	Working prototype or demonstrator
4	Product or service testing and concept refinement
5	Proven product or service
6	Deployment with early customers in real commercial environment
7	Product or service ready for testing in real user environment
8	Techno-commercial refinement of product or service
9	Ready for commercial deployment with real customers

Adapted from NASA Technology Readiness Approach.

We define these mTRLs as follows:

mTRL 0: This describes fundamental research activity before any potentially useful and validated science or technology has been established.

mTRL 1: This describes the technology maturity at the point at which the conceptual application of the technology has been defined in outline terms. At this point, there is a basic understanding of the potential use case and a rough idea of how the technology might make this possible; borrowing a term from the world of electrical engineering, we refer to this as early 'impedance matching'.

mTRL 2: The conceptual application has now been converted to a definition of the Product or Service which can potentially be offered using the technology.

mTRL 3: This is the level at which a working prototype or demonstrator has been built, embodying the technology or technologies in question.

mTRL 4: Following feedback from the initial 'Charter Customer' (the first real user of the technology), the new product or service is defined at this level.

mTRL 5: This is the level at which the product or service is ready at a functional level without the collateral around the product, including the method of deployment and the proposed business model.

mTRL 6: The product or service is now ready for use with early customers and so includes all the associated collateral, including a service infrastructure where relevant.

mTRL 7: At this level, early customer feedback has been used to define the modified product or service functionality, its required performance and critically, the chosen business model.

mTRL 8: The refined product or service is now ready for deployment with mainstream customers, not just the 'early' Charter Customers.

mTRL 9: The final product or service, with the full set of components, is now ready for commercial launch, including go-to-market collateral and proven business model, so the main challenge now is growing the mainstream customer base.

We discuss how mTRLs change with customer adoption behaviour in Chapter 17.

Chapter 2

Economic Paradigms
and the Meso-economic Environment

2.1 Why Economic Paradigms Matter

The commercialisation of science and technology does not happen in a value-free vacuum: in reality, the direction, trajectory, and outcome of commercialisation activities depend heavily on the prevailing economic paradigm.

In this context, when we talk about the economic paradigm, we mean the political, social, economic, technological, and financial environment in which individuals, organisations, and firms operate. The environment sets the broad context in which commercialisation activity is conducted. In particular, political ideology, economic policy, and the resultant operating environment can have a dramatic impact on whether and how science and technology ideas are commercialised.

While national and trans-national policies can set the tone within which this activity is conducted, we are concerned here with five broad areas where the prevailing paradigm can shape how opportunities are addressed.

Overall ideological narrative

Every market has an overarching narrative or 'story' which sets the backdrop for economic activity: this narrative includes views on the balance between the public and private sectors of the economy, the conditions required for wealth creation and how the proceeds of commercial activity are shared nationally and across geographical and political boundaries. This narrative typically shapes the areas discussed below.

Market structure

The structure of the market into which new products and services will be deployed is of fundamental importance, something which scientists and technologists sometimes ignore. We will be discussing this later in Chapter 5, but the key point to make here is that the paradigm sets the tone regarding how markets are segmented, how distribution channels work, and how regulation can impact the opportunity landscape.

Funding and investment

How the creation of new products and services is funded is probably the most critical question: the debate here is sometimes clouded by the broader narrative of economic policy including ideological arguments about public vs private investment. We discuss below how these debates have resulted in changing paradigms.

Capacity to innovate

The capacity to innovate new ideas, products and services, and business models is clearly central to our discussion, but paradigms can have a dramatic impact here, including how they deal with the ownership and exploitation of intellectual capital and how they contribute to the development of the human resources involved in this activity.

Boundaries

Paradigms typically have political, cultural and geographic boundaries, either explicit or implied, which create specific commercialisation systems. This can lead to interesting consequences, as commercialisation activities straddle regional and political boundaries. We will be exploring this later in the book, in particular, the challenges of cross-border commercialisation. Although these boundaries may be transparent or porous, there can be significant differences in commercialisation behaviour, even in connected systems, so the world is definitely not flat, contrary to Friedman's views![20]

2.2 The Evolution of Economic Paradigms

In order to understand the forces which shape the current dominant paradigms, we need to understand a little of the history of science and technology commercialisation since the industrial revolution. Environments typically evolve over time but, as Kuhn noted for scientific paradigms,[21] the change is not smooth but characterised by periods of relative stability interspersed with significant paradigm shifts. What follows is a very brief summary of the major paradigm shifts of relevance to science and technology commercialisation. We believe that knowledge of this history is critical to understanding the key drivers for science and technology-enabled innovation.

Despite the interesting perspectives on the early history of science and technology commercialisation in China and India before the 18th Century provided by Needham[22] and Dharampal,[23] the first clearly recognisable paradigm of relevance to us is probably that which developed during the Industrial Revolution in Europe between 1760 and 1840.

The Industrial Revolution

The Industrial Revolution embodied the first mechanisation-based system where labour and capital were disaggregated for the first time, as the power of craft-based industries was supplanted. This was reflected in Adam Smith's description of *The Invisible Hand* in 1779.[24] His publication laid the foundations for much of the economic theory in subsequent centuries and still appears to influence some thinkers despite its reference to 'invisible' agents, a metaphysical idea which sits strangely with talking about science and technology.

The Marxian[25] critique of this, first published in 1847, was based on the counter-Hegelian dichotomy between ideas and the material world, but the main relevance in the current context was its economic analysis. This discussed the contribution of labour in contrast with the supposed primacy of capital and so at least introduced the idea of human capital as a key component of new value creation. This idea was absorbed by Schumpeter, who discussed market spaces for commercialising science and technology formally for the first time.

Early Schumpeter

In the modern era, the first work to explicitly suggest a theory of economic innovation and the business cycle was Schumpeter's work on *Creative Destruction*,[26] first published in 1942. Schumpeter's analysis described the 'gale of creative destruction' or the 'process of industrial mutation that incessantly revolutionizes the economic structure from within, incessantly destroying the old one, incessantly creating a new one'.

Drawing on Marx, Schumpeter argued that the creative-destructive forces unleashed by capitalism would eventually lead to its demise as a system. Despite this, the term subsequently gained popularity within neo-liberal or free-market economics as a description of processes such as downsizing in order to increase the efficiency and dynamism of the firm.

The original neo-liberal paradigm

Despite or perhaps because of Schumpeter's work, a strong neo-liberal paradigm developed in the 1970s, which described the role and performance of corporations when commercialising science and technology-enabled innovation. This push was supported by empirical data from (mainly) large US corporations supported by a narrative about how they invested in research and development and how innovation required the right regulatory support and corporations with scale. This was the period when much of the work cited today on competition, value chains and market spaces was developed by thinkers such as Porter and Christensen.[27,28] Much of the literature about theories of the firm, including how they innovate, stems from this period.

In a direct rebuke to the idea of Adam Smith's 'invisible forces', Chandler[29] published a major review of how the different drivers affected the ability of firms (still large firms in the prevalent thinking then) to create and exploit new value. In *The Visible Hand*, Chandler argued the case for what he called managerial capitalism, where corporate managers were able to pull the levers to drive growth in competitive markets.

This neo-liberal paradigm dominated most thinking until the mid-1980s, setting the backdrop against which science and technology commercialisation initiatives were calibrated and judged — in particular, it accounts for Porter's zero-sum approach to competition where growth comes at the expense of others rather than 'growing the size of the whole cake' based on innovation.

The pseudo-neo-liberal agenda

The period since then has been characterised, particularly in the US and parts of Europe, by a 'new' neo-liberal agenda based on the unique primacy of capital and the role of the private sector in innovation. We refer to this as the pseudo-neo-liberal agenda to distinguish it from the original neo-liberal paradigm.

The critical aspect of this new paradigm has been the emergence of venture capital (VC) funding for commercialising science and technology. The role of VC and Private Equity has assumed such an importance in the minds of all players that it is practically seen as a prerequisite for successful commercialisation. This has also significantly affected the behaviour of many large corporations in the US and Europe, particularly their attitude to funding research and development and innovation. We will be exploring the role of VC in more detail later in terms of both the rhetorical intent and the reality.

In his critique of this new paradigm, Lazonick,[30] in particular, has argued that the *financialisation* of all sectors of the economy, especially in the US, has spawned the destructive ideology that firms should be run to maximise shareholder value. Firms have used the speculative stock market to attract finance in the form of VC, which can realise returns through a quick public offering on the stock market. Some firms who were market leaders in the 1970s have embraced this approach, but in the process have severely compromised their innovative capabilities and their overall positions as noted by Stiglitz.[31]

While the US has set the pace with this pseudo-neo-liberal agenda, the leakage of this mindset across other parts of the world has been mixed. Most European countries have embraced this agenda, as have many parts of Asia and Africa, in particular, China and India. The paradox, as Mazzucato[32] has noted, is that in the US, China and India, the neo-liberal agenda has not dissuaded the State from serious 'strategic' investment in key science and technology areas, so that the rhetoric of private sector supremacy is not matched by the reality when it comes to large investments, except in some European countries, notably the UK, where the state appears to be committed to withdrawing from strategic investments of this kind.

Systems approaches

This discussion of economic paradigms would not be complete without addressing the Systems of Innovation Approach which has been part of discussions on innovation policy since the late 1980s.[33] This 'mechanical' approach to understanding how innovative ideas are developed and commercialised builds on the theory of systems and system analysis; it has been used to discuss, for example, the operation of 'open innovation', where ideas are shared and exploited cooperatively with business models emerging later.

Edquist[34] has concluded that systems thinking has been characterised so far by an abstract approach with little empirical data to support its rationale. In practical terms, the difficulty in defining system boundaries and inputs and outputs explicitly means that this approach appears to have little practical utility in understanding science and technology commercialisation.

Evolutionary economics

Conventionally, economists have described environments at a very broad macro-economic level or at the micro-economic level where firms and their customers operate. The problem with this binary distinction is that it does not properly address the way in which these two levels are connected, which is precisely where many of the drivers of interest to us are located.

According to Nelson and Winter,[35] evolutionary economics deals with *the structures, processes and dynamics* which drive the behaviour of firms, institutions, industries, employment, production, trade, and growth. In particular, it can be used to understand the economics of science and technology-enabled innovation, especially the *non-equilibrium* behaviour which mainstream economics has been weak at addressing, given its static orientation.

This approach is based on defining a meso-economic layer which straddles the gap between macro-economic theory and micro-economic theory. Changes in structures and processes are manifested in the meso layer, which is why it is so useful when looking at how innovations can be commercialised. Although mainstream economists have been resistant to evolutionary economics, the *macro–meso–micro* model has been used over the last decade in particular to understand the key drivers of change.[36–38]

2.3 Unpacking the Meso-economic Environment

Given the need to understand the dynamics of new value creation, we use the evolutionary economics paradigm in order to understand the key drivers which shape the commercialisation of science and technology-enabled innovation. In doing so, we are trying to make explicit all the key forces which can enable or discourage this process. Our objective is to have a practical working model of the commercialisation environment, which can be used to understand how the key vectors operate. We then translate this understanding into a set of tools which can used to support the commercialisation process.

Figure 1 shows the working model for the science and technology commercialisation environment we have developed over the last decade, based on empirical evidence across different geographies, market spaces, and technologies.

The influence of the macro-economic environment is largely reflected in the ideological balance between the importance of the public and private

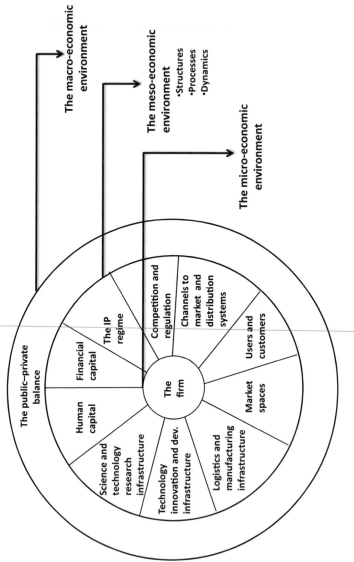

Figure 1:   The Meso-economic Environment.

sectors: this affects the overall climate for all the drivers in the meso-economic environment, especially in financial capital, market spaces, competition, and regulation. As we have noted in the discussions about economic paradigms, the shape and resilience of the commercialisation environment depends on the ideological backdrop. The prevailing political mantra sets this tone, whether it is an unrestrained free-market environment or where the state controls key elements of resource allocation in society. In specific terms, we need to understand the relative expected contributions of the public vs private sector, and also how public–private partnerships affect the climate for commercialisation. Tax-based incentives are clearly a part of this equation, but the attitude to risk is also important; for example, economists have commented on the difficulties where returns on capital are privatised while the risks are socialised.[39,40]

In practical terms, the meso-economic environment is shaped by 10 key components in the meso-economic layer: availability of financial and human capital, the science and technology *research infrastructure*, the infrastructure for technology *development and innovation*, the manufacturing and logistics infrastructure, the structure of market spaces, the behaviour of users and customers, channels to market and distribution systems, competition and regulation, and the regime for managing intellectual property (IP).

The provision of financial capital is a critical part of the overall environment. This not only includes diversity in the potential sources of funding, but also how this funding is made available at different stages of the commercialisation journey: we discuss this in more detail in Chapter 15, but appropriate funding is a key component of a successful environment.

The availability of human capital with the right skills is critical: while educational institutions have developed great expertise in imparting analytical skills, especially in science and technology, many environments lack the skills required for the *synthesis* of new ideas. Linked to the availability of skilled human capital is the need for a deep pool of experienced entrepreneurial talent with the right mindset and experience, which requires a vibrant industrial or consulting sector.

Access to skilled human capital and a pool of experienced entrepreneurs are not sufficient on their own: what is needed is a system which generates ideas and IP of sufficient quality and depth. In practice, this means the system must be capable of supporting strong basic and applied research, coupled with an IP regime which protects and enables this to be properly exploited. Science and technology innovation and the generation of intellectual capital are not sufficient: the meso-environment also needs to provide product and service innovation infrastructure and the ability to deploy and test new products and services.

The infrastructure required to support scientific and technical *research* is linked to but distinct from the infrastructure necessary for the *innovative development* of new products and services. The research infrastructure needs to provide the right environment and financial support for the generation of new thinking and ideas; as a result, it cannot easily be justified by reference to specific and existing market applications. In contrast, the translation of these ideas needs an infrastructure which supports the development of new products and services. Unfortunately, this fundamental difference between research and development activity is often ignored: conflating the two activities can lead to confusion as we can see in the professed remits of many national 'innovation' agencies. We explore this in more detail in Part IV of this book, where we discuss the translation journey in some detail.

The logistics infrastructure in a market space provides a key component of the overall meso-environment which supports science and technology commercialisation. This infrastructure also includes the provision of manufacturing, transport and communications resources, which typically depend on the attitude of the state to the balance between public and private provision.

The market space is a fundamental part of any commercialisation activity, in particular, how markets are structured, new value chains and the roles of the players within the market space. One of the big challenges is in understanding how market spaces are changing and morphing, sometimes as a result of science and technology-enabled innovation, for example, in new digital markets. We will discuss this in more detail later.

This leads us directly to users and customers: how they are segmented, their mindsets in terms of how they buy and consume new products and services, how they can be reached, in terms of the structure, capacity and effectiveness of distribution channels. We will be addressing the central role of customers in the commercialisation process in the next chapter.

Channels to market and related distribution systems can be important dynamic components of the meso-economic environment, since they can constrain or accelerate the deployment of new products and services.

Market spaces provide a useful framework for analysing the overall competitive environment, types of competitors, and how they can impact the success of a new product or service. How the market is regulated can have a significant impact on the trajectory and pace of commercialisation, especially where the role of state investment is critical for enabling infra-structure, for example, in the provision of communication networks.

Finally, the regime for managing and regulating IP is a key component of the meso-economic environment; we discuss this in more detail in Chapter 14.

2.4 Dominant Paradigms

We are acutely conscious that the firms in our research data, which covers the period from 1995 to 2015, have largely operated under conditions shaped by the pseudo-neo-liberal agenda discussed previously.

Most of the firms in the US and Europe have been shaped by this agenda. The main exceptions to this rule include firms in renewal energy and biosciences, particularly in the US, whose early growth has been supported by significant investment by the state in basic and applied technology development.

Firms in some parts of Europe have benefited from more systematic support based on public funding, both at national level and at the pan-European level. Despite the market rhetoric, the big economies in Asia and Africa have continued significant state-funded programmes to support the early stages of science and technology commercialisation, especially in China and India.

Detailed analysis of these environments is beyond the scope of this book, and in any case, the volatility of economic policies in this regard would make such an analysis difficult. We focus on the key meso-economic components discussed above and how they translate into the key vectors which affect the commercialisation journey, noting that the relative importance of these vectors can depend on the prevailing paradigm in some cases.

2.5 Translating Meso-economic Components into Vectors

Based on the meso-economic components defined above, we identify 12 key vectors which impact on the commercialisation journey for science and technology innovation-enabled firms. Ten of these vectors map directly onto the meso-economic components summarised in Figure 1. We define four vectors 'external' to the firm as follows:

The Market Spaces vector maps directly onto the market space component.

The Proposition Framing and Competitive Environment vector maps against Competition and Regulation.

The Customer Definition vector maps against the Users and Customers component in the meso-economic layer.

The Distribution, Marketing, and Sales vector maps against Channels-to-market and Distribution Systems in the meso layer.

We then define six vectors 'internal' to the firm as follows:

The Technology Development and Deployment vector maps against Science and Technology Research Infrastructure in the meso-economic layer.

The IP Management vector maps against the IP Regime in the meso layer.

The Product and Service Definition and Synthesis vector maps onto the Product and Service Innovation Infrastructure.

The Manufacturing and Assembly vector maps against the Manufacturing and Logistics Infrastructure.

The Funding and Investment vector maps against Financial Capital in the meso layer.

The Talent, Leadership, and Culture vector addresses the Human Capital component in the meso-economic layer.

Finally, we define two 'composite' vectors, covering Commercialisation Strategy and Business Models, which effectively act as the 'bridge' between the internal and external vectors, and hold the key to commercial success:

The commercialisation strategy vector effectively defines the commercial trade-off between external conditions and the internal response of the firm. We discuss this in Chapter 12.

The business models vector is linked to commercialisation strategy and is the key to creating commercially sustainable products and services and hence firms. We discuss this in detail in Chapters 4 and 13.

Chapter 3

The Triple Chasm Model

3.1 Theories of the Firm and Growth Metrics

Given the importance of science and technology-enabled commercialisation, there is great interest in understanding the key metrics describing how firms grow, especially from policy makers and investors. Entrepreneurs and start-ups are typically much more interested in the process and potential interventions as they try to manage risk at the level of the firm.

Unfortunately, most research at the level of the firm is based on data from well-established firms in stable markets and focused on transaction cost economics, organisation of the firm, and access to resources and capabilities[41–44]: there has been little structured analysis of the *commercialisation journey,* as firms grow from an initial idea to become serious market players. Evolutionary economists have started to look at more dynamic models for the firm,[45–47] but most of this work is still at a relatively abstract level.

There is a significant volume of research which looks at the *aggregate* behaviour of emerging science and technology firms, at regional and national levels, which is primarily of interest for policy makers. The available data can broadly be divided into two types: aggregate measures favoured by governments and intervention agencies, based on the idea of gross value added (GVA) or economic value added (EVA), or measures largely based on the role and impact of financial capital on firms over time.

While the capital-related measures can provide some indication of the progress of the firm, in reality, they are 'secondary' measures which depend on a number of other variables, and can be a poor guide to what is really happening. For example, one measure, often quoted by investors, policy makers, and even firms themselves, is the amount of capital raised by the firm along the path to growth. This secondary measure is a function not just of how the firm is developing, but depends on the market space it is in, the perceptions of investors which can vary significantly based on sentiment, and subjective perceptions of the value of the firm at any point in time based on multiple criteria. As a consequence, this measure is of limited value, since most firms actually grow through the use of internal resources (typically 1–2% of technology firms receive venture capital funding).[48]

The other favoured metric is the valuation of the firm based on the judgment of 'the market'.[49] This can be a notoriously unreliable measure, since most of the firms are still a long way from listing on markets which can validate the valuations. These valuations are at best the *opinions* of investors who may have a vested interest in the number. We will be discussing this later in Chapter 15.

3.2 Putting the Customer at the Heart of Our Analysis

Given these difficulties, when we started analysing how science and technology firms grow and what metrics we could use to characterise this growth, we realised that measuring how *customer numbers grow, at the level of the firm,* provided a powerful primary metric for assessing the development trajectory of a firm. We also realised, as we discuss later, that this data provided a strong basis for comparing the performance both of firms in the same market space and firms in different market spaces. This approach also allowed us to understand the relative importance of other variables, such as technology readiness and funding, in changing the trajectory of the firm. Subjective metrics such as company valuation then rightfully take their place as descriptors of the outcome of decisions based on tangible actions, rather than driving the process.

We need to add an important qualification here: we define customers in this context as customers for a single definable product or service, not aggregate customers for a portfolio of products. In practice, the growth in customers may be quite different for different types of products. For example, customer growth numbers and the timescales for take-up can be very different for the different products in the product range of a typical consumer electronics company. In practice, this matters little because most early stage firms are focused around a single product or service innovation. Where we deal with firms launching families of products early in their commercialisation journey, we divide the data into separate components for analysis. In practical terms, we also segregate the data where a firm radically changes its strategy from selling to consumers to selling to other firms: clearly in this situation, we are looking at quite different behaviour. We discuss the performance of multi-product firms in Chapter 20.

Much of the analysis and the insights in this book are the consequence of placing the customer at the heart of our analysis: this approach allows us to evaluate the development of firms in a variety of market spaces across the world and also to draw conclusions independent of any particular ideologies about the role of private vs public investment, except to the extent that this can become one of the factors affecting the performance of the firm.

The research for this book spanned the period 1995–2015, covering different technologies, many different market spaces and around 300 firms in Europe, North America, and Asia. In virtually all cases, we collected both quantitative and qualitative data to support our analysis and insights. In all cases, the primary quantitative data was based on measuring customer numbers.

3.3 The Three Chasms

Our initial examination of customer growth data in the media and entertainment, software, systems and computational tools, and telecommunications market spaces showed three significant discontinuities in customer growth numbers. When we extended this to studying data from firms in other market spaces, including engineering and healthcare, we saw the same qualitative pattern where customer growth appeared to stall at three different points as firms grew.

When we ran a series of focus groups, round tables and other industry fora, we were surprised to discover that most executives confirmed that these patterns resonated with them. Broadly speaking, these three discontinuities in the growth of customers appeared to relate to three distinct points in the growth of the firm: the transition from a concept to a working prototype, the creation of a product or service with a sustainable business model, and the point at which early success was translated into building serious scale in customer numbers.

The first discontinuity did not surprise us, given our experience with a wide range of technology start-ups over the last three decades. When we looked at the third discontinuity in more detail, we realised that this was something that Moore had talked about in his book, *Crossing the Chasm*,[50] without providing much empirical evidence at the time. The existence of the second, middle discontinuity surprised us and started us thinking about the need for more detailed insights into this phase of a firm's growth, which had been previously ignored and buried in dark descriptions of the 'valley of death', a singularly unhelpful metaphor.

Drawing on Moore's approach, we decided to adopt the term 'Chasms' to define these three discontinuities. We believe the use of this word is justified on two counts.

Firstly, the chasms correspond to periods when the number of new customers added falls steeply as others have also noted,[51,52] often to zero, which shows up visually as a 'chasm' when the number of customers added is plotted against time; in a plot of cumulative customer numbers against time, the equivalent visual representation is a 'saddle'. This behaviour is illustrated in Figure 2, which is taken from real data for one of the firms in our data set.

We also believe the idea of a chasm provides a powerful *metaphor* to describe the challenges of crossing this gap. Later in the book, we discuss the concept of vectors, which describes the variables that can be adjusted to improve the chances of crossing a chasm, much in the way that a climber or runner needs to optimise their strategies for overcoming gaps and hurdles in their path.

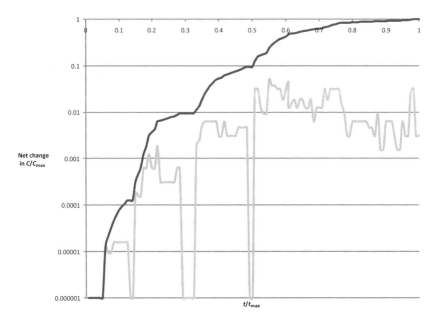

Figure 2: **Characterising Chasms.**

Following from the above, we formally define the three chasms firms need to cross in their commercialisation journeys as follows:

Chasm I: This describes the transition from the product or service concept to a working prototype.

Chasm II: This describes the transition from an early product or service to a fully functional product or service with a commercially sustainable business model.

Chasm III: This describes the transition from early customers to the main body of customers as the firm scales significantly.

Our early empirical insights into the existence of the three chasms led us to a more critical examination of previous work on the importance of diffusion theory when looking at science and technology-enabled innovation. We discuss this in Section 3.4.

3.4 Empirical Generalisations and Diffusion Theory

As we tried to make sense of the empirical data that we have been collecting over the last 20 years, we looked at two different ways of modelling our data: agent-based modelling techniques and aggregate-level diffusion models. Agent-based models, for example Monte Carlo methods, typically need large data sets and were harder to validate. Although diffusion models can provide less direct insights into key drivers, they typically need less data and can provide good overall insights. More importantly, we realised that the diffusion theory-based approach pioneered by Rogers, Bass and others, coupled with treating customer growth as a primary variable, provides a powerful way to understand how science and technology-enabled innovation is commercialised.

In his seminal work in 1942, Schumpeter first talked about creative destruction and the potential to use diffusion theory to understand how ideas are commercialised. The first quasi-quantitative treatment of this was provided by Rogers in 1962,[53] when he suggested that market adoption of new ideas, based on the number of customers, could be described by the diffusion equation: he suggested that this take-up could be represented by a normal distribution. Rogers also proposed that there were five categories of adopters: the different categories were represented by one and two standard deviations on either side of the peak for the normal distribution. This work still provides the basis for the simple model used by technology marketers where the five categories are referred to as innovators, early adopters, the early majority, the late majority and laggards, but the Rogers classification rested on the assumption that the rate of innovation remains constant with time, which is manifestly not true.

The theoretical model to represent cumulative distribution of adoption over time for new products was first presented by Bass in 1969.[54] Bass relied on diffusion theory to model the timing of adoption that leads to a specific S-shaped growth pattern for new technologies or products. Bass did not concern himself with the underlying processes that generate this shape of take-up but provided some empirical data in support of this model.

Since the publication of the Bass model, there have been hundreds of papers and real-world applications of this model with refinements, extensions and applications, supported in many cases with empirical data from a range of industries. Mahajan *et al.*[55] reviewed and attempted to classify this broad data set in 2010. There are three observations in their review that particularly interest us, given that we have adopted a similar approach: most of the published work related to market growth following take-off with little interest in the earlier phases of growth; the market data showed some evidence of 'saddles', where customer addition either slowed significantly or stopped for a period of time, suggestive of Moore's postulation of a chasm at the point before significant scaling; the data suggested some potentially significant patterns in the way in which values of the internal and external diffusion coefficients changed with product or service maturity.

3.5 Our Approach to Data Modelling

Our earlier insights into the presence of these chasms, where customer growth stalls for a period of time at various points in the growth of the firm, led us to systematically analyse the customer data we had gathered in the course of our work with a wide range of firms at different stages of their growth.

Our data covered firms in 12 market spaces which we discuss in detail later: media and entertainment; telecommunications; software, systems and computational tools; electronics and computing hardware; aerospace engineering; automotive engineering; oil and gas engineering; healthcare services, medical devices and regenerative medicine; red, white, green and blue biotechnology; energy and lighting; financial and information technologies and services; and education, skills, recruitment, and training.

In all these market spaces, our data covered four different types of customers: businesses, governments, consumers, and knowledge workers with appropriate business models. Typically, firms with business-to-business (b2b) business models had smaller customer numbers than firms with business-to-consumer (b2c) business models. Our data also showed

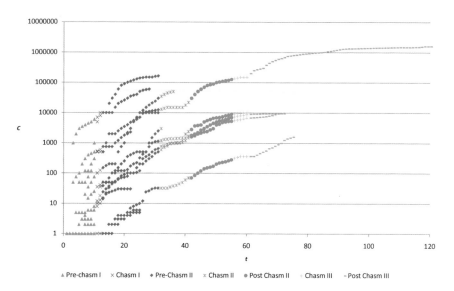

Figure 3:   Customer Growth for Media and Entertainment Market Space.

variations in the length of time required to reach the maximum number of cumulative customers, which we discuss in Chapter 5.

Figure 3 shows how the cumulative number of customers, C, varies with time, t, for a number of firms in the media and entertainment market space; we discuss different market spaces in Chapter 5. The customer numbers on the y-axis are plotted on a log scale: they clearly show that the overall pattern of behaviour is the same, both for firms with small numbers of business customers and for firms with much larger numbers of consumers, albeit with different growth timescales. Our data displayed similar behaviour across a wide range of market spaces, which provided the basis for generalising our results, as discussed later in this chapter.

Our data harvesting activity was constrained by several factors: it was not always possible to follow the entire progression of a firm from idea to maturity, given that firms started at different times; some of the firms we monitored failed at one of the chasms, usually Chasm II (more on this later), and the overall timescales varied significantly with market space, so some of the firms in the media and entertainment market space went from idea to maturity in 3–4 years, while for some engineering firms, the time to maturity could be 12–15 years.

When we first started with this programme of research, we speculated on how significant the effects of market space and geographic location would be on any conclusions we could draw, for example, is the behaviour of media and entertainment firms in the US significantly different from that of similar firms in China? As we examined the data, we rapidly came to the conclusion that the geographic location of the firm was less important than the prevailing paradigm in the market space, so that all firms showed broadly similar behaviour with noticeable differences restricted to the overall timescales for maturity.

Based on the factors discussed above, we decided to aggregate all the data for media and entertainment firms into a single data set. In order to do this, we needed to normalise the data to take account of the wide variations in the absolute number of customers in a firm and the different times taken to reach maturity by different firms.

For customer numbers, we normalised the data by computing the ratio of the cumulative number of customers, C, at any point in time to the maximum cumulative number of customers achieved by the firm at maturity, C_{max}. For the time axis, we used the same approach, where we computed the ratio of the actual time, t, to the total time required by the firm to reach maturity, t_{max}. This resulted in normalised values of C/C_{max} in the range from 0 to 1.0 and normalised values of t/t_{max} in the range from 0 to 1.0.

Figure 4 shows the results of our normalised data for the media and entertainment market space based on the same raw data presented in Figure 3: this illustrates the point that normalising the data in this way allows the behaviour of firms to be represented by a single curve.

Quite early in our analysis, we realised that the success of this normalisation approach depended on the accuracy with which we *estimated* C_{max} and t_{max}, given that the precise values of these variables could not always be measured. The availability of other collateral data on technology adoption, firm valuation, and industry dynamics, for example from proxies, helped us to make reasonable estimates for C_{max} and t_{max}. Mahajan, in his major review paper referred to above, also commented on the importance of estimating C_{max} and t_{max} correctly, where marketers are using this approach to plan their activities.

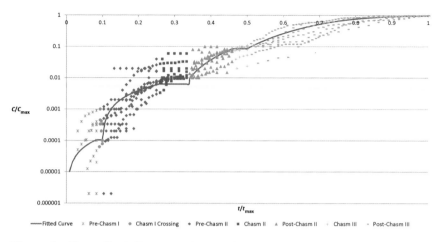

Figure 4: Normalised Customer Growth for Media and Entertainment Market Space.

3.6 The Triple Chasm Model

Detailed examination of our data suggested that we could generalise our approach to describe the behaviour of *all* science and technology firms in a single composite view. As a result of this assessment, we decided to aggregate all the data, covering different market spaces, geographies and technologies into a single data set where we could explore the generic challenges facing all science and technology firms.

The aggregate normalised data revealed seven different segments of behaviour. Three of these segments covered the three chasms, of variable duration. Chasm I was the shortest, in terms of elapsed time, followed by Chasm III. Chasm II was the longest duration chasm as Table 3 illustrates. These differences in the duration for each chasm confirmed the anecdotal evidence from the firms participating in our qualitative research, which suggested that the challenge of establishing a viable business model to underpin the sale of products to customers is a key factor that contributes to the extended duration of Chasm II.

The other four segments in our aggregate model covered the time period before crossing Chasm I, the time period between Chasms I and II, the time period between Chasms II and III, and the time period post Chasm III until the maximum number of customers is reached.

Table 3: Typical Duration of Chasms.

Segment	t/t_{max} Start	t/t_{max} End	Duration
Chasm I crossing	0.09	0.1	0.01
Chasm II crossing	0.26	0.34	0.08
Chasm III crossing	0.46	0.50	0.04

Taking our cue from the Bass approach to diffusion modelling dis-cussed above, we modelled the last three of these segments using the formulation below:

The probability of customer adoption at time t given that adoption has not yet occurred $= v_e + v_i \times$ (*cumulative fraction* of adopters at time t).

If $f(t)$ is the probability of customer adoption at time t and $F(t)$ is the cumulative customer distribution, then this proposition can be writ-ten as

$$f(t)/\{1-F(t)\} = v_e + v_i F(t).$$

This approach of course reflects the fact that adoption behaviour var-ies across the different stages of the commercialisation journey and that the trajectory over time depends on the impact of the coefficients, v_e and v_i, which we define as the external and internal influences, respectively, on adoption behaviour.

For all three segments described above, the curve fitting was based on solving the diffusion equation: the values of v_i and v_e were computed to get the best fit as reflected by the r^2 correlation coefficient based on using the portion of the overall solution based on the estimated values of t_{max} and C_{max}.

Table 4 shows how the values of v_i and v_e vary across the different chasms. In particular, they highlight the consistent increase in the external coefficient, v_e, as commercialisation proceeds, consistent with increased awareness of the new product or service in the market. The results also highlight the significant increase in the internal coefficient v_i across Chasm II, consistent with the significant resources required to cross

Table 4:   **Variation in Diffusion Coefficients Across Chasms.**

Segment	t/t_{max} Start	t/t_{max} End	v_e	v_i
Pre-Chasm I	0	0.09	0.00001	0.009
Transition from Chasm I to II	0.1	0.26	0.0003	0.009
Transition from Chasm II to III	0.34	0.46	0.0025	0.08
From Chasm III to max customers	0.50	1.0	0.005	0.08

Chasm II. Figures 5 and 6 illustrate the results of this multi-segment curve fitting approach for the aggregate data set. They confirm a number of key findings of our research.

Science and technonology innovation-enabled firms all display similar patterns of behaviour irrespective of the precise area of technology under consideration: they all exhibit three significant discontinuities or chasms in the growth curve where customer growth stalls for a period of time.

The *shapes* of the diffusion theory-based curves change as the chasms are crossed; these shape changes are reflected in changing values of v_e and v_i across the chasms. Changes in the 'external' coefficient v_e are a reflection of the changes in the customer environment, representing in

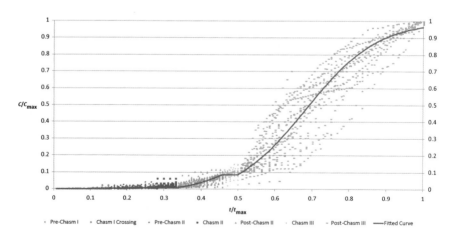

Figure 5:   The Triple Chasm Model (Linear-Linear Axes).

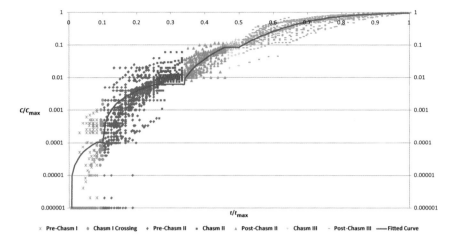

Figure 6:   The Triple Chasm Model (Log-Linear Axes).

particular the heterogeneity in customers; this is consistent with the observations of Rogers, Bass, and others. Changes in the 'internal' coefficent v_i are a reflection of the inputs required in order to facilitate chasm crossing; in practice, this includes changes in technology readiness, deployment tactics, investment, management, and other resources deployed by the firm.

While firms in different geographies and different market spaces take different lengths of time to achieve maturity, the time taken to reach a particular point, expressed as a ratio of the total time to maturity, fits into a similar and predictable range for all firms: the values of t/t_{max} at Chasms I, II and III are roughly the same for all firms.

The modelling activity raised a number of interesting questions about how the value of v_e and v_i varies with time, the nature and duration of the chasms, and the implications for potential interventions at the chasms. This is discussed in Chapter 4.

3.7 The Triple Chasm Model vs Rogers and Bass

The general consensus based on the work of Rogers, and those building on his work, is that the commercialisation of innovation is a continuous diffusion process. Rogers assumed that the rate of innovation remains constant across the whole journey, which is manifestly not true; Bass extended this treatment, introducing two diffusion parameters, which govern the external and internal forces driving the rate of innovation. Our results reveal that the diffusion process is not continuous but has three important discontinuities across which the diffusion parameters can change.

Rogers postulated different customer categories along the commercialisation journey, which have become part of marketing wisdom: innovators, early adopters, and the early majority. Our results show no evidence of this kind of customer segmentation. Instead, our results reveal different customer behaviours consistent with the three chasms: the first customers help validate early product or service prototypes in crossing Chasm I; crossing Chasm II involves signing up Charter Customers who help substantiate the business model; crossing Chasm III leads to mainstream customers.

Rogers, Bass, and others following in this tradition all overestimate the rate of customer growth in the early stages of commercialisation. At the point at which Chasm II has been crossed, our results show that the number of cumulative customers corresponds to *roughly 1% of the total*, much smaller than the numbers projected by both Rogers and Bass. Around Chasm III, where the mainstream market can be accessed, this figure rises to 10% *of cumulative customers*, compared to Rogers and Bass who suggest figures between 40% and 50% for the number of cumulative customers.

More critically, since it impacts time to market, our data show that, in general, *only* 10% of all customers are signed up *after* 50% of the commercialisation journey is complete! Rogers suggests that 50% of customers are signed up after 50% of the journey is complete; Bass suggests the customer numbers are slightly less than the Rogers prediction.

Figure 7 summarises these differences by comparing the variation in C/C_{max} vs t/t_{max}, as predicted by the simple Rogers model, the Bass model and data, and the data underpinned by the Triple Chasm Model.

Both Rogers and Bass are overly optimistic when projecting early growth in customer numbers. Our data suggest that all science and

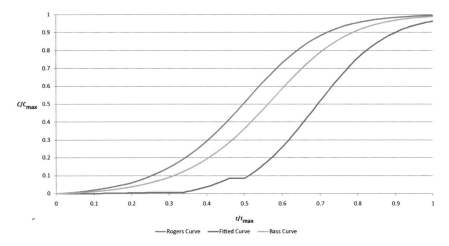

Figure 7: **Rogers, Bass, and the Triple Chasm Model.**

technology-enabled firms take a lot longer to achieve meaningful early traction than has been generally assumed; this clearly has implications for the level of resources required for success.

We explore the practical implications of this for the growth of science and technology firms in the next chapter.

Chapter 4

Chasm-crossing and Commercialisation Vectors

4.1 Defining Vectors

Vectors are usually defined either as a force with magnitude and direction or more generally as a quantity with more than one element. We define commercialisation vectors in the latter spirit, so that we can articulate the forces affecting the commercialisation process.

We define a commercialisation vector as a quantity consisting of several individual sub-vectors. For example, the commercialisation vector for Technology Development and Deployment consists of the following sub-vectors: commercialisation options, base vs application technologies, technology platforms, applications and tools, integrated products, and contingent technology deployment which compares deployment options.

We extend this approach to define 12 commercialisation vectors, and their sub-vectors, which together enable the finer granularity of analysis, required to model and understand the commercialisation process. The vectors and sub-vectors are discussed in detail in Chapters 5–16. Figure 8 shows the complete set of vectors: we group these into *internal* and *external* vectors, as follows, consistent with the aggregate internal and external diffusion coefficients v_i and v_e discussed in Chapter 3, and two additional

Vectors	Sub-vectors
Overall commercial management	
	Commercial proposition overview
	Maturity assessment
	Multiple propositions
Market spaces	
	Defining market spaces
	Market space-centric value chains
	Chasms vs market spaces
	Characteristic times vs market spaces
Proposition framing and competition	
	Proposition framing
	Competition
	Partners and suppliers
	Regulation
Customer definition	
	Customer typologies
	Consumers
	Affinity and knowledge-centric users
	Businesses
	Market sizing
Distribution, marketing, and sales	
	Go-to-market key issues
	Channels to market
	Positioning, branding, promotion
	Service-centric delivery
Commercialisation strategy	
	Strategic ecology
	Weighting-based priorities
	Priorities vs maturity
	Managing disruptive changes
Business model development	
	Architecture
	Components
	Revenue models
	Business model metrics
Ip management	
	General ip issues
	Ip typology for S&T firms
	Ip maturity management
	Ip mngt for market spaces
Manufacturing and assembly	
	Manufacturing unpacked
	Scaling for manufacture
	Process innovation
	Integrated manufacturing delivery
Product definition and synthesis	
	Synthesis unpacked
	Voice-of-the-customer approaches
	Technology-mapping approaches
	New approaches to synthesis
	Proposition deconstruction
	Service definition
Tech. development and deployment	
	Commercialisation options
	Base vs application technologies
	Technology platforms
	Application and tools
	Products and services
	Managing technology deployment
Talent, leadership, and culture	
	Talent and entrepreneurial intensity
	Teams and roles
	Org structure and management
	Leadership
	Culture, behaviours, and rewards
Funding and investment	
	Sources of funding
	Funding vs maturity
	Early stage funding
	Venture capital
	Customer funding
	Firm valuation

Figure 8: The 12 Vectors and Sub-vectors.

composite vectors, which effectively describe the trade-offs between the internal and external vectors.

The *external* vectors are as follows:

Market Spaces: This vector is concerned with understanding the target market space for the idea under development. This means we need to understand the overall shape of the market space, the key players in the space, their roles, and where the opportunities are for new products and services. In particular, it requires a clear formulation of the market space-centric value chain. We discuss our approach to defining market spaces in Chapter 5.

Proposition Framing and Competitive Environment: Probably, the most critical vector when it comes to commercialising technology-based innovation is framing the overall customer proposition in the context of the competitive and regulatory environment defined by the market space. This focuses on understanding the gaps in current provision, thinking about where new products and services can be deployed, and the strategy for the value added by the new proposition delivered to the end-customer. We also need to understand the typical timescales for introducing new ideas into this market space. We discuss this in detail in Chapter 6.

Customer Definition: The customer vector involves a clear understanding of customer typologies, in particular, the types of customers to be targeted: consumers, affinity and knowledge-centric groups, businesses or government. We can then refine the overall customer proposition, which in turn enables us to estimate the size of the potential market. We need to understand the different ways of profiling consumers and how they buy and use products. For affinity and knowledge centric groups, we need to understand the potential difference between the buying customer and the actual user. The behaviour of business customers is usually strongly shaped by the size, complexity and position of the firm in the market space. We discuss our approach in Chapter 7.

Distribution, Marketing, and Sales: We need to understand how the new product or service is taken to market, including positioning, branding, channels, promotion, partners, and methods of distribution. This also includes pricing, margin structures and how commercial yield is managed. Many science and technology-enabled firms do not commit sufficient resources to understanding, developing and executing go-to-market plans: enthusiasm alone is not sufficient for taking new ideas to market. We discuss our approach in Chapter 11.

The *internal* vectors are as follows:

Technology Development and Deployment: This vector is clearly at the heart of science and technology innovation-enabled firms, but includes an understanding of base vs application technologies, as discussed in Chapter 1, technology platforms, applications and tools, integrated products and the options for technology deployment. There are many ways to commercialise new technologies, and part of the challenge is in understanding the key attributes of interest for potential customers, which is not always obvious. The key development issues, including technology readiness, and deployment options are discussed in Chapter 8.

Product and Service Definition and Synthesis: Most scientists, technologists, and engineers are trained in the analytical tradition, not in synthesis, so this is a critical vector, where the product proposition for customers is clearly defined and the corresponding service proposition is clearly set out. This is probably the biggest challenge for science and technology-enabled innovation because there are multiple ways to encapsulate the technology and to package it into the right product and service envelope. We discuss this in detail in Chapter 9.

Manufacturing and Assembly: Some technologies, for example, in digital content, face relatively simple manufacturing challenges such as replication and packaging; however, many technologies need to address the manufacturing and assembly challenges of getting products into the marketplace. This vector addresses a number of key issues: scaling technologies for manufacturing, innovations in manufacturing processes, supply chains, and integrated approaches to design, simulation and manufacturing. We explore this in Chapter 10.

Intellectual Property Management: Intellectual property (IP) creation, management and exploitation are critical for the successful exploitation of any new innovation. In addition to the generic IP management challenges, we need to understand and apply a broader definition of the sources of IP value. Firms also need to understand how the IP management priorities can change with firm maturity. We discuss this in Chapter 14.

Talent, Leadership, and Culture: This is a critical vector because the success of any commercialisation depends on the quality and effectiveness of the human resources, not just in technology but particularly in product management, marketing and sales. Technology firms need to understand how the required talent, core competences, composition of teams, leadership and culture need to develop as firms grow; this can be difficult in the face of sometimes ill-judged interventions from investors who may not always understand the challenges specific to technology firms. We discuss our approach in Chapter 16.

Funding and Investment: As discussed earlier, capital is one of the critical vectors in the commercialisation process, although not with the primacy that some neo-liberal economists might claim. We are particularly concerned with the form and timing of this vector in the context of the three chasms. As we will discuss later in Chapter 15, there are many types of potential investment and it is important to separate the rhetoric from the reality when dealing with potential investors and also understanding their investment rationale, including the timing of potential returns.

The *composite* vectors are as follows:

Commercialisation Strategy: Most approaches to the development of commercial strategy over the last 30 years have focused either on market positioning or resources and capabilities; these approaches have also been applied mainly to large firms in relatively stable markets. Given our interest in rapidly growing firms in dynamic markets, this is a critical vector for us, which addresses the trade-offs between the internal and external vectors. We discuss our approach to this challenge in Chapter 12.

Business Models: This is a critical vector often ignored by science and technology-enabled firms, partly because it acts at the interface between internal and external vectors. The business model fundamentally determines how the product or service is sold, managed and serviced, the commercial viability of any proposition, and its sustainability. For most new technology-enabled products and services, there is a wide range of potential business models which depend on the market space, the customer, the 'distribution' of value across the market space value chain, and cost and speed to market. Understanding the business model ecology in terms of target customers and channels is critical: often, multiple iterations are required before a sustainable business model can be implemented. We discuss our approach in Chapter 13.

4.2 Relative Importance of Vectors when Crossing Chasms

One of the key drivers for our research was to understand the relative importance of the commercialisation vectors at different points in the commercialisation journey.

We started by conducting in-depth discussions with leaders in the firms who provided most of our customer data in order to understand their views on the key vectors and obstacles for their firms as they tried to grow. Our research then enabled these qualitative insights to be underpinned by quantitative data by generating aggregate scores which allowed us to understand the relative importance of the vectors at each of the three chasms. This in turn led to the development of the Workbench described in Chapter 21 of this book, which provides practical guidance for firms along the commercialisation pathway.

Figure 9 summarises our findings. Chasm II represents the broadest challenge with the need to address all 12 vectors. This analysis was corroborated by the anecdotal evidence we gathered subsequently in the sessions we conducted with leaders of a very wide range of science and technology firms in many geographic locations across the world.

Our research clearly shows that the relative importance of the vectors changes across the three chasms. When crossing Chasm I, the most important vectors are Proposition Framing and Technology Development and Deployment, which shape the transition from concept to prototype. At this stage of development, the other vectors are less important, which clearly has implications for resource deployment priorities.

Empirical Data on Chasm Intervention

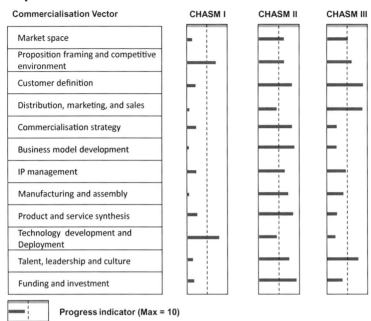

Figure 9:   Relative Importance of Vectors Across the Chasms.

Chasm II is a critical part of the journey and requires attention to all the vectors. Although the technology vector is now less important, all the other vectors need to be addressed in parallel. This is manifestly the most complex part of the journey: this is where the highest proportion of technology firms fail, which we discuss later.

When crossing Chasm III, the relative importance of the vectors changes again. Customer segmentation, distribution, marketing and sales activities take centre stage at this point as the primary focus moves to customer scale-up.

Given the change in relative complexity, the risk of failure is very high around Chasm II, which means the funding sources at this point are critical. Unfortunately, as we will discuss later in Chapter 15, there is a gap between the rhetoric and reality when it comes to investor attitudes, especially around Chasm II.

4.3 Diffusion Modelling and Vectors

As we noted in Chapter 3, previous work on analysing customer growth based on diffusion theory has largely focused on the later stages of the commercialisation process. However, the published data provides some evidence of systematic variation in the values of the diffusion coefficients with customer numbers.[56–61] In analysing our data, we were particularly interested in the variation of the diffusion coefficients v_e and v_i at the early stages of commercialisation, and to understand whether this variation could be linked to the commercialisation vectors.

The diffusion theory-based curve fitting approach to our data led us to the conclusion that the aggregate behaviour of the vectors can be represented by the diffusion coefficients v_e and v_i in the Triple Chasm Model, as shown in Table 5.

The impact of the first four market space-centric external vectors is represented by the coefficient v_e; the aggregate effect of the other six internal vectors is represented by the coefficient v_i. The relative importance of these 10 vectors in crossing each of the three chasms, as discussed above, is reflected by changes in the values of v_e and v_i across the chasms.

The diffusion parameter v_e, encapsulates the four vectors external to the firm, covering market spaces, proposition framing and the competitive environment, customer definition, and distribution, marketing and sales. The value of v_e grows steadily as the commercialisation progresses. In particular, the value of v_e increases 30 times on crossing Chasm I; across Chasm II, the value increases by over eight times; and the value of v_e doubles on crossing Chasm III. The parameter v_e effectively governs the slope of the customer growth curve, so these findings are very valuable in helping firms to understand their relative maturity on the commercialisation journey and hence the challenges they face.

The diffusion parameter, v_i encapsulates the six vectors internal to the firm, covering IP management, manufacturing and assembly, product and service definition and synthesis, technology development and deployment, talent, leadership, and culture, and funding and investment. This parameter does not grow significantly across Chasms I and III, but the value of v_i increases by about nine times across Chasm II. This is

Table 5: Variation in v_e and v_i Across the Three Chasms.

Vector	Diffusion Coefficient	Pre-Chasm I	Chasm I	Pre-Chasm II	Chasm II	Pre-Chasm III	Chasm III	Post-Chasm III
Market spaces								
Proposition framing								
Customer definition	v_e	0.00001		0.0003		0.0025		0.005
Distribution, marketing, and sales								
IP management								
Manufacturing and assembly								
Product and service synthesis	v_i	0.009		0.009		0.08		0.08
Technology development and deployment								
Human capital								
Funding and investment								

consistent with the qualitative evidence that internal interventions are critical at Chasm II.

Given how the parameters v_e and v_i control the conditions which affect the growth trajectory, we can see the importance of actively 'driving' the appropriate vectors to increase the likelihood of commercial success, rather than accepting that this is the natural order of things, and succumbing to passive metaphors such as the 'valley of death'. These results highlight the critical importance of the internal vectors for successful commercialisation.

4.4 Crossing Chasm I

Crossing Chasm I is the first hurdle for all science and technology entrepreneurs. The challenges of stimulating innovation and generating new conceptual ideas should not be underestimated: indeed, there are many parts of the world where this starting point is particularly problematic, partly because of historic underinvestment in building science and technology and innovation capacity. Even in environments where the innovation infrastructure is strong, the Chasm I challenge can present a major hurdle. In our experience, there is rarely a shortage of innovative ideas: the big challenge is in turning them into something viable, even when the generation of new ideas and testing of prototypes can be done relatively quickly and cheaply.

Our results show that, at Chasm I, the biggest focus needs to be on the technology itself combined with framing the overall proposition in the context of the competitive environment. Understanding potential customers and defining the product in outline terms can also be important at this stage. The other vectors are much less critical at this stage, provided there is a sufficient supply of innovative ideas. In particular, external funding at this stage is less important than some popular perceptions would suggest, *provided there is investment in research activity prior to tackling Chasm I.*

Given the small teams usually deployed at Chasm I, issues of organisational structure and leadership are rarely an issue, but a culture which nurtures the talent required to invent new ideas and innovate to create new value is critical at this point.

Funding requirements at this stage are relatively small compared to the next stages of the commercialisation journey.

4.5 Crossing Chasm II

Our evidence points to Chasm II being the most complex part of the commercialisation journey for two main reasons: there is insufficient understanding of the existence of this chasm and how it impedes growth, partly because of the popular narrative centred on subjective notions about how commercialism happens, and Chasm II also corresponds to the highest area of commercial risk, which is reflected in the reluctance of most investors to fund firms at this stage.

This difficulty is reflected in the importance of all the vectors at this point in the commercialisation journey, starting with the need to understand the market space into which the new product or service will be deployed. Framing the proposition more precisely in the competitive and regulatory environment, in particular, where it fits into the market space value chain, can be critical for crossing Chasm II.

It is also important at this point to define customers more precisely and to understand the relative importance of different types of customers especially if the proposition has wide potential, which can often be the case for science and technology-enabled innovation. This in turn can provide better insights into go-to-market strategies and tactics, in particular, the broader issues around manufacturing and deployment, direct vs indirect business models, the role of channels and the nature of distribution networks.

Technology development and IP management are important at Chasm II, but the most critical task is shaping and packaging the right product or service, which can often involve multiple iterations and requires the support of patient funding. For some types of products, the manufacturing and assembly vector can also be very important. The product or service iteration in virtually all cases also includes development of the right business model: even when the product or service is stable, it can take several iterations of the business model and usually involves several rounds of market testing. This can be a real challenge as the popular notion is that firms develop a clear view of this upfront and may at most need a single alternative, as for example, Mullins *et al.*[62] suggest, before they get this right. In our experience, it can take five or six iterations of the business model before a viable approach emerges.

Chasm II usually requires specific talent and leadership, organised in the right kind of teams, distinct from Chasm I, where structure is less important. In particular, dealing with multiple vectors in parallel requires close attention to processes and roles. This is different from Chasm III, where the organisational structure and leadership is more in keeping with that typically projected in classical theories of the firm.

Probably the most problematic challenge in crossing Chasm II is the funding and investment challenge. Unfortunately, this high risk part of the commercialisation process is poorly supported: the rhetoric of venture capital (VC) is rarely matched by the reality; most financial investors actually want to invest post Chasm II, as their term-sheets make only too clear, and yet, many firms spend (waste) a lot of time and resources in their usually fruitless search for VC. We discuss this in more detail in Chapter 15.

4.6 Crossing Chasm III

Once Chasm II has been crossed, the Chasm III challenge is primarily a scaling one, with success dependent on clarity of objectives, understanding and focusing on the right priorities, and deploying the right level and volume of resources.

Crossing Chasm III requires precise definition of target customers and users; this involves understanding user behaviour and product adoption in detail and tuning the marketing and sales messages appropriately.

The go-to-market tactics are critical at this stage, focused on manufacturing and packaging optimisation, the development of channels to market, including negotiating the right distribution deals and incentives, and product and services promotion.

Talent, leadership, and culture of the firm becomes critical for success now and requires detailed attention to organisational structure, teams and how they are organised and motivated; in particular, it is critical that marketing and sales teams are adequately resourced and organised effectively.

Investment is less of an issue now, unlike Chasm II, because working capital is easier to obtain with clear evidence of commercial traction.

These insights from the Triple Chasm Model have enabled us to design a set of practical tools aggregated into a Workbench to help firms to increase the likelihood of crossing all chasms successfully. We discuss this later in Chapter 21.

Part II

Customers, Propositions, and Synthesis

Chapter 5

Market Spaces

5.1 Limitations of Conventional Market Segmentation

The conventional approach to quantifying markets depends on market segmentation based on several criteria including geography, demographics, psychographics, and customer behaviour.[63–65] While this approach can provide useful data on the overall structure and size of a market it does not always provide sufficient insight into the real nature of the opportunity. In particular, the dramatic escalation in the number and range of new technologies creates problems with using conventional segmentation and market measurement techniques[66,67] for science and technology-enabled innovation. The OECD *Frascati* classification scheme for technologies, which we discussed in Chapter 1, faces a similar challenge, which is why it is subject to regular revision, but the problem remains: conventional approaches to market segmentation are inadequate when it comes to understanding science and technology commercialisation.

Conventional methods may not adequately describe market segments based on end-users because *technology often creates new categories of activity*. For example, how do you distinguish between markets for biotechnology-enabled products and services targeted at plant, animal and human targets, which have all historically been part of entirely different industries? Do we treat these as distinct markets when it may make more sense to treat them in a new aggregate category?

Market segmentation typically *reflects existing industry value chains*, so that firms in current delivery systems are seen as being part of that segment. How do we deal with new firms which radically reshape value chains but may be active across multiple conventional markets? For example, communications technology firms may impact markets in telecommunications, energy, lighting, and healthcare: how do we decide which market category they are best associated with?

Digital technologies have dramatically blurred the boundaries between market segments. For example, media, publishing, and telecommunications firms are now competing for the same customers, sometimes with the same product sets. Should a new digital media firm be seen as a content firm or a telecommunications firm in terms of market segments? This lack of clarity even allows some investors to classify social media network firms as technology firms when they are simply users of ubiquitous technology products also used by other firms across the entire marketplace.

The *move from products to services, with different business models,* also creates difficulties in using conventional market segmentation. For example, innovative new firms may provide technology-enabled services to firms active in both healthcare and publishing markets. In this case, which market segment do we assign them to?

So, why does this matter to us? How marketers overcome these classification challenges is beyond the scope of this book, but we need ways to characterise the qualitative and quantitative nature of potential markets for new products and services based on new technologies. In particular, we need a practical and consistent approach which enables us to *understand the relative importance of the major factors* at work in the market spaces of interest to us.

5.2 Defining Market Spaces

Our practical solution to this problem is based on defining *market spaces*, which enables us to group firms into categories which display *common structures, processes and dynamics,* in the spirit of the meso-economic approach described in Chapter 2. This should enable us to understand the challenges of commercialising science and technology-enabled firms in a more structured way.

Our approach to defining market spaces consists of the following elements:

We start with historical definitions of markets based on conventional 'homogeneous' approaches to market segmentation.

We then adopt a 'heterogeneous' approach to market definition by identifying all the key players relevant in this market: this includes typical players derived from conventional segmentation; we then add players from 'adjacent' market segments, who are now active in the new market space; and finally, we add the new or emergent players who did not previously exist, but are active in enabling new functionality, new products and services, and new business models.

We define new market space-centric value chains which incorporate the heterogeneous approach discussed above and the changing, or completely new, value relationships between the players who constitute the market space.

The new market spaces typically encompass a broad range of potential customer types and relationships: business customers, consumers, 'knowledge users', business-to-business-to-consumer (b2b2c) relationships, and governments as customers, for example, in defence.

They also typically support a range of business models for products, services and extended support, for example, software as a service propositions.

This approach allows customer overlaps to be handled systematically, so that the same customers can be assigned to different market spaces; for example, some customers may appear in both the media and entertainment market and healthcare market spaces, depending on the thematic focus.

5.3 Market Space-centric Value Chains

Porter[68] first introduced the concept of value chains in 1985 with a strong focus on the firm and its relationship with suppliers and customers. This *firm-centric value chain* has been used extensively to understand the structure and organisation of well-established firms. It has been particularly useful in analysing situations where the firm operates in a well-established market and the locus of interest is internal to the firm. The approach has been extended over the last three decades to create *supply-chain-centric value chains*, where the wider market environment around the firm can be modelled. It has been particularly helpful, for example, when looking at firms which provide product or service components to other firms, outsource some functions, or operate in cross-border environments: but it is still largely a view which places the firm at the centre of the analysis.[69–71]

Firm-centric value chains have several important limitations: because they are centred on the firm, they usually present a static, 'backward-looking' historic perspective on the role of the firm within the *existing* market space; this means that the processes and roles are defined by the existing paradigm, which reduces their potential value in understanding how technology or other factors can generate new processes and new players; they also provide limited insight into the reshaping of relationships with existing and new players and the creation of new business models. In summary, firm-centric value chains are of limited value when exploring science and technology-based innovation, especially where there is large potential for radical change.

Our response to this challenge has been to develop market space-centric value chains, which start from an *external* perspective, first visualising the new broader set of processes and the relationships between them. We then identify potential roles for players in this new market space, which can be fulfilled by existing players, new players, or players who can morph to fulfil new and different roles. This approach allows us to identify gaps, potential opportunities, competitors and threats; it can also provide insights into future commercial, resource and regulatory challenges. We illustrate this approach to market space-centric value chains by looking at the media and entertainment market space, as shown in Figure 10.

This highlights how a market space-centric value chain can provide insights into markets which are not available from conventional market segmentation: for example, players previously active in the devices space now need to understand and be involved in content-management, advertising and payment systems, with different customers, business models and

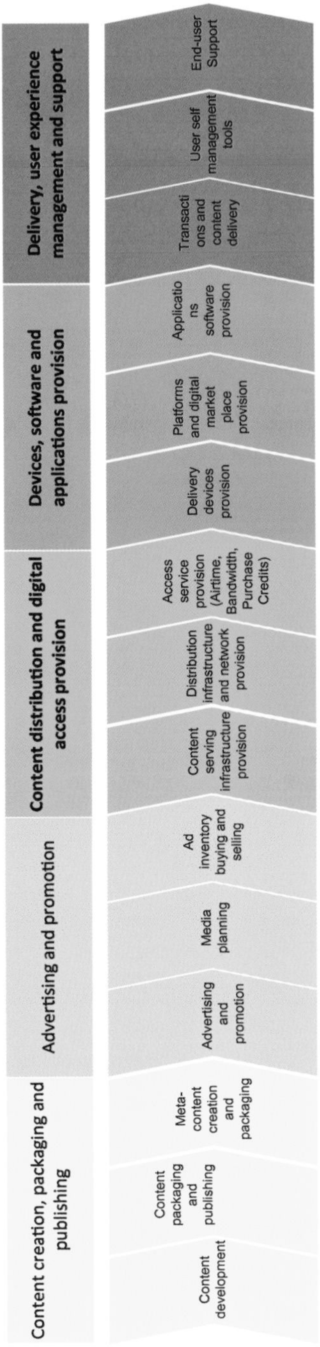

Figure 10: Value Chain for Media and Entertainment Market Space.

partners; telecommunication firms now need to provide different products and services and manage different customer relationships; firms need to make strategic decisions about where in the value chain they focus their energies and where they partner; and some firms may take on roles where they manage end-to-end-customer relationships without having a major technology-based position in any single part of the overall value chain.

This complexity is not restricted to the media and entertainment market space. For example, new market space-centric value chains in healthcare services can show even more complexity. We have observed and mapped this behaviour in all the market spaces studied during our research: we provide further details in the Workbench summarised in Chapter 21.

5.4 Key Market Spaces

Our experiences over the last decade have led us to segment the firms in our data set into 12 different market spaces where we have systematically studied science and technology-enabled innovation: this grouping is largely based on key relationships, behavioural similarities and continuity with historic market segments, as discussed earlier in this chapter. We describe these 12 market spaces below:

Media and entertainment

This market space includes all the firms involved in the creation, distribution and delivery of content and related services: firms involved in the conventional market segments of radio, television, film, and advertising; all digital forms of static and dynamic content; electronic delivery devices; new content formats; meta-content management and delivery; mobile and internet-based content; and interactive products and services, including gaming. Digital technologies have had a dramatic impact on the shaping of this market space.

Telecommunications

The telecommunications market space includes a wide range of communications technologies, including digital radio, internet technologies, devices such as cells, hubs, routers and switches, network management technologies, and signalling protocols. While there is a close relationship between the media and entertainment and telecommunications market spaces, we treat them separately because the level of technology complexity, development timescales, and deployment issues result in important differences between these two market spaces.

Software, systems and computational tools

While software, systems and computing technologies play major roles in many other market spaces, we treat them distinctly because they constitute a major market space in their own right. For example, new software languages and tools may be applied in the media and gaming industries or in energy and lighting. We also include firms creating computational tools in this category, for example, analytics engines, which can be used in customer profiling by media firms or by energy firms to manage usage. New software operating systems and applications software are also included in this grouping, but firmware is grouped with electronics and computing hardware.

Electronics and computing hardware

The electronics and computing hardware market space includes firms involved in creating new display technologies, computing platforms, architectures and chipsets and also includes firms providing specialised hardware used in the design and manufacture of these, for example, new lithographic techniques. This space includes new forms of data sensing, storage and processing elements. This is also the market space where firms in the emerging quantum engineering area will eventually be located. We specifically exclude application-specific devices from this category, for example, assigning firms working on glucose monitoring devices to the healthcare market space, even though they clearly include electronic hardware and software elements.

Aerospace engineering

This market space covers all those firms involved in the design and manufacture of airborne platforms and the ground-based operations needed to sustain these platforms; it also covers the firms in the extensive supply chains which provide the wide range of technologies and services required, including, for example, materials, aerostructures, propulsion systems and avionics. Historically, this space has been characterised by the dominance of a relatively small number of very large players, but our research revealed the emergence of many smaller players providing smaller lower cost platforms such as nanosatellites and unmanned aerial vehicles.

Automotive engineering

The automotive market space covers all ground-based transportation including different types of vehicles and the wider infrastructure which supports their deployment and use; it also covers the extensive supply chains necessary for their design, manufacture, and operation. This space is similar to aerospace engineering, but the market space-centric value chain shows a much wider group of players with less concentration of power and influence in the hands of a small group of very large players. This space is also likely to change more dramatically with the introduction of electric vehicle propulsion technologies.

Oil and gas engineering

The oil and gas market space consists of a number of areas typical of the extractive industries, covering upstream areas concerned with exploration and extraction and downstream areas concerned with processing and refining; it also includes the larger supply chains which cover specialist areas such as sub-sea engineering, drilling, and monitoring. It is not clear what the future shape of this market space will be, given the pressures on fossil-fuel use, but it is currently a major market area.

Healthcare services

The healthcare services market space includes firms involved in the diagnosis, therapy and monitoring of human health. This category includes a wide range of firms involved in primary, secondary and tertiary healthcare, including medical devices, drug delivery and regenerative medicine.

It also includes firms involved in the delivery and management of clinical practice, including for example, new m-health services, prescription management, and healthcare insurance management systems. This market space is being radically transformed by the emergence of personalised medicine enabled by developments in, for example, gene therapy and synthetic biology.

Biotechnology

The biotechnology market space covers four different types of biotechnologies and includes firms which usually cover one, or sometimes several, of the following areas:

- **'Red' biotechnology**, which covers medical processes and organisms which produce new drugs, or new gene-based therapies: for example, using stem cells to regenerate damaged human tissues and perhaps regrow entire organs.
- **'White' biotechnology**, which covers new bioprocess-based industrial processes: for example, the production of new chemicals or the development of new biofuels for vehicles.
- **'Green' biotechnology**, which includes the development of pest-resistant grains or the accelerated evolution of disease-resistant animals: for example, in secondary agriculture, sometimes referred to as livestock; it also includes nutraceuticals and environmental applications.
- **'Blue' biotechnology**, which builds on processes typically found in marine and aquatic environments; for example, using algae to control the proliferation of noxious water-borne organisms, or to generate small amounts of energy.

Biotechnology market space-centric value chains have developed dramatically over the last decade, as lab-scale trials are converted to commercially scalable processes.

Energy and lighting

The energy and lighting market space covers all aspects of the generation, storage, distribution, use and management of energy, often combined with lighting products, services and solutions. This space is changing significantly, as micro-generation, especially from renewable energy sources, takes off and energy storage and distribution management become more sophisticated. Firms in this space have to navigate relationships with new types of emerging players, as previously monolithic value chains are rapidly disaggregated.

Financial services

The financial services market space is moving rapidly from highly integrated, often large, monolithic environments to a much more distributed environment which involves digital transactions: e-commerce players have already transformed the retail industry; new firms are emerging dealing in micro-payments, real-time transactions, trust management, and an expanding need for sophisticated information services, including managing meta-transactions based on large volumes of data and metadata. Electronic currencies are part of this space and will require re-engineered value chains

Education, skills, and learning

The education and skills market space has changed rapidly with the move from 'physical' to electronic delivery and 'blended learning', which is changing the market space-centric value chain with the emergence of completely new players. This space includes all aspects of the skill management process, including skill assessment, skill development, education, recruitment and training: for example, it includes firms involved in scaling delivery mechanisms and the design and deployment of new business models.

5.5 Chasm Behaviour Across Market Spaces

The aggregate Triple Chasm Model results discussed in Chapter 3 showed that the behaviour of all firms, irrespective of the market space, can be generalised into a single overall model provided that customer adoption and timing data is normalised in an appropriate way.

Previous research has identified systematic variations in the behaviour of firms from different market spaces.[72–82] We used our large normalised data set to establish the presence of the three chasms for different market spaces, to explore any systematic variations in the location and duration of each chasm, and to assess any significant variations in the diffusion coefficients v_e and v_i across the chasms for data from different market spaces.

We concluded that, to the level of accuracy of our data, the multi-segment curve fitted to the composite data from all market spaces was a good fit for the data sets from each of the 12 market spaces. In all cases, there was clear evidence of the three chasms, and the locations of the three chasms were approximately the same for all market spaces in terms of the values of t/t_{max}. The duration of Chasm II appeared to be slightly longer for some market spaces, especially in healthcare and biotechnology. We speculated whether this was due to more complex regulatory hurdles at Chasm II for these market spaces, but the volume of our data did not justify any detailed assessment of this behaviour, given that it appeared to be a relatively small effect.

5.6 Comparing Timescales for Different Market Spaces

The normalised cumulative customer data for the different market spaces showed very little variation across the different market spaces. The actual time series data, however, showed significant variation in the time, t_{max}, required to reach the maximum number of cumulative customers C_{max}, although the *relative* positions of the chasms, as a % of the total time, t_{max}, remained roughly constant.

Our data showed significant differences in t_{max} across the 12 different market spaces: this 'time to maturity' is clearly a function of the market space. We define this as the *Characteristic Time*, which is the *mean* time to reach the maximum number of cumulative customers for all the firms in our data set for each market space. These mean values provide useful insights into how long it takes to build successful firms in different market spaces.

Figure 11 shows the differences in the characteristic times for the 12 market spaces in our data set.

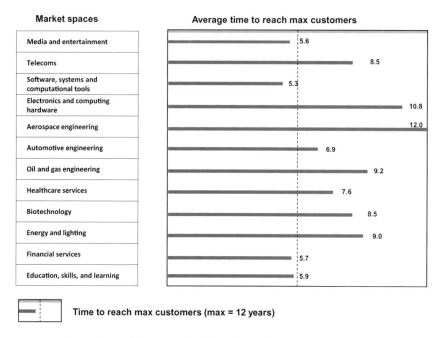

Figure 11:   **Characteristic Times for Different Market Spaces.**

The characteristic time has important implications for all those involved in building science and technology-based firms because of the resources required to build these firms. In particular, this can have a very big impact on the attitudes of investors. It also means that firms operating in market spaces with longer characteristic times need to be addressing larger potential markets to justify the increased resources required. In this context, it is not surprising that the mean time taken to reach maximum customer numbers for media and entertainment and financial services firms is half that typically required by electronics and hardware firms: this partly explains investor interest in media, software, education and learning and financial services firms. It is also worth noting that telecommunications firms take longer to reach maturity, on average, than media firms: it is harder to build the infrastructure to move data than it is to create the data. We discuss the practical implications of these differences in our Workbench, using case studies from different market spaces.

Chapter 6

Proposition Framing
and the Competitive Environment

6.1 Proposition Framing

Moving from general market definition to estimating the potential market in a structured way requires the customer proposition to be framed explicitly. As discussed previously in Chapter 5, market space-centric value chains provide a powerful way to frame the overall commercial proposition for science and technology-enabled firms.

Figure 12 illustrates how the media and entertainment market space-centric value chain can be used to frame products and services for a smartphone device provider. This approach to framing not only allows the device provider to focus on its core competences, to understand other players in the market space, their roles and positioning, and the opportunities and challenges associated with offering new products and services. It also enables firms to understand if and how they can provide a wider range of products and services, or change their positioning radically: for example, device manufacturers can use this to assess the potential for becoming providers of content-based services.

The approach can be applied to a wide range of market spaces, particularly where technology is changing the nature of products, services and business models: for example, in the generation, distribution and delivery of renewable energy products and services or the delivery of new therapeutic interventions in healthcare. Some of the most disruptive

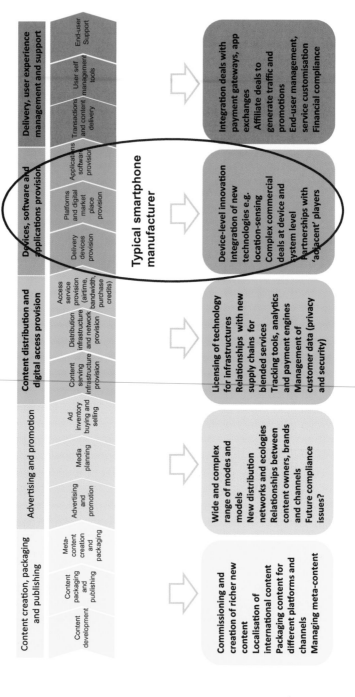

Figure 12: Proposition Framing in the Media and Entertainment Market Space.

innovations often depend on changing the frame of reference: the new framing can dramatically influence the business model more than the direct impact of a new technology. Market space-centric value chains for a range of market spaces are discussed in the Workbench summarised in Chapter 21.

6.2 The Competitive Landscape

Taking a new product or service to market requires clarity about the broader commercial environment, in particular, the potential competition and an understanding of any regulatory constraints. This is critical for a wide range of market spaces from telecommunications to biotechnology and healthcare.[83,84]

We use the same market space-centric value chains introduced in Chapter 5, and used for proposition framing above, as the basis for conducting this analysis. Our overall approach consists of the following elements.

We first build the relevant market space-centric value chain for the new product or service. We then populate this value chain with all the key players active or potentially active in this space. Finally, we examine this 'populated' value chain from three different perspectives: market drivers, technology drivers, and regulatory drivers.

We illustrate how this approach works by way of an example using the media and entertainment market space-centric value chain. The example shown in Figure 13 is a *composite* view based on a number of new products and services from different firms in the media and entertainment market space, so we can illustrate the power of this approach. In practice, of course, a single firm will typically be mapped into a smaller number of areas, but this approach can enable them to understand exactly where they play relative to others in the market space.

Specifically, this approach can help identify potential customers, suppliers, partners, competitors, and barriers to entry. This kind of 'framing' is the key to using value chains to shape strategic thinking and decision-making and to define the resources and capabilities required to compete effectively.

Value chain groups (top banner):

Content creation, packaging and publishing			Advertising and promotion			Content distribution and digital access provision			Devices, software and applications provision			Delivery, user experience management and support		
Content development	Content packaging and publishing	Meta-content creation and packaging	Advertising and promotion	Media planning	Ad inventory buying and selling	Content serving infrastructure provision	Distribution infrastructure and network provision	Access service provision (airtime bandwidth, purchase credits)	Delivery devices provision	Platforms and digital market place provision	Applications software provision	Transactions and content delivery	User self management tools	End user Support
Market drivers →														
New content players				New intermediaries			New entrants	Pricing pressures			Potential lockout from majors			Pay-per-view
Technology drivers →														
Content format management		Cross-channel EPG			Ad inventory management		Fixed mobile convergence	FTTC and Hybrids, devices		Multi-device O/S		User management tools	Subscription manager	
Regulatory drivers →														
Sports rights		Navigation for premium content		ASA compliance		Release window management		Spectrum licensing			Third party carriage requirements	Transaction handling		

Figure 13: Market, Technology and Regulatory Drivers — *Composite View for the Media and Entertainment Market Space.*

Specific features worth observing in this particular example include the following:

Market Drivers: Positioning and roles of new content creators, new intermediaries, and new distribution players; changes in the behaviour of users as they 'consume' new services.

Technology Drivers: In this market space, new content and meta-content formatting approaches, new data transmission techniques, platforms and infrastructures, and new payment technologies have the potential to redraw the competitive landscape.

Regulatory Drivers: Regulations governing data storage, transmission and delivery, including the licensing and allocation of radio spectrum for distribution, rules around privacy and cyber-security, and regulations around content copyright and advertising.

Our research showed similar but different impacts in other market spaces; for example, the energy and lighting market space has complex market drivers based on the tension between market forces and the principle of universal access, which also has strong regulatory implications.

We discuss the broader applicability of this approach in the Workbench summarised in Chapter 21.

6.3 Sources of Competitive Differentiation

The approach to framing propositions and mapping competition and regulation onto the same market space-centric value chain provides a powerful way of shaping and refining new products and services. It also provides useful insights into three different aspects of competitive differentiation for new products.

Differentiation based on focusing on a single or on adjacent parts of the value chain

New products and services can be differentiated on the basis that they provide new or different *functionality*, the way or *form* in which this is provided, whether this functionality is delivered more *effectively,* or whether it is provided more *efficiently.*

For example, a new type of medical diagnostic product may measure a property not previously measured, or may do it differently (for example non-intrusively), or do it more efficiently so that it does not require specialist staff to operate the equipment, or it may do this at a lower cost.

This is consistent with conventional ways of describing product or service differentiation.

Differentiation based on overall value chain impact

Competitive differentiation of this kind depends on the product or service occupying *new or broader parts of the value chain*, the effect of which is to deliver integrated functionality for users and customers, often with improved effectiveness and efficiency.

For example, smart phone providers can provide additional services such as music on the phone or enable real-time mapping and navigation services using the same device. This can be used to differentiate the core product from competitors who do not provide these additional services.

The ultimate expression of this kind of competitive differentiation, of course, is for the new product or service to assume a *gatekeeper role in the value chain*, which controls the provision of other products and services. This depends on a strategic dominance based on controlling a key part of the value chain. An obvious example of this, of course, is the role played by conditional access systems in television, where the provider can control access to content and associated services from other players, based on controlling the distribution system.

Differentiation based on reframing the value chain

The most radical competitive strategy is for a firm to effectively reframe the overall value chain which governs relationships between the various players in the market space. This can lead to the creation of new types of customers, new types of market space players and the need for new roles in this new environment. It can be used to create new products and services, new business models and to change the rules for competition.

An example of this kind of redrawing of the market space and the associated market space-centric value chain is what is happening in the energy and lighting market space: the previous market space based on concentrated power generation in conjunction with an integrated power distribution system is being supplanted by a market space in which power generation, storage and distribution are highly distributed. This is radically changing the nature and role of the firms engaged in the market space, business models and the nature of competition and regulation.

6.4 Partners, Suppliers, and Collaboration

Analysis based on market space-centric value chains provides a powerful basis for framing the overall customer proposition and the opportunities for 'co-creation' with partners and suppliers to deliver an integrated proposition for the customer. We use the same media and entertainment market space discussed earlier in this chapter to illustrate this, as shown in Figure 14.

In this scenario, customers may want the provision of an integrated product and service offering, which includes the device, content, for example, music or digital maps, and applications which provide navigation capability on the device. In addition, making this more affordable to the end-user may require the integration of advertising functionality on the device, which enables brand advertisers to effectively subsidise the provision of other services.

One strategic option for the firm providing the device in this case may be to expand its capability to provide all these services. An alternative strategic option is for the firm to collaborate with other firms with the relevant expertise to deliver the full functionality of interest to the end-user and customer. This collaboration can take two obvious forms: a partnership where the complementary firm shares in the commercial risk and reward in offering the broader service to the customer, or a more conventional supplier arrangement where the device firm procures the additional services from another firm on a commercial basis.

In some market spaces, the collaboration may be based on a mixture of partner and supplier arrangements. These arrangements may also be made between firms who are otherwise competitors, leading to situations

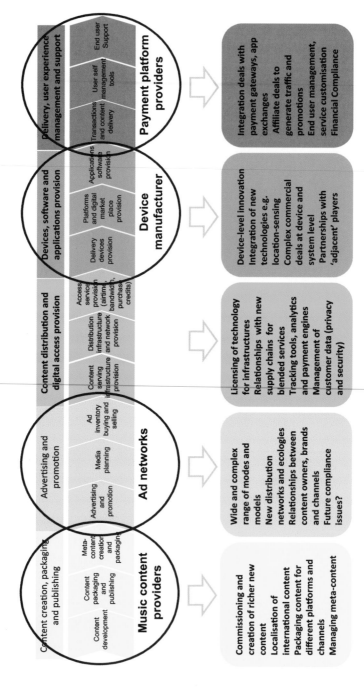

Figure 14: Partners, Suppliers, and Collaboration in the Media and Entertainment Market Space.

where the 'collaborate–compete' relationship is quite dynamic and changes with types of customers or geographic territories.

The market space-centric value chain provides a powerful generalised basis for exploring these options during the commercialisation journey for all market spaces discussed previously. We explore this in detail in the Workbench summarised in Chapter 21.

Chapter 7

Customer Definition

7.1 Typology-based Customer Targeting

We discussed the limitations arising from conventional market segmentation in Chapter 5, where we made the case for an approach based on defining market spaces more clearly. The challenge faced by many firms is that this lack of clarity often flows into customer definition and sizing. In particular, some of the firms we researched were unclear, especially early in their commercialisation journeys, about the nature of their potential customers and hence their business models. This problem has been recognised by Kotler[85] and others[86,87] in the last decade, but the challenges remain.

One of the issues facing firms built on science and technology-enabled innovation is focusing clearly on the identity of the customer for the new proposition. This is particularly difficult because the natural tendency for technology entrepreneurs is to focus on the science or technology innovation. Customer targeting depends on understanding two key parameters: the nature of the customer and the potential number of customers for a particular product or service.

Our research has identified four distinct types of customers, based on how customers *decide* to use the product or service, how they *actually use* it, how they *benefit* from it and how the product or service is *paid* for. The key aspect of interest to us in defining the customer clearly is to understand the overall environment in which the customer operates and the ultimate end-user of a product or service. This has a direct impact on the type of business model used to generate revenues from the product or service, which is discussed later in Chapter 13. We define the four customer types as follows:

Business customers are essentially firms or businesses who buy and use a product or service. These firms will typically use the product or service in a number of different ways: it may be incorporated into their own product or service or be used to run their own businesses; we discuss this in some detail later.

Governments and other related organisations are typically buying products for use in their own activities. Their buying behaviour is often characterised by a large disconnect between those making the buying decision and the actual users of the product or service. This usually leads to long purchasing timescales, and complex and sometimes opaque decision criteria; but governments can be powerful charter customers, who can facilitate the crossing of Chasm II.

Consumers are individuals who buy and use a product or service in a number of different ways, ranging from entertainment to carrying out specific tasks. In some situations, products and services used by consumers may be provided free or paid for by third parties, such as advertisers; we discuss consumer behaviour and segmentation later.

Members of knowledge or affinity-based groups or communities who use products or services based on the sharing and use of knowledge within the group. Knowledge or affinity-based users may act as individuals, but their behaviour is shaped either by a group affinity or a need to access specific knowledge. For example, a clinician in a hospital is a knowledge-based user, even though the clinician may operate in a corporate environment. Social media users in 'closed' groups also behave in a similar way.

Once we have a way of clearly defining customer types, we can estimate the number of customers for a specific product or service in order to understand the scale of the potential commercial opportunity. The data from the firms we studied enabled us to make some general observations: typically, products aimed at consumers had the largest number of customers, followed by products and services targeted at knowledge and affinity centric groups; products aimed at governments had the smallest number of aggregate customers. Typically, the 'yield' per customer was smallest for consumers, rising for knowledge-based groups and highest for business customers. This has significant implications for product design, branding and positioning, channels to market and business models, which we discuss later in the book.

Figure 15 shows the customer typology we have developed to support this characterisation. This illustrates the broad coverage for different customer types.

Typical customer numbers for the four types of customers are significantly different (note the log scale on the customer numbers axis): the key point to note is that knowledge and affinity-based users display both consumer and business user-type behaviour.

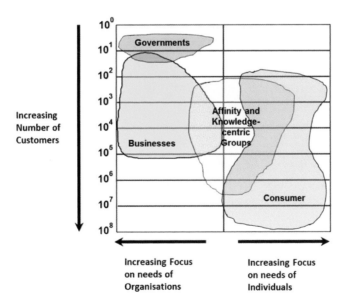

Figure 15:   Customer Typology-based Targeting.

The business models deployed with these different customer groups are usually quite different. Products and services delivered to other businesses or firms typically deploy several types of business-to-business (b2b) models; where these business customers then sell these products and services onto end consumers, the business models may reflect the business-to-business-to-consumer (b2b2c) chain.

Products and services delivered directly to consumers will deploy business-to-consumer (b2c) business models and the pricing of these services will reflect perceptions of value by the actual user of the service, for example, the purchaser of a mobile phone.

Products and services delivered to knowledge-based or affinity-centric groups of users are likely to have complex (b2k) business models because users of these products may be different from the customers who actually pay for them. For example, the users of clinical databases may be medical professionals, but payment for these services may actually come from private healthcare providers or public hospitals.

Products and services sold to governments depend on (b2g) business models, which can have very different structures, based on the end-use case. These business models may display aspects of all the other types of models discussed above.

These distinctions between the four major types of customers matter, particularly when business models depend on indirect funding, for example, based on sponsorship or advertising. These differences are discussed in detail in Chapter 13.

7.2 Consumers

The challenge firms face in understanding consumer segmentation and profiling to target customers for their products and services is not the paucity of approaches and techniques but the difficulty in deciding *which* approach to adopt when there are so many different, and sometimes conflicting, methods available. When trying to understand the challenges faced by the firms in our data set, we looked at several sources which reviewed and compared available techniques[88–92] but concluded that what science and technology-enabled firms needed at the earlier stages of commercialisation was an aggregate approach which combined the different ways of profiling consumers.

Table 6 shows our integrated approach to consumer profiling. Before discussing this integrated approach, it is worth reviewing some of the methods which have been advocated over the last decade. For a long period of time, the conventional approach to profiling consumers was based on socio-demographic categories which segmented consumers into groups based on social class and spending power. As digital technologies gained traction in the late 1990s, this was augmented by techno-demographic categories which augmented socio-demographic categories based on willingness to use new technologies. In the last decade, generational ideas of behaviour have become more prevalent, with frequent references to millennials (where unfortunately this definition can refer to individuals with a range of birth dates from 1980 to 2000, depending on the source!), Generation X and Generation Y, although it is clear that these kinds of ideas can be rather short-lived in their utility. There have also been attempts to resurrect socio-demographic categories by recasting and extending the older categories. While these different approaches can provide some useful insights, at the earlier stages of commercialization, firms need a way of profiling target customers and estimating potential markets and revenues. We describe the approach we have adopted to do this in Table 6.

Our integrated approach is based on combining three different ways of describing consumers. The first component is the weighted

Table 6:   Integrated Approach to Consumer Profiling.

Behavioural	Psychographics	Socio-demographics
Usage behaviour	Values	Demographic
Sample-based usage data	Focus groups	Age, gender, Gen X, Gen Y data
Purchase behaviour	Attitudes	Social groups
Sample-based purchase data	Focus groups	Conventional socio-demographic data
Benefits sought	Lifestyles (typical archetypes)	Geography
Survey data	VALS types	Geo-location data
Weighted behavioural average (WBA)	Weighted psychographic average (WPA)	Weighted socio-demograhic average (WSA)
Weighted aggregated consumer (WCA) profile		

socio-demographic average profile: we start with socio-demographic descriptors, which cover demographic approaches based on age, gender, and generational descriptors; we then add descriptors based on socio-demographics and then geo-location data, which is increasingly important with the wider availability of location information, especially from location-aware mobile devices.

To this first component, we add the weighted psychographic profile which integrates information on Values (derived from focus group discussions), Attitudes (also derived from focus groups) and Lifestyles (based on archetypes generated from historic consumption of similar products and services). This second component is similar to the VALS-type approach developed by Mitchell *et al.*[93]

The third component of our integrated approach is the weighted behavioural average, which is based on the behaviour of existing users or customers for similar products or services: we start with usage behaviour, then add in purchase behaviour (so we get some idea of propensity to buy) and then add in information about the typical benefits desired by the customer when making the buying decision.

We then combine these three components to create the weighted aggregate consumer profile, which enables us to estimate the potential number of customers for a particular product or service. The techniques for doing this can be found in the Commercialisation Workbench which we summarise in Chapter 21, but the key point to make here is that this approach gives us a rational technique for estimating consumer numbers.

7.3 Business Customers

Compared to the multiplicity of approaches dedicated to estimating the number of potential consumers for a product or service, little attention has been paid to systematic techniques for estimating the number of business customers.[94,95] What there is does not appear to address some of the key issues which drive usage and buying behaviour by businesses.

Based on the data from our research, we can make some general observations about business customers:

Business markets have historically been segmented into 'vertical' domains based on conventional market segments; this is being undermined by changing market spaces, as discussed in Chapter 5.

The size of a business can be a critical determinant of behaviour, especially as technology enables a dramatic rise in the number of small and medium size enterprises. The consequential fragmentation of business customers is changing the pricing and competitive landscape.

The buying behaviour of businesses is becoming more sophisticated as access to information and decision-making tools improves. In particular, *consumerisation* of business customers is likely to become a major challenge, as smaller corporates behave like quasi-consumers with similar service and pricing expectations.

Dramatic growth in technology development and deployment is creating new opportunities and threats for all businesses as market spaces and value chains are being dramatically reordered. Promotion of 'currently fashionable technologies' by suppliers can obscure the ability to understand their relevance and impact: for example, catch-all terms such as 'big data', 'cloud' and 'mobile application technologies' provide very little insight into customer numbers. Content-centric businesses especially need to understand and exploit a wide range of technologies across all parts of their value chain.

In the context of this, there are two key variables which determine how we estimate the potential size of business customers: the size of the target business customer, and the way in which the new technology, product or service is deployed by the corporate customer.

Figure 16 shows our simple model for segmenting firms by size, based on the number of employees in the firm; analysis of our data shows this is the best measure of the size of a firm because it affects the organisational behaviour of the firm, its capacity to absorb new products and services, and its ability to 'deploy' the product or service purchased. Firm size based on the number of employees is a much better indicator of the buying behaviour of a firm than its turnover or profitability.

The model shows five different categories of size-based businesses; the smallest firms, classified as micro-companies employ less than nine staff, the very largest employ more than 500 staff. This segmentation is consistent with the organisation behaviour of firms based on size,[96] which we discuss in Chapter 16.

When it comes to looking at the ways in which a product or service is deployed by a business customer, we need to understand the three different ways in which new technologies can impact business customers.

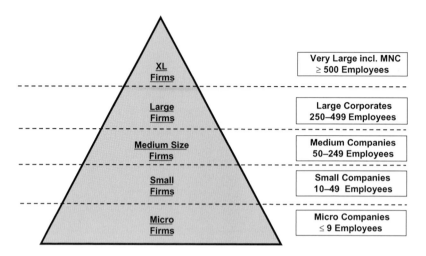

Figure 16:   Business Segmentation by Size.

In order to address this in a structured way, we need to segment all firms, irrespective of their size into three categories:

Technology firms, who integrate technologies in the products and services they supply to their customers. Good examples of this include most engineering companies, firms who make and sell mobile devices and medical device firms: all these firms are characterised by what we may describe as high levels of technology intensity in their operations.

Technology-enabled firms, with a lower level of technology integration, which do not sell products with embedded technologies, but depend critically on using technology to enable their operations. Examples of this includes e-commerce and social media firms, which are not technology firms but whose fundamental existence depends on the use of enabling technologies.

Non-technology firms, whose products and services do not have any embedded technologies, and whose existence does not depend on enabling technologies; these firms may use technologies to improve their efficiencies, for example, the use of document management systems by law firms.

It is clear that this distinction is not absolutely clear-cut and indeed some firms may straddle these categories, but it is important to understand these broad categories because it affects how they behave as customers.

When looking at the behaviour of firms as customers for technology products, we also need to understand the types of technologies these firms typically acquire. We separate technologies into three categories, based on their impact on firms:

Efficiency technologies which essentially cover process automation and improvement tasks; they are largely used inside businesses and are likely to be procured from external providers.

Pervasive technologies which affect all aspects of the function of a firm, from research, product design and sale to customer engagement. Typically, these technologies affect all parts of the value chain: mastering pervasive technologies is particularly critical for content-centric businesses.

Focal technologies affect the core or key elements of a product or service; they are typically accessible to and utilised only by specialised users.

Figure 17 shows the relationship between the types of firms discussed above and how they harness these three different types of technology.

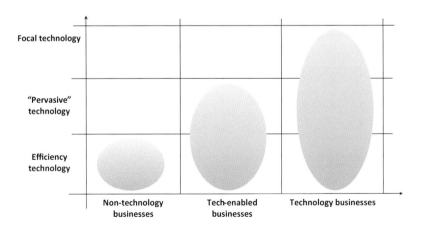

Figure 17:   Usage of Technology by Businesses.

Where firms sit in this framework can be a key factor in how they behave as business customers, including their buying behaviour, their perception of value and hence product and service pricing. We discuss this in Figure 17.

We discuss frameworks and tools for estimating customer numbers in the Workbench summarised in Chapter 21.

7.4 Affinity and Knowledge-centric Groups

Most literature has focused on consumers with some research on business customers, but there is hardly any recognition of the third type of customer in the literature. Our research shows that this is an important group of customers with attributes significantly different from consumers and businesses. Affinity and knowledge-centric customer groups display some attributes found in both consumers and businesses and also exhibit some unique characteristics. This matters in a wide range of knowledge-centric industries which have been transformed by digital technologies, for example, medical publishing, as well new affinity groups enabled by social media, such as members of private clubs or communities with business models distinct from conventional business paradigms.

There are three different types of knowledge and affinity-centric groups: knowledge and expertise-mediated groups, affinity-based groups, and hybrid groups, combining affinity and knowledge.

The knowledge and expertise mediated groups can be sub-divided into 'deep knowledge', 'practicing knowledge' and 'shallow knowledge' groups, which display the following characteristics:

Sophisticated knowledge users are moving from consuming 'data only' products to demanding 'value-added' services, as many media and technology firms in our data set have experienced.

Specialised domain knowledge remains important for knowledge users although buying behaviour is becoming simpler, and more transparent as users are empowered to buy direct from suppliers.

There is significant pressure on pricing and service levels as the number of suppliers proliferates and some large knowledge publishers make efforts to adopt 'gatekeeper' roles, and to occupy wider roles in the value chain, as we discussed in Chapter 6.

Low technology barriers to entry will enable knowledge 'gurus' to drive in the opposite direction, creating focused interactive knowledge communities.

Affinity-based groups have grown dramatically, especially as a result of digital technologies including the internet and mobile voice and data services. Customers can be grouped into three sub-categories: peer-to-peer groups, curated groups, for example, professional membership associations, and special interest groups. Many of these customers are behaving in new ways which affect service delivery, management and pricing.

Finally, we have hybrid groups, which combine the characteristics of knowledge-centric and affinity-based groups, with sub-groups characterised by their primary interest in content, transactions or special areas of interest.

Tools for profiling these customers are included in our Workbench.

7.5 Estimating Market Potential

Successful technology commercialisation depends on identifying the right markets, customer segments and building a realistic estimate of the market potential for the technology, product or service. For some technologies, the addressable market may include all four types of customers discussed above, albeit with different product and service packaging and business models. For example, audio recognition technologies have been used to provide music recognition services to consumers and also used to provide copyright management tools for businesses and organisations who want to extract maximum value from their music rights portfolios.

When it comes to estimating market potential for some technologies, the problem is that we may be trying to estimate the size of markets which do not yet exist. Where markets exist already for similar or relevant products, it is possible to use well-structured data based on actual market measurements. Where the new market is not dramatically different from current markets, we can make estimates by treating these as derivative markets, based on understanding where the key differences lie and how they might affect customer behaviour. For example, some of the early estimates for online digital content channels were based on treating them as derivatives of existing print magazine products. However, this is not always possible, especially where we are looking at the market potential of entirely new markets with no obvious proxies. For example, when in-vehicle satellite navigation systems were first created, there were no obvious parallels to guide estimation of how big this market would become, or indeed that the biggest group of customers would be individual consumers.

For all three types of markets, existing, derivative and completely new markets, our research suggests that we need a structured approach to market estimation. We present tools for doing this in the Workbench summarised in Chapter 21.

Chapter 8

Technology Development and Deployment

8.1 Characterising Technologies

The firms in our research addressed a wide range of technologies covering all the areas summarised by the *Frascati* criteria in Chapter 1. Given this technology diversity, we needed to develop a generic approach to classifying technologies, so we could explore the broader challenges of how technology is deployed, irrespective of the specific characteristics of a particular technology.

Prior to developing this generic approach, we conducted an extensive review of published work on the deployment of new technologies. There is a large body of literature on the subject of 'technology transfer' which underpins a technology transfer industry dedicated to understanding how technology is 'transferred' from research institutions and laboratories to commercial environments.[97,98] Most of this work is concerned with the generic ways in which universities, for example, can commercialise their research. We discuss this later in Chapter 14 where we address the role of IP-generating organisations and agencies in transforming technology innovation into commercial value.

However, there has been little systematic assessment of the *ways* in which technologies are subsequently deployed to generate this commercial value. Rosenberg[99] and Christensen[100] have investigated the *disruption* engendered by new technologies, but not all technology-based transformations are disruptive. There is also a small body of literature on optimising technology deployment, based on operational research methods, but it appears to be limited to technologies and firms in the information technology industry and does not present any general conclusions.[101–103]

Based on the evidence from our data, there are three broad challenges in commercialising science and technology-enabled innovation: understanding which aspects of the technology are most relevant, how these technologies are 'packaged' into usable components, and how this impacts the relevant market space.

The approach we developed and tested to address these three questions is based on the different ways in which a technology can be taken to market, as illustrated in Table 7.

We start with the initial 'building blocks' based on fundamental developments in a particular scientific or technology area, the *Base technologies*, as discussed in Chapter 1. This requires detailed understanding of the precise features and granularity of the technology under consideration. Base technologies may have applications across a wide range of market spaces, but the way in which they are 'packaged' into application technologies usually reflects the types of applications deployed in different market spaces.

Table 7:   Technology Deployment Model.

Technology Layer	Characteristics
Base technologies	Fundamental 'building blocks' with applicability across multiple market spaces
Application technologies	Aggregation of different base technologies
Platforms	Integration of different application technologies to enable new functionality
Applications and tools	Functionality aimed at end-users based on application technologies and platforms
Products	Integrated functionality for users based on base and application technologies, data, metadata and applications and tools
Services	Integration of products and associated services, including on-boarding, usage and support

The next layer in our technology deployment model is based on *Application technologies*. Application technologies are typically an aggregation of one or more base technologies with additional components which may facilitate commercial exploitation: they will usually reflect the requirements of one or more market-specific application spaces. Several application technologies can also be assembled to address specific market needs.

The *Platform* layer is often critical in deploying novel new technologies: this layer consists of platforms and infrastructures where a number of application technologies are integrated in order to provide new functionality for users in a number of different ways. This integrated functionality also enables new business models for commercialising the technology, which we discuss later in Chapter 13. The platform layer is important in most market spaces; apart from the integrated functionality it offers, it can also play an important role in hiding underlying technology complexity from users where this would be an impediment to adoption.

Users often interact with technologies at the level of *Applications and Tools*, which typically depend on an underlying platform which enables the delivery of value to end-users. The applications and tools layer depends strongly on the data and metadata associated with the application area. We discuss this in Chapter 9 when we explore the synthesis of new products and services. This layer can be particularly important in content and data-centric market spaces, where, for example, new mathematical algorithms can play a critical role.

The *Product* layer is where a new technology can be most explicitly perceived by end-users and customers, based on the functionality the product provides. Typically, in a wide range of market spaces, new technologies may form the core of a new product, for example, a new drug based on a new compound or a new display technology which enables a new form of projection system. However, as our data confirmed, frequently, a new technology may only form part of a new product, which has important implications for thinking about how technology is commercialised. We will be discussing the synthesis of new products in Chapter 9 and the business model implications in Chapter 13, but for now, we need to recognise that this is only one way in which new science or technology can be deployed.

The *Service* layer typically builds on the product layer and is specifically concerned with how technologies can be deployed to deliver services to customers. Technologies associated with services can have very wide market application: for example, algorithms associated with data visualisation or analytic tools can be applied in many market spaces, ranging from healthcare to media and entertainment, where large data sets create opportunities for analysis, inference, and interventions.

8.2 Base vs Application Technologies

The key to understanding how base technologies can be deployed for maximum impact is to understand the linkage between base and application technologies. This linkage depends strongly on the market space where the application technologies will be applied. Indeed, our data show that this coupling between base and application technologies is different, even for the same base technologies, for different market spaces: for example, a base technology concerned with computer architectures will be manifested in different application technologies when applied in media and entertainment applications vs 'smart' grids for power management.

Even within the same market space, base technologies can act in different ways to impact on different functional areas. This point is illustrated in Table 8, where we map base vs application technologies for the media and entertainment market space. It shows how a wide range of base technologies can be reflected in different application technologies. The same base technologies may be packaged differently to provide application technologies applicable to different market spaces, for example, in the energy and lighting market or in regenerative medicine. A systematic analysis of base vs application technologies, for all the market spaces which constitute our data set, is beyond the scope of this book but is included in the Workbench we summarise in Chapter 21.

8.3 Technology Platforms

Application technologies can be deployed successfully in many ways, but the ability to integrate these technologies into a coherent platform can often provide a very powerful way to deploy enhanced functionality

Table 8: **Mapping Base vs Application Technologies for Media and Entertainment Market Space.**

Base Technology	Application Technology						
	Creation, Manipulation and Packaging	Content Storage Retrieval and Management	Transaction and Customer Management	Distribution and Delivery	Usage	Research Planning and Promotion Management	Integration and Process Management
Input/output	•••	••	•	•	•••	••	•••
Processor	•••	•••	•••	••	•••	••	••
Storage	••	•••	•	•	•••	•••	••
Software languages and tools	•••	•••	•••	•	••	••	•••
Software engineering	••	•••	•••	••	••	•••	•••
Compression	•	••	••	•••	•	•	••
Encryption	•	•	•••	•••	••	•	•
Communications	•	•	•••	•••	••	••	••
Authentication	•	••	•••	•	•••	•	•
Agent technology	•	•••	•••	•	•••	••	•

Note: • Low impact, •• medium impact, ••• high impact.

for customers with a more sustainable business model. For example, some of the application technologies identified in Table 8 for the media and entertainment market space can be combined to provide a platform which enables dynamic real-time rights management for the music industry.

Integrated platforms can operate at three different levels of complexity: *integration of technology functionality* which, for example, can also enable synchronised management of content and data, *functional integration* which can deliver a wide set of functions in a seamless way, and *commercial integration* which enables functionality with an integrated business model.

In a variety of market spaces, technology deployment via platforms can create the potential for new classes of defensible, sustainable, and powerful services. The firms in our data set provided many such examples, where they were able to occupy powerful new roles in previously fragmented markets. We can illustrate this based on a platform which enables the management of loyalty schemes over multiple digital distribution channels. The platform designed for the media and entertainment market space shown in Figure 18 delivers integrated functionality to a set

Figure 18:   Platform for Multi-Channel Loyalty Programmes.

of customers who would otherwise have to use a wide range of technologies in order to achieve the same functionality.

Our Workbench summarised in Chapter 21 provides examples of firms adopting this approach across a wide range of market spaces, including for example, platforms to deliver integrated patient care in clinical settings.

8.4 Applications and Tools

Many technologies are deployed as discrete applications and tools: in fact, our data showed that this was a common way of rapidly deploying technologies in a focused and demonstrable way. A topical example of this approach, of course, is the deployment of digital technologies and content over social media platforms, where the connection with customers is more immediate and the value of the technology can be tested more quickly than by other means. However, this relies on the availability of delivery platforms provided by other players. As a consequence, our data suggested that this method of deployment is more common for technologies based on incremental improvements over existing solutions: this was rarely seen as an attractive deployment strategy for more radical technologies capable of significant disruption.

Table 9 illustrates a wide set of health-related applications and tools deployed for different types of customers. These applications and tools were developed by a large number of small firms: they used a common data set and the applications were deployed over a wide range of different platforms operated by players from several market spaces, including media and entertainment, telecommunications and healthcare services. Some of these applications were developed and deployed rapidly using publicly available delivery infrastructures; more complicated applications required the development of sophisticated algorithms and the use of specialist data sets. What this demonstrates, however, is the different ways in which applications and tools can be deployed from a commercial perspective.

8.5 Products and Services

For many firms, the ultimate expression of their technology is the creation of a new product (and less frequently a service) enabled by the

Table 9: Health-related Applications and Tools.

Products and Services	Users and Customers								
	Organisations and Businesses			Knowledge Workers			Consumers		
	Health	Education	Travel	STM	Health	Travel	TV and Film	Print	Social Media
Mobile websites	Ref info.	Surveys	Price comp.	Journals on mobile	Online/handheld reference content	Guides	Films	News	Alerts
Downloaded apps and content	Fitness tracking	Study materials	Deal alerts	Search and locate articles	Clinical apps	Mapping	Catch-up	Alerts	Update
Packaged, customised interactive services	Health advice	Tutoring, mentors	Location-based services	Online journals	Expert opinions	Travel advice	Listings and prog.	Subs	UGC, sharing and advice

technology. For firms starting with a new base technology, this involves first understanding the relationship between base and application technologies for a chosen market space, then understanding how these application technologies can be applied to different parts of the appropriate value chain in order to 'shape' the new product or service and to understand its potential commercial impact.

Creating a new product depends on the ability to integrate a wider range of components, including data and metadata; for example, a new medical diagnostic device based on a new sensing technology requires other complementary technologies such as data processing and computing technologies, plus clinical information enabling the results to be interpreted and presented in a helpful way. We discuss the challenges of synthesising new products and services later in Chapter 9, but the point we want to make here is that there are several different ways to take technologies to market, with different complexities, costs, rewards, and timescales for each approach.

8.6 Technology Deployment Strategies

Firms and innovators focused on commercialising their technologies and related concepts need to understand the different ways in which their intellectual property (IP) can be commercialised and the advantages and disadvantages of each deployment approach.

Few of the firms in our research data addressed this question systematically: most of them identified potential opportunities for their technologies in a broad market context and then proceeded to develop solutions based on their best instincts. While this approach was successful for some of these firms, there were many situations where the initial deployment strategy had to be modified once the scale and complexity of the challenge became apparent, and in some cases, the wrong choice of deployment strategy led to dramatic consequences for the firms.

Our research identified a number of broad attributes which can shape technology deployment strategies, as illustrated in Figure 19.

The *depth of technology expertise* required, relative to the other attributes, declines gradually as the deployment strategies become more market-centric.

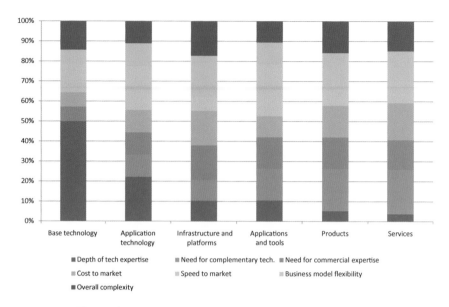

Figure 19:   Comparing Technology Deployment Strategies.

The need for *complementary technologies*: This matters very little where the commercialisation approach is based on licensing or selling the base technology directly to other firms, but increases gradually as the deployment strategy involves greater integration with other product and service components.

The need for *broader commercial expertise* is the highest for situations where platforms, products and services are delivered to end-customers: the approach requires greater affinity with the end-customers than for strategies based on selling base or application technologies.

The *cost of technology deployment* is the highest for platforms, products and services, given the need for not just complementary technologies but also the need for much broader commercial expertise.

The *speed to market* is the quickest where the technology is encapsulated in applications and tools. Deployment strategies based on complete end products and services are slower given the complexity associated with product development and packaging. Interestingly, approaches to licensing or selling base technologies are also much slower because of the need to choose the right application spaces and educate potential customers. Platform deployment typically has the slowest speed to market.

Infrastructures and platforms provide the greatest *flexibility in business models*, especially based on new service-based delivery; we discuss this in more detail in Chapter 13.

The *overall complexity* is the highest for strategies based on platforms compared to all other technology deployment strategies.

There are some important broad conclusions to be drawn from this analysis: the evidence does not support any inherent advantage based on choosing any particular strategy for technology deployment: but it shows that these choices can have significant implications, particularly in terms of cost, complexity, speed to market, and the trade-offs between risk and reward.

Making the right decisions about technology deployment strategies is particularly important where major new technologies have been developed with the potential to not just disrupt a supply chain, but to impact a number of broader areas, to significantly alter the shape of the overall market space, to change the nature and roles of players within the space, and also how they interact with each other.

The firms in our research data made different decisions based on the material conditions affecting them at different points in time. We also saw several examples of firms which changed their approach over time, driven mainly by execution and funding implications. There were several instances where firms pursued alternative approaches in parallel, for example, developing products at the same time as licensing the base and application technologies to other firms designing their own products.

Not all the firms in our research started with strong base technologies, but where they did, we saw a wide range of approaches with mixed results. For example, 3D printing has the potential to fundamentally transform the activities of materials, manufacturing and distribution firms, creating opportunities to develop new platforms, new tools and applications, and to provide new products and services. The challenge for firms in this environment was to maintain focus and to understand the practical constraints when deciding on a single or on multiple deployment strategies.

We found several examples of firms in our research who struggled with similar challenges in areas as diverse as genome sequencing techniques, plastic electronics, lighting and display technologies, and quantum engineering.

The key insights to emerge from our analysis are: firms need to match the chosen strategy to market conditions, to understand their capacity to execute based on the availability of appropriate resources, and to be aware that hubris can be a serious risk especially where firms believe they are inventing a new future.

We provide more detailed insights on contingent technology deployment strategies for different technologies and market spaces in the Workbench summarised in Chapter 21.

Chapter 9

Synthesising New Products and Services

9.1 The Synthesis Challenge

Creating new products and services can be a major challenge for scientists and technologists because their typical mindset is influenced by the analytical tradition, reinforced by an educational system which largely ignores synthesis skills. Most scientists and technologists subscribe to the narrative of continuous evolution and development of scientific knowledge in spite of the work of Kuhn *et al.*,[104,105] who recognised the importance and impact of discontinuities in knowledge paradigms.

New product and service creation needs to be rooted in a creative and entrepreneurial mindset.[106] This requires the ability to rapidly recognise and connect problems to their solutions by identification of non-obvious associations and reforming or reshaping available resources in a non-obvious way. Unfortunately, these skills can be in short supply. The ability to synthesise new products and services depends on clarity of market needs or value sought and the capability to create value, which is not part of the usual skill set for scientists and technologists. Situations where the value sought, or the value creation capability is not clearly identifiable, require creative and entrepreneurial approaches to match the two and create new value, which is even harder.

Several different approaches have been developed to tackle this challenge: we discuss these in Section 9.2.

9.2 Ideation: Approaches to Concept Generation

There are three broad approaches to generating new product and service concepts: customer-centric approaches based on the 'voice-of-the customer', technology-centric approaches based on 'technology mapping', and approaches based on synthesising customer-centric and technology centric approaches. Synthesis approaches are strongly influenced by the complexity of new and emerging market spaces, which we discussed in Chapter 5. Figure 20 compares these three approaches.

In broad terms, there are three types of techniques based on the voice-of-the-customer:

Methods based on detailed research into the behaviour of consumers. The rationale is that detailed *customer research* will yield insights into their behaviour and needs and hence guide thinking on the functions and features of new products or services; this implicitly assumes that the behaviour of existing customers can be used to represent future customers.

Approaches based on customer *focus groups* are widely used because they enable deeper insights than conventional consumer research. The effectiveness of these approaches depends on the way in which the members of the focus group are chosen and the way in which the groups are

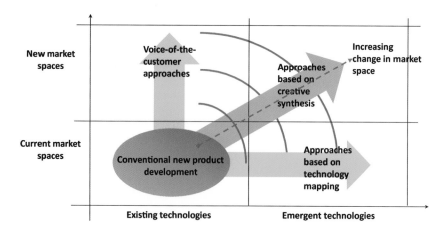

Figure 20:   Synthesising New Products and Services — Generic Approaches.

curated; for example, the level of detail provided for any concepts and how the interactions and discussions are framed.

Key user analysis relies on the idea that there are key groups of users for any product or service, and that engaging with these groups will yield the best insights on functions, features and benefits. This technique is of limited value for significantly new products where, for example, it may be very hard to identify key potential users; the technique has been quite effective in driving changes to existing products where the customers are well known.

Voice-of-the-customer approaches can be very effective where the behaviour of existing customers can be 'extrapolated' into their behaviour towards new products and services.

Approaches based on technology mapping are quite different from voice-of-the-customer approaches, since they focus on the capabilities and potential of technology to shape new products and services, in particular, new and emerging technologies which can enable new functions, features and benefits.

In broad terms, there are three types of technology-mapping approaches:

Techniques based on a strong *functional* focus, which explore how a particular technology, or a group of technologies, can enable new functionality in products and services; this functionality may be targeted at existing customers or at new customers attracted by the enhanced functionality.

Approaches with a strong *applications* focus, where technologies do not just enable new functionality but offer the potential to create new applications for customers.

Techniques based on how technologies can *impact all or parts of market space-centric value chains*, which we discussed in Chapter 5, to offer the potential for innovations greater than techniques based on functional and applications foci.

In many situations involving science and technology-based innovations, voice-of-the-customer and technology-mapping approaches are inadequate, especially where the technologies can enable significant changes to market spaces. In these situations, as Figure 20 illustrates, we need approaches which synthesise the customer and technology view points to create innovative new products and services.

There are three levels of synthesis, consistent with increasing levels of market space complexity and impact:

Outcome driven innovation championed by Ulwick[107] is built around the theory that customers buy products and services to get jobs done. The approach is based on identifying important but poorly served outcomes, with a focus on customer-desired outcomes rather than demographic profiles in order to segment markets and offer well-targeted products.

Methods based on *design thinking*, an approach initially proposed by Kelley,[108] where design thinking is used to invent, prototype and test radically new ideas, where there is not a clearly defined user need in the beginning or only a technology concept.

Creative synthesis approaches, which build on design thinking, but critically integrate potential business models with customer and technology perspectives when creating new products and services.

Table 10 summarises these different approaches to product and service concept generation.

Table 10:   Overview of Approaches to Concept Generation.

Voice-of-the-customer approaches	Customer research and insights
	Customer focus groups
	Key user analysis
Synthesis-based approaches	Outcome driven innovation
	Design thinking
	Creative synthesis
Technology mapping	Functional focus
	Applications focus
	Market ecosystem-centric value chain focus

9.3 Approaches Based on Technology Mapping

There are a number of approaches to creating new products and services based on technology mapping with a focus on either functions or applications.[109–112]

All these techniques can be quite effective, especially where the technology has a focused impact, for example, as we discussed in Chapter 7 for business customers. In some market spaces, we need a more sophisticated approach to understand and map potential technology impact when designing new products and services. We have developed and tested an approach based on mapping detailed market spaces, so we can understand the potential technology impact at a level of granularity which supports sensible product and service design. Figure 21 illustrates this approach for the media and entertainment market space, which we discussed in Chapter 5. This map shows how currently 'fashionable' technologies, such as semantic technologies and technologies associated with the internet of things, can actually impact the creation of products and services in a discernible way beyond general sentiments of their utility.

Discussion of how this approach can be applied to other market spaces can be found in the Workbench summarised in Chapter 21.

9.4 Creative Synthesis

The voice-of-the-customer and technology-mapping approaches described above provide powerful ways to think about new products and services but have been criticised for their 'mechanical' approach which underplays the importance of creativity.

There have been several attempts to understand the importance of creativity and to suggest how this could be systematically integrated into product and service design. Most of these attempts, however, have a very strong abstract focus,[113] which makes it difficult to apply them in any practical context.

There is general acceptance that new product and service creation needs to be rooted in a creative and entrepreneurial mindset. This requires

Content Creation, Manipulation & Packaging	Content Storage, Retrieval & Management	Processing & Computing Technology	Transaction & Customer Management	Research, Planning and Promotion Management	Messaging, Distribution & Delivery Technology	Usage Environments
Capture	Databases	Processing Architectures	Rights Management	Monitoring Tools	New Voice technologies	Print
Simple Synthesis	Logical Structuring & Tagging	Computing Platforms	Micro-payment Technologies	Sales and Transaction Tracking Tools	sms and derivatives	Mobile Phones & Other Personal (Wearable) Devices
Virtual Worlds	Semantic Tools	New Algorithms	Transaction Management Technologies	Analysis & Modelling Tools	e-mail and related technologies	Large format Computing Devices
Transformation	Search			Media Buying and Selling Technology	Broadcast radio & TV	New Digital Displays
Authoring	Standardisation	Simulation	Billing and Payment Systems	Promotion Management	Narrowcast including IPTV	Re-profiled Consumer Equipment
				Ad-serving Technologies	m2m technologies	
Editing & Proofing	Maintenance & Optimisation				Small cell & related technologies	Operating Systems & Tools
Resource Optimisation & Management						
Workflow technologies						
Security						
Platform Technologies						
Technology Integration Tools						

Overlay theme labels: **Very Low Cost Data**, **Semantic Technologies**, **Micro Transactions**, **Social Media**, **Mobile Devices**, **IOT**, **Virtualisation**

Figure 21: Technology Mapping Applied to Media and Entertainment Market Space.

the ability to rapidly recognise and connect problems to their solutions by identification of non-obvious associations and reforming or reshaping available resources in a non-obvious way. The ability to synthesise new products and services depends on clarity of market needs or value sought and the capability to create value. Situations where the value sought or the value creation capability is not clearly identifiable require creative and entrepreneurial approaches to match the two and create new value.

We have already described outcome-driven innovation which involves 'matching' technologies vs markets in order to develop an idea at an intermediate point between the 'impact' of these two variables, but this is only helpful in the initial formulation of a new product or service.

Design thinking has been used extensively over the last decade to provide a systematic approach to synthesis, where customer attitudes can be matched against technology capabilities, using a structured approach.[114] Although it has been suggested that design thinking can be used more broadly, for example, to design new organisations,[115] its real strengths lie in the conception and design of new products and services where solutions need to optimise customer and technology trade-offs which impact form and functionality.

If design thinking as currently applied has a weakness, it is that it does not explicitly address market spaces and business models which enable products and services. This is becoming increasingly important in some situations, for example, in new products based on the 'internet of things', where the shape of a new product or service can be determined not just by the relationship between customers and technology but also by the prevailing market space and the business model required for a commercially viable proposition.

Figure 22 shows the *creative synthesis* approach we have developed to tackle this challenge. The approach essentially combines the three drivers of new product and service synthesis: customers, technologies, and market spaces.

Details of how we apply this model can be found in our Workbench which is summarised in Chapter 21.

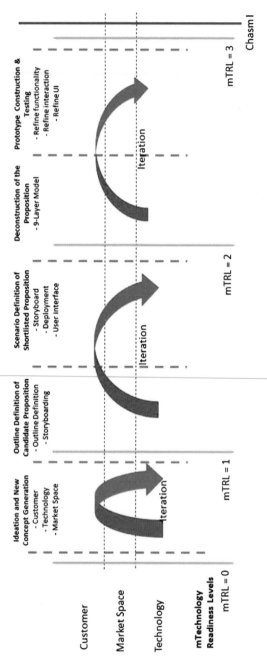

Figure 22:   **Creative Synthesis.**

9.5 The Proposition Framework

The approaches described above enable a new product and service to be synthesised at a broad proposition level, where the customer focus, the enabling technologies and the overall business model are defined. The next challenge is to look in detail at the shape of the constituent components of the product or service.

Using the data and insights from the firms in our data set, coupled with our experience over the last decade, we have developed the Proposition Framework shown in Figure 23 which enables us to 'deconstruct' a new product or proposition into the nine key components which can be used to describe it.

The Proposition Framework consists of the different technology layers, which we discussed in Chapter 8, the customer layer we discussed in Chapter 7 and layers dealing with data, or content, and metadata, linked in a cascade from base technologies all the way through to customers.

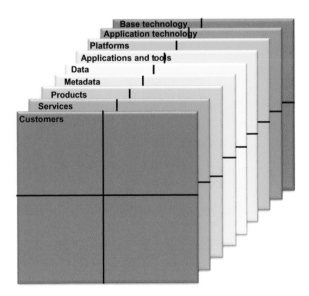

Figure 23:   The Proposition Framework.

The nine layers of this model are as follows:

Base technologies provide the 'building blocks' based on fundamental developments in a particular scientific or technology area. Base technologies may have applications across a wide range of market spaces, but the way in which they are 'packaged' into application technologies will often reflect the types of applications deployed in different areas.

Application technologies are typically an aggregation of one or more base technologies with additional components which facilitate commercial exploitation: they will usually reflect the requirements of one or more market-specific application spaces.

The **platform** layer consists of platforms where a number of application technologies are integrated in order to provide new functionality for users in a number of different ways. The platform layer is important in most market spaces.

The **applications and tools** layer depends fundamentally on data and metadata; it is particularly important in content and data-centric market spaces in a number of market spaces.

The **data** layer consists of the content, which can be manifested in a number of ways, either as highly structured data, for example clinical data describing a disease pathology, or lightly structured data such as a video feed of a musical concert.

The **metadata** layer is critical in many cases because it essentially forms a look-up table which provides a guide to the content layer; the metadata layer may also cover information, for example, which enables the functioning of a platform provided directly to customers.

The **product** layer is where a new technology can be most explicitly deployed especially in the minds of customers. New technologies may form the core of a new product, but typically, most products are an aggregation of all the layers preceding it, described above.

The **service** layer usually builds on the product layer and is specifically concerned with how technologies can be deployed to deliver services to customers; in a number of situations, however, services may be delivered to customers without any product being involved.

The **customer** layer is critical because it helps clarify who uses the product, service or component of a product or service (where the customer is an 'intermediate' firm); this layer can help illustrate the impact of focusing on consumers vs corporate customers vs knowledge-centric customers in terms of which other layers then become operative.

It is important to note that not all nine layers in this model are relevant for all products and services: in some cases, the starting point for a new idea may well be a new application or tool; in other cases, the offering may consist of metadata only, for example, an index which links to content in a different product; or in many cases, there may be no service involved, just a product consumed by an end-customer. Part of the value of this model is in understanding which components are relevant to a customer; indeed, the model can also be used to elucidate different variants of an offering for different types of customers.

The Proposition Framework is important for a number of reasons. Technology-enabled businesses need to understand the complex relationship between the different 'moving parts' captured in each of the layers. The model helps visualise the relative importance of these 'moving parts' and the key relationships between them for a particular set of products and services. It can also be used to qualitatively compare different product and service options quickly. The model shows how technologies, content and end-user services can interact to provide the qualitative basis for existing and new business models and therefore identify opportunities for future products and services.

Chapter 10

Manufacturing and Assembly

10.1 Generic Challenges

Many of the advances in manufacturing over the last two decades have been driven by advances in automation resulting in higher quality products, lower costs, better use of materials, and greater flexibility in processes and supply chains. These changes have had a greater impact on some market spaces than on others. The impact has been highest in two areas in particular: in high volume products targeted at consumers, where these changes have enabled relatively sophisticated products to be produced at very low cost utilising global supply chains, as for example, with smartphones or new drug therapies, and in the manufacture of complex products targeted at businesses, where the volumes are typically lower, but the manufacturing processes involve the integration of design and simulation technologies with materials processing and sophisticated assembly techniques, as for example, in the manufacture of new energy generation and storage products.

10.2 Manufacturing Unpacked

Detailed discussion of the generic manufacturing challenges is outside the scope of this book. Our research confirms the continuing importance of these automation-based improvements but reveals three particular areas of relevance for science and technology firms in terms of manufacturing, assembly, and packaging.

Technology scaling is critical, so that performance measured in research and development environments can be replicated in real production and delivery environments. For example, manufacturing yields in bioprocesses or materials in electronics manufacturing sometimes do not scale linearly when moving from pilot plants to full-scale manufacturing.

Adapting existing processes and designing new processes which are required to manufacture new products and services cost effectively is the second critical area technology firms need to address. In some situations, the success of a technology innovation may depend more on the ability to manufacture cost effectively rather than the technology innovation itself, a factor which is sometimes ignored by scientists and technologists.

Designing and implementing *new approaches in the logistics and deployment* of new products and services has become more important as business models move from a product orientation to providing the same functionality on a managed service basis. This clearly affects the design and management of distribution systems but can also have significant impact on manufacturing and assembly.

Table 11 shows the relative importance of these three attributes for different levels of product and service innovation. Conventional products mainly face logistic challenges, while completely new products need to address technology scaling, process innovation and logistic challenges.

Table 11:   Deconstructing Manufacturing Challenges.

Innovation Intensity	Attributes			
	Technology Scaling	Process Innovation	New Logistics	Examples
Conventional products and services	✓	✓	✓✓✓	Integrated automation, e.g., just in time
Hybrid products and services	✓	✓✓✓	✓✓✓	Application of silicon-based processing to LEDs
New products and services	✓✓✓	✓✓✓	✓✓✓	3D printing, nanomaterial processing

10.3 Scaling for Manufacture

Our research highlights the importance of technology *scaling* in a number of market spaces and associated technologies. The problem fundamentally relates to the challenge of 'reproducing' results obtained in development laboratories when it comes to production environments, sometimes because of unforeseen nonlinear effects which prevent 'extrapolation' of techniques to high volume production environments.

We observe these difficulties particularly when dealing with biological technologies or with new processes in the electronics industry. The nature of this challenge is illustrated by an example from the 'white' biotechnology industry, as shown in Figure 24.

This example shows the development of new process technology related to the creation of new chemicals from agricultural produce based on the application of different inputs, including new enzymes, to enable the transition. While this process can be demonstrated in a laboratory setting, scaling up for manufacture cannot depend on extrapolation, since the processes do not scale in a simple linear fashion. This effect is also encountered by those working on the development of new gene therapies and associated bioprocessing for healthcare therapies.

The impact of this on commercialising new technologies can be significant. In the examples we encountered in our research, the problem led to the need for further technology deployment late in the day, and in several cases also impacted the potential commercial viability of new products and services in ways that had not been anticipated. This scaling challenge is not restricted to biotechnology and healthcare market spaces.

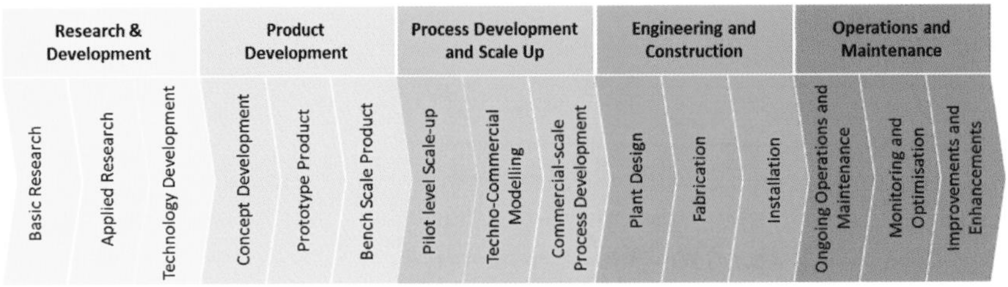

Figure 24: Technology Scaling Challenge — Example from the 'White' Biotechnology Market Space.

We also observed difficulties in technology scaling in several firms involved in building new electronics hardware and in the semiconductor industry where the commercial viability of products and services was significantly affected, when scale-up for manufacturing led to much lower manufacturing yields.

10.4 Manufacturing Process Innovation

There have been many advances in manufacturing process innovation over the last three decades in particular, with several different philosophical approaches based on common principles but emphasising slightly different outcomes, including *just-in-time* manufacture aimed at optimising the supply chain, and more recently *lean manufacturing*, focused on resource optimisation. Detailed discussion of these is beyond the scope of this book.

In our research, we looked in particular at areas where firms need to adapt or develop entirely new processes to manufacture, package or deploy a new product or service. Many firms focus strongly on the key enabling technologies but underestimate the practical challenges of creating or embedding new processes when taking their ideas to market.

We identified three different approaches to manufacturing process innovation adopted by the firms we examined in our research. The majority of firms focused on generic approaches based on *lean manufacturing*, reflecting the emphasis on resource optimisation over the last two decades.

Some of the firms in our data set adopted a *cross-fertilisation* strategy based on utilising tried and tested manufacturing approaches used in other market spaces. This enabled them to not only use proven methods but also enabled more cost-effective use of equipment originally developed for other uses with modest changes to reflect the new need: for example, adapting products and technologies used in the printing industry to effectively 'print' new solar panels for use in solar arrays. The changes involved replacing printing inks with new organic molecules used in the solar receptors but maintaining the core print engine responsible for positioning and driving the printing heads. Another example was the use of manufacturing processes originally designed for electronic chip manufacturing and assembly to manufacture new structures based on nanomaterials which can be deployed in equipment to enable bedside bioprocessing.

In a small number of cases, firms with innovative technologies also focused strongly on *innovations in the manufacturing processes* required to take their products to market. Many of these attempts failed, illustrating the complexity of simultaneously innovating both the technology and the manufacturing processes required to take it to market. Probably the best example of this was a firm which tried to develop new plastic electronics technologies and the new manufacturing processes required to deploy the technologies, in effect trying to build an entirely new market space in the process. The message here is to not underestimate the complexity involved in creating an entirely new market space.

10.5 Integrated Design, Simulation, and Manufacturing

Probably the most common deployment challenge for technology companies identified by our research relates to the integration and logistics of manufacturing, packaging, and deployment. Cloud computing firms provide a good illustration of this challenge. The technologies for secure data processing, storage and distribution are well developed, but the logistics of how products and services based on these technologies are deployed remains a major challenge; for example, the logical and physical rules for how cloud platforms and infrastructures operate, how they interact with customers and the business models which support these offerings.

These logistic challenges are becoming more acute with the proliferation in more granular data, very large volumes of data, very fast response networks, and more sophisticated end-user functionality in the hands of customers. Proposed new 'internet of things' services are starting to highlight this, where the challenge is not in the enabling technologies, but in the logistics of product and service deployment, which requires a more integrated approach to go-to-market strategies.

These challenges are not just restricted to firms active in the media and entertainment, telecommunications, electronics and hardware and software and computing market spaces. The same logistic challenge is fundamental to the design of new products and services enabling gene therapy for patients in the healthcare market space; for example, in our research we encountered several firms struggling to address this challenge when designing new forms of personalised bedside bioprocessing and treatments.

This integration challenge is now being addressed under the umbrella of a global initiative labelled *Industry 4.0*, which promotes the wider computerisation of design, simulation and manufacturing[116]: this reflects the view that the first industrial revolution mobilised the mechanisation of production using water and steam power; the second industrial revolution then introduced mass production with the help of electric power, followed by the digital revolution and the use of electronics and information technologies to further automate production. This new fourth phase is based on four design principles:

Interoperability: The ability of machines, devices, sensors, and people to connect and communicate with each other via the 'Internet of Things' or the 'Internet of People'.

Information transparency: The ability of information systems to create a virtual copy of the physical world by enriching digital plant models with sensor data. This requires the aggregation of raw sensor data to provide more valuable contextual information.

Technical assistance: The ability of assistance systems to support humans by aggregating and visualising information comprehensibly for making informed decisions and solving urgent problems. This is based on the ability of 'cyber physical' systems to physically support humans by conducting a range of tasks that are unpleasant, too exhausting, or unsafe for their human co-workers.

Decentralised decision-making: The ability of these 'cyber physical' systems to make decisions on their own and to perform their tasks as autonomously as possible. This also includes a decision-making hierarchy, where any exceptions, interferences, or conflicting goals, are delegated to a higher level of decision-making.

Overall, our results confirm the importance of addressing the manufacturing and assembly vector in any commercialisation strategy.

Part III

Strategy, Funding, and Go-to-Market

Chapter 11

Distribution, Marketing, and Sales

11.1 Generic Go-to-Market Challenges

When we embarked on our research, we realised early on that we needed to distinguish between the generic challenges faced by all firms and those *issues particularly relevant to science and technology firms*. The generic go-to-market challenges for firms have been described in detail by various authors over the last 20 years. We refer interested readers to the excellent primers by Kotler *et al.*[117,118] Over the last decade, there has also been interest in building more agile go-to-market systems[119–121] which may be particularly relevant for science and technology firms, given how technology development has accelerated changes in many market spaces.

To maintain a coherent overall perspective on go-to-market challenges, we start with a brief overview of the generic issues *all firms* need to address, as summarised in Table 12. Later, in this chapter, we discuss the relative importance of the different issues for technology firms along the commercialisation journey.

The product and service management challenges include not only the management of product categories and product portfolios, but life-cycle management of products and services. To this, we need to add: pricing issues, including strategy, tactics and dynamic pricing; product sales and marketing challenges, including positioning, branding and demand

Table 12:   Go-to-Market Challenges.

Product and service management	Category management Portfolio management Life-cycle management
Pricing	Pricing strategy Pricing tactics Dynamic pricing
Product marketing and sales	Positioning and branding Marketing and promotion Demand generation and sales
Channel management	Channel mix Resource management Performance management
Post-sales management and support	Customer support Customer management Product and process improvement

generation; management of channels and salesforces including channel mix, resource deployment and performance management; and finally, post-sales management and support, including product and process improvement and customer management and support, which has become particularly important for services based on subscription business models.

Our research confirmed that these generic challenges all apply to firms enabled by science and technology innovation. However, the research highlighted the following areas of particular importance for technology firms, which we discuss in detail below: channels-to-market; and positioning, branding, and promotion.

11.2 Channels-to-Market

The generic challenges surrounding channels-to-market have been extensively discussed and summarised over the last decade,[122–124] but technology companies face some specific issues. Our research showed that many of the technology firms started with a 'default preference' for direct sales

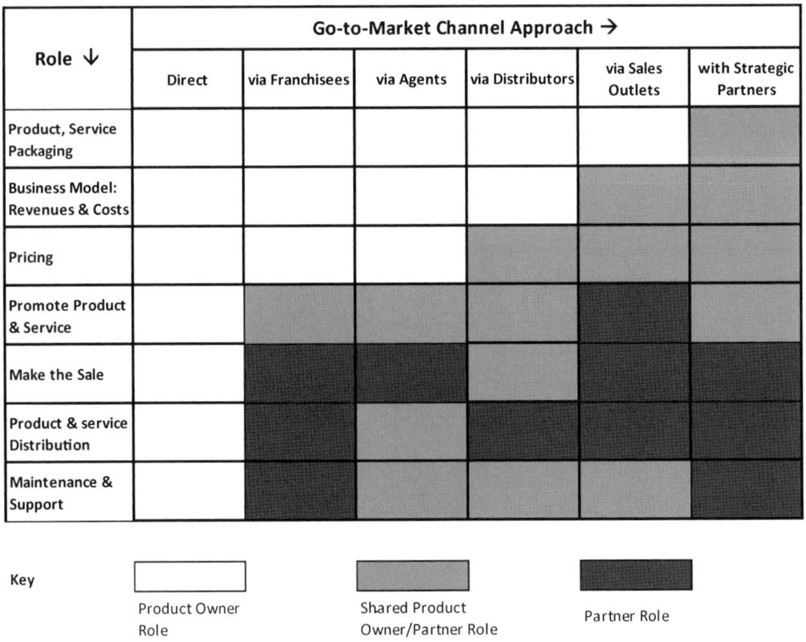

Role ↓	Go-to-Market Channel Approach →					
	Direct	via Franchisees	via Agents	via Distributors	via Sales Outlets	with Strategic Partners
Product, Service Packaging						
Business Model: Revenues & Costs						
Pricing						
Promote Product & Service						
Make the Sale						
Product & service Distribution						
Maintenance & Support						

Key

Product Owner Role   Shared Product Owner/Partner Role   Partner Role

Figure 25:   Comparing Channels-to-Market.

to customers, even where an objective analysis would have pointed to the importance of using 'third party' channels. We believe this may stem from a management bias towards associating channel-based delivery with lower levels of innovation and the assumption that strategic control requires direct methods of distribution. Most of these firms turned to serious consideration of channel-based strategies only after several attempts at direct selling. Our data illustrates the need to have a clear understanding of potential go-to-market channels and their benefits and disadvantages. Figure 25 compares different approaches based on the results of our research.

The comparison provides an overview of the typical options firms need to consider when reviewing potential channels-to-market for their products and services. The two basic approaches of course are to go to market direct or to harness a range of potential channels with different business models. The key factors in making the decision on the direct route vs third party channels depend on who performs the following roles: product or service packaging; the business model, in particular revenue and cost models; product or service pricing; promoting the product or service; making the sale; distribution of the product or service (physical, electronic, and 'blended'); and product and service maintenance and ongoing support.

Science and technology-enabled firms need to tackle all these elements when addressing the ways in which their products and services are taken to market, but our research highlights several key areas which are critically important.

Working with strategic channel partners typically requires the greatest flexibility because the partner can be involved in all the roles described above, but this flexibility can bring important benefits in terms of customer knowledge, shared risk and bigger rewards (albeit shared). Our research shows that strategic channel partners can be particularly valuable when taking sophisticated products and services to new markets, for example, partnering with a major medical device company to take a sophisticated new diagnostic technology to market.

Franchise-based channels are attractive because they provide strategic control of the product or service proposition and the ability to pass many of the go-to-market costs to the franchisee. The degree of control over the franchised proposition can vary (loose vs tight franchisees), but for technology products, the evidence suggests that this kind of coupling produces better results.

The use of agents is typically favoured for less complex products, especially for selling into distant or emerging markets provided the post-sales support and maintenance arrangements can be handled adequately, for example, for portable solar energy products. For technology products, agency arrangements tend to be used for short term or *ad hoc* arrangements when first taking products and services to market.

The use of distributors can bring powerful benefits especially when selling in larger volumes. Distributors can perform a range of tasks, including providing guidance on product packaging and pricing. Distributors can also handle 'local' logistics such as storage, delivery and compliance with regulation and taxation. Distributors can be useful for selling to both businesses and consumers, for example, for selling smart-phones or diagnostic medical equipment.

Retail sales outlets, where products and services can be purchased directly by consumers, are important for high volume products and services and associated consumables, for example, computing and communications devices such as laptops and mobile phones, routers and television receivers. Retail sales outlets can be important across a wide range of markets.

Technology companies need to assess these different channels-to-market before deciding on the 'best' options consistent with the overall commercial strategy, the risk-reward profile and the level of investment required. Tools for doing this systematically are included in our Workbench, which is summarised in Chapter 21.

11.3 Positioning, Branding, and Promotion

The challenges around positioning, branding, and promotion have been well described for firms in general, see for example, Kerin *et al.*[125] Some of the specific issues for technology firms and their products and services, have been addressed more recently by the Kellogg team,[126] who capture the overall issues in terms of simplified models, starting with the 4Ps, now extended to 7Ps, where the Ps represent the key variables of relevance.

Based on our research, we have defined a modified version of the 7P's model for science and technology innovation-enabled firms, which we characterise as the m7P's model. We have used this model to assess the strategies for the firms in our research data set. We discuss our insights after defining our modified m7Ps as follows:

Product: This defines the wider product and service envelope, the core of the product, and the key components of the overall product offer.

Positioning: This defines the overall positioning of a product or service, clarifying the value added and differentiation compared to competing products and services.

Price: This defines 'baseline' pricing for the product core as well as the pricing for additional components, including additional services and add-ons such as maintenance.

Place: This describes how and where product or service is delivered, for example, for physical products such as electronic devices, this might be retail stores, but for media and content-based products, this could include locations such as online stores and e-commerce platform.

Promotion: This covers how products and services are promoted, including advertising, marketing campaigns, and digital promotions across a wide range of media.

Process: This includes how the product or service is delivered and consumption processes for users, but covers all the processes associated with taking products and services to market, for example, the sales management process. Defining process can be especially important for value-added service delivery of software and computational products and services.

Partners: For many products and services, the role of partners can be critical for go-to-market; this variable is concerned with defining the types of partners and the associated commercial implications.

The relative importance of the m7Ps varies, depending on the product or service, the market space and the target customers for the offering.

Product	▬	Product and service configuration for target audience
Positioning	▬	Desired positioning; differentiation based on *core proposition* and *service wrapper*
Pricing and packaging	▬	Packaging and pricing based on business model, including service-tiering where appropriate
Place	▬	Service delivery and interaction environment Physical, digital or 'blended' places
Promotion	▬	Marketing campaigns for lead generation PR campaigns including multiple media types Direct mail and e-marketing campaigns Visibility with target audience based on optimal positioning
Process	▬	Streamlined sales process with appropriate sales resources
Partners	▬	Partners: Strategic, tactical, and operational

▬ Relevance indicator (max = 10)

Figure 26:   Relative Importance of the m7Ps — An Example.

When a firm is planning its strategy and tactics for taking a new product to market, it needs to understand the relative importance of each of these m7Ps, so it can allocate the appropriate level of resources for each of the m7Ps. Our research showed that these variations in the relative importance of the m7Ps can have a significant impact on the overall success of a go-to-market plan.

As an example of this, Figure 26 compares the relative importance of the m7Ps for a new digital online service which provides analytical, computational, data storage and visualisation services for business customers in corporate environments.

11.4 Key Issues for Science and Technology-enabled Firms

When investigating the distribution, marketing and sales challenges faced by the firms in our data set, we turned to the work published by Moore, which we hoped would provide some useful insights for our assessment. However, we faced three challenges: Moore's work provides some qualitative insights with little empirical data to draw on; the work also builds on Rogers' idealised definition of different customer categories, which, as we noted in Chapter 3, is at variance with real customer adoption data; as a consequence, the precise location of the 'Chasm' which Moore refers to is not always clear.

Instead, the approach we adopted was to use the detailed commercialisation canvas described in Chapter 17 in order to understand the relative importance of the sub-vectors which influence distribution, marketing and sales.

Figure 27 summarises the results of our research, based on surveying the firms in our data set. This shows how the distribution, marketing and sales mix, based on the 15 variables grouped into five areas, change as the commercialisation journey proceeds. These results highlight the key issues for fast growing science and technology firms. In particular, they show that there is a gradual build-up of the importance of the variables as the journey progresses. The biggest change in the number of variables actually happens around Chasm II with subsequent changes reflecting the

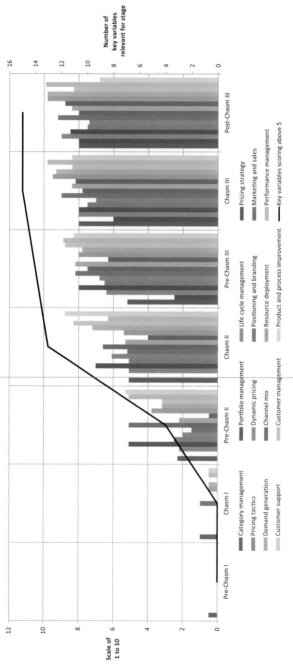

Figure 27:   Relative Importance of Go-to-Market Vectors on the Commercialisation Journey.

gradual and increasing importance of all the variables without any significant discontinuities around Chasm III. This has important implications for the success of commercialisation: the issues which enable successful scaling actually need to be addressed earlier in the journey, around Chasm II, not Chasm III. We discuss this later in Chapter 17. More detailed guidance based on these insights can be found in our Workbench, which we summarise in Chapter 21.

11.5 Integrated Service Delivery

Over the last decade, developments in digital technologies have turned some product companies into service companies; this gradual move from selling products to providing services which includes the provision of these products, has revolutionised business models in some market spaces. The move to service provision has also changed the way in which corporate customers consume products and services with a tendency to imitate consumer behaviour: this 'consumerisation' of corporate markets has changed the wider packaging and support requirements for new services.

As a consequence, brand positioning is now seen as a powerful way to create differentiation from the competition and disciplined, practical market planning has become critical. Firms need a strong customer-focused culture and organisation with a clear business model which focuses the firm's activities on specific customer segments and clarifies what value is created and how.

In this service-oriented environment, the emphasis of customer marketing activity moves from a 'transactional' focus to a 'relational' focus. The attraction of new customers, *customer acquisition*, becomes the first step in the marketing process. The relationship marketing has to focus on attracting, maintaining and enhancing customer relationships, *customer retention*. Long-term customer retention becomes the goal, and customer lifetime value a key measure of success.

The interesting paradox observed by others and confirmed by our research data is that while the product core of an offering typically represents 80% of the total cost of a service, it only contributes to 20% of the customer impact. The converse is true: although the expenditure on the 'service wrapper' typically only reflects 20% of the total cost of an offering, it can be responsible for 80% of the perceived customer impact.

This paradox has major implications for technology commercialisation strategies, and also for the development of new service-based business models which we discuss in Chapter 13. It emphasizes the importance of surrounding the core product offering with smaller additional functions and features, which may simply be commodities with little or no innovation in themselves, but when added to the core, create an offering with a strong cluster of tangible and intangible features and benefits; good examples of this include new online entertainment services and medical diagnostic products which include clinical insights which increase the perceived value of particular diagnostic measurements for a specific patient.

Chapter 12

Commercialisation Strategy

12.1 Strategic Ecology and Drivers

Any systematic assessment of commercialisation strategy needs to start with a clear understanding of the strategic ecology: understanding the overall commercial environment and the key drivers is critical when assessing the position and trajectory of a firm. The drivers in this ecology also need to reflect the key parameters relevant for firms enabled by science and technology innovation.

Our definition of this strategic ecology is based on the 12 vectors already discussed in Chapter 4.

The four external vectors in this ecology are as follows:

Market spaces: This defines the overall shape of the market space, the key players in the market space and their roles. It also includes articulation of the associated market space-centric value chain.

Proposition framing and competitive environment: This frames the overall customer proposition, in the context of the competitive and regulatory environment. It focuses on understanding the gaps in current provision and the value added by the new proposition delivered to the end-customer.

Customer definition: This defines the types of customers to be targeted: consumers, affinity and knowledge-centric groups, businesses or government. It allows us to profile target customers and to estimate the size of the potential market.

Distribution, marketing, and sales: This describes how the new product or service is taken to market including positioning, branding, channels, promotion, partners, and methods of distribution.

The six internal vectors in the strategic ecology are as follows:

Technology development and deployment: This characterises the type of technology, how it is deployed and its potential impact. It includes an understanding of base vs application technologies, products, services, and technology platforms.

Product and service definition and synthesis: This covers the definition of new products and services, in particular, the adaptation of existing products or the synthesis of entirely new solutions.

Manufacturing and assembly: This covers the usual manufacturing challenges and also the scaling technologies for manufacturing, innovations in manufacturing processes, supply chains, and integrated approaches to design, simulation, and manufacturing.

Intellectual property (IP) management: This addresses the issues associated with defining, protecting, and exploiting IP, which includes registered, unregistered and 'open' rights.

Talent, leadership, and culture: This covers the quantity, quality and effectiveness of human resources, not just in technology but particularly in product management, marketing and sales. It includes core competences, composition of teams, leadership and culture firms need to develop as they grow.

Funding and investment: This addresses the form, quantum and timing of investment. It includes the different types of potential investment and the conditions bounding such funding.

To these 10 vectors, we add two composite vectors, which are critical to the overall strategic ecology affecting the firm:

Business models: This acts at the interface between internal and external vectors. The business model fundamentally determines how the product or service is sold, managed and serviced, the commercial viability of any proposition, and its sustainability.

Commercialisation strategy: This effectively covers the choices made regarding the importance of the other 11 vectors. Most approaches to the development of commercialisation strategy over the last 30 years have focused either on market positioning or resources and capabilities. Given our interest in rapidly growing firms in dynamic markets, this is a critical vector for us, which addresses the trade-offs between the internal and external vectors. We discuss how our approach to strategy formulation differs from previous approaches in Table 13.

12.2 Approaches to Strategy Formulation and Development

Any literature search will reveal many hundreds of approaches and tools addressing the challenges of strategy formulation, development, and testing. The challenge in comparing the validity and usefulness of these tools is that they are based on a number of different approaches with varying relevance and accuracy.

Table 13:   Strategic Ecology.

Type of Vector	Vector
External	Market spaces
	Proposition framing and competitive environment
	Customer definition
	Distribution, marketing, and sales
Internal	IP management
	Manufacturing and assembly
	Product and service definition and synthesis
	Technology development and deployment
	Talent, leadership, and culture
	Funding and investment
Composite	Commercialisation strategy
	Business models

Broadly speaking, these approaches differ in several important ways: how the challenge is framed, the granularity of the approach, and whether it provides insights at a broad industry level or at the level of an individual firm.

There are seven main approaches to framing: the provision of general insights at an industry level; firm-level insights; positioning-based 'external' approaches drawing on Porter's work;[127] competence-based models drawing on the resources of the firm, the most well-known being Prahalad and Hamel's work[128] on core competences; organisational models, in particular, Teece's work[129] on dynamic capabilities; game theory-based approaches; and integrated dynamic approaches, for example, Burgelman's work;[130] and Johnson's approach based on the economics of strategic diversity.[131,132]

However, that is only part of the picture: these framing approaches reflect different levels of granularity of assessment of the challenges. Some of them provide insights based on simple influence models; the firm-specific insight models are based on selected attributes, which are more useful, but these attributes are usually generic groupings of several 'internal' and 'external' forces, such as for example, the SWOT model, which looks at Strengths, Weaknesses, Opportunities and Threats. This makes them more useful as broad education and communication tools, rather than analytical tools which can help understand the strategic drivers.

These are all typically 'static' tools which can be used to explore relatively stable conditions onto which the impact of radical change can in theory be overlaid. Teece's work on dynamic capabilities looks at the processes involved in building the capabilities to compete in dynamic markets, but lacks the more granular insights which could provide more practical guidance for firms. Burgelman and Grove have started to address the challenge of systematically integrating heterogeneous forces, but the work is based on a single case study. More recently, Johnson has recognised the importance of looking at competitive strategy with greater granularity in an integrated way, but the work is still at a relatively abstract stage.

There is one other important limitation of these approaches which concerns us: most of these strategy formulation techniques have been developed using data from large, mature firms, with very few insights into the earlier stages of high-growth firms which concern us, especially around Chasms I, II, and III.

Detailed treatment of these issues is beyond the scope of this book, but we summarise the differences between these approaches in Table 14.

This gap in understanding led us to the development of a new approach to strategy formulation and development, building on our data and insights, which we describe in Section 12.3.

We believe our new dynamic approach based on commercialisation vectors addresses the main problems with most existing approaches: it allows the relative importance of external and internal vectors to be handled in an integrated way; it provides the level of granularity and detail required to sensibly develop firm-level commercialisation strategy; it enables the approach to be applied consistently to the firm at different points in its commercialisation journey; and finally, it can also be used to model and assess the impact of significant market, technology and operational innovations, even for mature firms.

12.3 Dynamic Vector-based Approach to Commercialisation Strategy

The deficiencies in existing approaches to strategy formulation and development led us to create a new dynamic vector-based approach to commercialisation strategy. Our approach has the following broad attributes: it enables the impact of external and internal vectors to be treated in an integrated way based on an explicit framework and architecture; the approach can be used for firms of all sizes, as they grow from concept to full commercialisation, including the strategic changes when crossing Chasms I, II, and III; it can be used to assess disruptive strategic changes; and finally, the approach is underpinned by data from a large number of firms at different levels of maturity across different market spaces, which provides a significant body of normative data.

Figure 28 summarises how this vector-based commercialisation strategy tool operates. The tool is included in our commercialisation Workbench, summarised in Chapter 21, where we provide further details of how the tool can be used.

Table 14: Approaches to Strategy Formulation and Development.

Strategic Approaches	Strategic Imperatives			
	Influences	Attributes	Processes	Drivers
Industry insight models	PESTEL 3Cs			
Firm-specific insight models		SWOT ANSOFF matrix BCG matrix GE-McKinsey matrix		
Positioning-based models		Generic strategies (Porter) Disruptive technologies (Christensen)		5 Forces + firm-centric value chains (Porter)
Competence-based models				Core competences (Prahalad and Hamel)
Organisational models			Dynamic capabilities (Teece et al.)	
Game theory-based approaches		Gaming approaches (Nalebuff et al.)	Options theory	
Integrated dynamic approaches		Strategy dynamics (Burgelman and Grove)		Economics of strategic diversity (Johnson) Commercialisation vectors (Phadke et al.)

Vector-based Commercialisation Strategy
Strategy Formulation and Development
Identify position along commercialisation journey *Use Triple Chasm Model* *Verify against mTRLs* Identify key vectors of relevance at this level of maturity *Focus on key vectors at this point in the commercialisation journey* Examine potential influence of key vectors *Look in detail at vectors and sub-vectors to assess relative importance* Assign weights to key vectors based on *commercial* impact *Score the vectors based on simple 0–10 scoring range: 0 = no impact; 10 = maximum impact*
Strategy Testing and Refinement
Identify execution capacity of the firm for all vectors *Look in detail at the firm's current or planned capacity to execute vectors* *Assign weights to this execution capacity* Determine weighted impact of vectors on strategy *Compute aggregate weights based on relative importance and ability to execute* 'Tune' strategic focus *Examine weighted impact* *Explore opportunities for modifying strategic priorities based on relevance and execution scores*
Strategy Deployment and Dynamic Management
Monitor performance *Evaluate deviations from strategic intent* Strategy refinement *Identify opportunities for course correction* *Design and test incremental changes to strategy* Strategic pivots and radical new strategies *Explore strategic pivots towards different eco-systems, customers or business models* *Radical changes to Strategy involving many vectors*

Figure 28: Vector-based Commercialisation Strategy Formulation.

In order to illustrate how the tool can be used, we show a typical output which defines the relative strategic importance of the different vectors for a single firm from our data set. Figure 29 shows the strategic focus for a firm in the media and entertainment market space, at the point in its

Figure 29:   Typical Commercialisation Strategy for a Post-Chasm II Firm.

commercialisation strategy where it has crossed Chasm II and is poised to cross Chasm III. These results help shape strategic priorities and plans aimed at improving the likelihood of crossing Chasm III effectively. What is clear from this is that the tool can also be used in order to investigate different strategic scenarios and to optimise decision-making.

12.4 Changing Strategic Priorities as Firms Grow

Most approaches to strategy development have focused on corporates, or larger firms, where detailed research on a small number of firms has been used to derive generic conclusions about the factors important for competitive strategy. This has generated a number of 'strategy schools' as discussed earlier in this chapter. There is a risk that this kind of case study approach can focus on outlier firms (extreme successes and failures), but the bigger challenge is that very little attention has been paid to strategic priorities on the commercialisation journey, in particular, the early stages. In fact, most approaches have ignored this problem; Burgelman, for example, refers to this only with a passing reference to the 'valley of death', a metaphor which we have referred to elsewhere in this book. The reality, however, is that strategic clarity is just as important, if not critical, at the earlier stages of growth, especially given the shortage of resources typically affecting these firms early in their lives.

We illustrate how our vector-based dynamic model can be used to understand changes in strategic priorities along the commercialisation journey in Figure 30: the data relates to the same firm in the media and entertainment market space, and the results show the changing priorities for the firm as it tackles Chasms I, II, and III.

In particular, these results show the importance of a relatively small number of commercialisation vectors at Chasm I; the number of relevant vectors increases significantly at Chasms II and III. In this particular case, the differences between Chasms II and III can be seen clearly with a greater focus on distribution and business models around Chasm III. Clearly, these patterns depend on the specific conditions affecting an individual firm, which can be quite different across different market spaces, but the results show the power of this new approach in terms of strategy formulation and development.

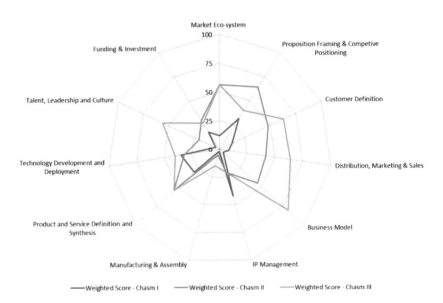

Figure 30: Changes in Strategic Priorities with Firm Maturity — An Example.

12.5 Strategic Responses to the Competitive Environment

The dynamic nature of this vector-based approach means it can also provide far greater insight into the strategic planning and behaviour of larger mature firms facing significant changes in their market environment.

In particular, there are three types of challenges where we have applied this approach and generated case studies and data across the 12 market spaces which form the basis of research for this book:

Firms operating in relatively stable environments, where this approach can be used to design and implement changes in strategy based on small incremental changes to the importance of several, sometimes many, vectors, to 'fine-tune' performance.

Significant changes in market spaces, where the overall shape of the market space is dramatically altered by changes in technology or regulation, for example. This may result in the need to target different customers and use new distribution channels, which requires a major *strategic* 'pivot', affecting several vectors including technology, product synthesis, and business models.

Disruption in technology, business models and distribution channels can significantly impact many vectors driving overall commercialisation strategy; our approach can provide insights at a far greater level of granularity than general models talking about disruption as an aggregate effect. It can also be used to assess opportunities for the creation of radically new product and service categories, which can impact all the vectors described in the model. This kind of radical transformation does not happen often, but requires a broader strategic response based on understanding the new sources of competition and new product opportunities.

Chapter 13

Business Models

13.1 Why Business Models Matter

Our research revealed that a critical vector for most firms is the development of a robust business model, which is seen as the key to building a sustainable firm. Despite the importance of this vector, our qualitative and quantitative data showed that many firms do not adopt a systematic approach to business model generation, often relying on *ad hoc* approaches in the hope that some kind of business model will emerge eventually.

We discuss how firms can address this challenge in a structured way based on the following key elements: we define business models and their components; we then explore the narratives around different business models and the sources of revenue associated with them; we discuss the relationship between different market spaces and business models as revealed by our research; and finally, we discuss the different types of business metrics required to underpin the different models.

13.2 Defining Business Models

At the most basic level, the business model can be defined as 'how the firm plans to make money,' but a review of the literature shows a variety of ways in which business thinkers use the concept.[133] The early foundations for defining business models were set out by Drucker,[134] who explored the key assumptions and components required to articulate a business model; in particular, he was interested in making explicit the assumptions underlying the operations of a firm and how they influence commercial success. In our view, probably the best description of a business model is that proposed by Teece[135] who wrote that 'a business model articulates the logic and provides data and other evidence that demonstrates how a business creates and delivers value to customers. It also outlines the **architecture** of revenues, costs and profits associated with the business enterprise delivering that value.'

Magretta[136] has noted that the term 'business model' first came into widespread use with the advent of spreadsheets which enabled the various components to be modelled and tested; as a consequence, most firms now equate business models with spreadsheets which make explicit the assumptions and components for a firm and compute the relationships between these variables.[137]

Spreadsheets, however, are only part of business models and provide the basis for making explicit and testing the key elements of a business plan, which include the following key components: customer value proposition, the profit formula, key resources, and key processes.[138] The key objective of a business model is to link the 'narrative' for a firm to the actual numbers associated with this narrative, which is why a series of books and papers have conflated the different assumptions and hypotheses associated with the overall narrative (or 'story') of the firm with the quantitative data describing the 'profit formula' for the firm.[139-141]

In our view, this conflation can obscure the key drivers underpinning the business model, especially for science and technology-based firms. Our approach is based on treating the business model as a unique vector, as described earlier in Chapter 4, so that we treat the development of a business model as a distinct task, which reflects the impact of the other vectors, but allows the impact of changes in these other vectors to be reflected in the design of a business model in an explicit way, rather than under general categories such as processes or resources. It is worth noting that this approach applies to firms of all maturities, not just nascent or emerging firms.

Our structured approach based on 'deconstructing' the vectors allows the development of business models in a more systematic way than with some previous approaches which, for example, conflate customers and channels with resource costs. This can be particularly problematic for science and technology-centric firms where success can depend on comparing different commercialisation options based on *different narratives* for a firm. For example, content-centric businesses face major challenges to their business models because technology developments have enabled the creation of new products and services, the delivery of more granular services to customers, and better targeting of micro-customer segments. The consequential lowering of barriers to entry for new smaller, more agile players has enabled the creation of radically new business models. Content businesses focused on consumers have already felt the brunt of these changes: newspapers have had to radically alter their business models and become online-centric in their approach as new entrants have damaged advertising revenues for the incumbents. These changes are not restricted to just content businesses. Virtually, all the market spaces described in Chapter 5 are subject to significant changes in business models from energy and lighting to biotechnology and healthcare services.

13.3 Business Model Components

Our structured approach to business model definition is based on segmenting the business model vector into the following components, as shown in Figure 31.

Business models are shaped by the *Overall Narrative*, which effectively describes the 'design choices' made about the shape of the target market space, target customers and the product or service proposition; we have already discussed new product and service synthesis in Chapter 9, but the selected overall narrative depends on understanding and articulating the linkages between the proposition, customers and the shape of the target market space, as discussed previously in Chapter 6.

The qualitative view of the business model needs to be quantified, which depends on clarifying the key *assumptions* behind the narrative: this includes making explicit the key drivers and the underlying logic and key metrics including customer types, numbers and pricing. It is these explicit assumptions which typically drive the business model spreadsheets discussed previously.

Business model vector deconstructed	
Overall narrative	Target marketspace
	Target customers
	Proposition
Assumptions	Narrative-based drivers, logic
	Customer numbers
	Pricing
Revenues	Primary
	Secondary e.g. advertising
	Distribution-adjusted
Costs	Technologies, materials
	People
	Third parties e.g. legal, acct services
Revenue and cost allocation logic	Parametric dependencies
	Time-based variation
Margins	Product and service basis
	Time basis
Cash flow	Leading and lagging criteria
	Time-based variation
Intellectual property	Registered rights
	Unregistered rights
	'Open' rights
Other assets	'Hard' assets
	'Soft' assets
Funding	Customer revenues
	Debt
	Equity
	Gap analysis
Scenarios	Alternative narratives
	Scenario generation
	Modelling
Sensitivity analysis	Base case
	Pessimistic scenarios
	Optimistic scenarios

Figure 31:   Business Model Components.

The most critical component of any business model is an assessment of the potential *Revenues* generated by the product or service; this includes primary revenues generated by sales, secondary revenues generated by associated activity, such as advertising, and clarity on the actual revenues accruing to the firm after adjustment for distribution costs. We explore this in more detail in Table 15.

Table 15: Business Model — Potential Revenue Sources.

Component	NRE	Licenses Perpetual	Licenses Time-bound	Royalties	Leasing	Outright Sale Core	Outright Sale Consumables	Commission	Match-maker	Transactions	Subscriptions Time-metered	Subscriptions Value-metered	Proxies Advertising	Proxies Sponsorship
Services	✓								✓	✓	✓	✓	✓	✓
Products					✓	✓	✓	✓		✓				
Meta-content				✓		✓							✓	✓
Content				✓		✓		✓			✓	✓	✓	✓
Apps, tools and processes	✓	✓	✓	✓							✓	✓	✓	✓
Technology platforms	✓	✓	✓		✓	✓					✓	✓		✓
Application technologies	✓	✓	✓	✓										
Base technologies	✓	✓	✓	✓		✓								

The *Costs* associated with creating, making and distributing products and services need to be made explicit; this includes the costs associated with technology development, materials, 'third' party costs associated with legal, financial and accounting services, and people costs for permanent and *ad hoc* human resources.

Accounting policies and conventions can determine *Revenue and Cost Allocation Logic*, but revenues and costs need to be allocated to specific activities. This ensures that aggregate revenues and costs are modelled consistently within the chosen assumptions and logic describing parametric dependencies and time-based variations in revenues and costs.

The difference between revenues and costs, usually described as the *Margin* or surplus, needs to be computed based on segmenting products, services and associated activities, such as support, on a time-varying basis. Setting out the underlying logic explicitly enables this margin to be optimised on the basis of modifying the relative importance of the underlying variables.

Cash flow is one of the criteria sometimes neglected by science and technology firms; the difference between cash generation and achieving margins can sometimes be the difference between success and failure. A systematic approach to the business model enables the potential cash flow implications of different strategies and tactics to be compared. In particular, the leading and lagging criteria for cash generation and how they vary over time can be used to 'optimise' the cash required to grow and run a firm; this in turn can affect the level of external funding or investment required, which we discuss in Chapter 15.

The value of the *IP and other assets* can have a crucial bearing on the selection of a business model. IP does not just cover registered rights such as patents, but also unregistered and open rights, which can impact how a business model reflects the exploitation of these assets in a broader way, not just through revenue generation; we discuss this in Chapter 14.

The *Funding* required by a science and technology firm depends not just on the projected cash flow but also on the level of ambition, the need to invest 'ahead of the curve', and the need to address specific time-limited opportunities. We discuss the balance between customer, debt and equity funding in Chapter 15.

Well-structured business models enable firms to explore different *scenarios* based on developing alternative business narratives with small or large changes in the underlying assumptions; these scenarios may simply involve changing the values of key parameters such as the number of customers or they may involve significant changes in business logic, for example, moving from a product paid for by the end-customer to a service paid for by advertising.

Once a narrative and business model has been established, it is still important to understand the impact of deviations from the assumptions in the values of the key business model parameters. *Sensitivity analysis* allows firms to look at variations from the base case, and to explore more pessimistic or optimistic outcomes. This can be particularly important when introducing radically new technologies where the potential take-up cannot be easily predicted before launch.

13.4 Business Model Narratives and Revenue Generation

Business model narratives are shaped strongly by the way in which revenues are generated. There is a wide range of ways in which technology firms can generate revenues which are summarised in Table 15. The *x*-axis of this table shows the potential revenue sources, the *y*-axis shows the different product and service components based on the Product Characterisation Framework discussed in Chapter 9. The entries in the grid indicate the relevance of different types of revenue for the different product components.

The principle revenue sources identified in Table 15 are as follows:

Non-recurring engineering (NRE) revenues: When a science or technology firm provides its technologies to another firm, there may be a need to provide additional engineering expertise to enable more effective use of the technology, usually on a one-time basis, hence the notion of non-recurring costs for the acquiring firm and sales revenues for the supplying firm.

Technology can be licensed to customers for use under defined conditions and defined timescales; *licenses* can either be in perpetuity (for use indefinitely) or time-bounded in various ways (for example, for monthly or annual use). Technology licensing usually requires very clear definitions covering usage domains and methods of usage.

Royalties are payments made for the use of a technology (either stand-alone or integrated with other technology); typically, royalty payments are made on the basis of the volume of usage, for example, the number of product units the technology is deployed in or the number of customers using a particular service. For example, if the design of a processor chip is used in a new smartphone device, then the royalties are calculated on the basis of the number of devices sold. Royalty payments can also apply to usage of copyrighted material; for example, digital images may be provided to firms or consumers, in which case the royalties may be proportional to the number of times the image has been used, or in some cases, linked to the number of users.

Leasing of technology products follows the usual rules of leasing, where the customer, a firm or a consumer, is allowed to lease and use a product for a fixed period of time, during which ownership remains with the supplier; at the end of the leasing period, the product is returned to the supplier. Leasing has also been applied to technology platforms with a wide range of functionality, not just products.

The *outright sale* of a technology, content or product follows the usual rules governing the sale and transfer of ownership implied by the sale. Where products may require consumables so that they can function at all, there are some interesting opportunities for different business models, which are commercially sustainable. For example, many printers today are sold for less than the cost of making and supplying them, based on the manufacturers making much larger margins on the ink, the consumable, to offset the losses on selling the core product. These core + consumables business models may also incorporate subscription-based additional services to reduce the risk to the business model.

Where products and content are sold to firms or consumers by third parties in the channel, these firms will have revenue models based on earning *commissions* on the sale of these products.

Transaction revenues have become more relevant for technology firms, as payment technologies enable smaller transactions to be carried out effectively; this approach can be used by firms to collect small amounts of revenues from a large number of customers, for example, media and entertainment firms providing content, applications and tools to consumers.

Matchmaker revenues apply where services are provided which typically involve connecting buyers and sellers; these can be charged as fixed fees or as a percentage of the revenues resulting from the matchmaking activity.

Subscription revenues have become very important for technology firms over the last decade, 'metered' by either value or time. In particular, the development of digital technologies and infrastructures has dramatically increased the scope of subscription-based services across a wide range of applications, including the provision of content, computing resources, energy and engineering functionality. We discuss the different metrics required to measure the effectiveness of these approaches later in this chapter.

Proxy methods of revenue generation, where advertisers or sponsors effectively subsidise the consumption of products and services, have grown dramatically over the last decade, as providers of content, applications and technology search for ways to develop sustainable business models.

In Chapter 9, we discussed the different product and service components. Table 15 also shows the potential sources of revenues for the different ways in which technology can be taken to market. In particular, it shows the following:

Base technologies can typically generate revenues based on the provision of non-recurrent engineering expertise, technology licensing, royalty payments and sometimes, the outright sale of the technology itself.

Application technologies offer the same revenue generation opportunities, except it is much harder to sell application technologies outright because they typically may include licensed-in third party technologies.

Technology platforms can generate non-recurrent engineering revenues, and platform licensing and leasing revenues, and can sometimes be sold outright, but the most significant opportunities may be in the provision of subscription-based services.

Applications, tools and processes attract the same revenue opportunities as base and application technologies, and also offer the opportunities to generate revenues from advertising and sponsorship.

Content and meta content can typically generate revenues from royalties or outright sale, especially to consumers, and also have the potential to generate significant advertising and sponsorship revenues.

Technology-based products typically generate revenues from sales of products and consumables; in some situations, these products can also generate commission-based revenues from other firms in the sales channel.

Technology-based services usually generate revenues from subscriptions, and associated activities including transactions, advertising, and sponsorship.

Service-based revenues have become increasingly important, especially over the last decade, as firms which previously sold products and consumables, are now providing the same or enhanced functionality as subscription-based services. For example, medical devices or consumer electronic devices can now be provided on the basis of service-based revenue models. This creates new opportunities for innovation based on business models.

Developing sustainable business models for new products and services is difficult. Our data show that success often requires multiple iterations of the model; some of the firms in our data set had been through 5–6 iterations before they established a sustainable business model. This is in sharp contrast to popular literature which emphasises the importance of having an explicit business model at the outset and assumes that this model can be implemented successfully, although there is acknowledgement that in some situations, it may at least be necessary to have a Plan B.[142]

13.5 Business Models and Market Spaces

The development and application of the different business models discussed above depends strongly on the target market space and customer type, as observed by Robbins-Roth,[143] Kornberg,[144] and Coles *et al.*[145] Our own research yielded the following general insights about firms in different market spaces:

Media and Entertainment: For both consumers and business customers, the main business models deployed are based on licensing and subscription with some firms involved in the outright sale of packaged content; proxy methods of revenue generation are very common, especially for products and services aimed at consumers.

Telecommunications: For consumers, the main business models are based on subscriptions and transaction-based revenues, again with strong proxy revenues based on advertising and sponsorship; for business customers, licensing models are common.

Software, Systems and Computational Tools: Licensing and subscription-based models are most common for firms in this market space, but some business models include leasing and transaction revenues for business customers and consumers, respectively.

Electronics and Computing Hardware: Firms in this marketplace deploy licensing and royalty models focused mainly on business customers with outright sales of core products and consumables for consumers.

Aerospace Engineering: Firms in our data set were exclusively focused on selling to business customers with business models focused on NRE, licensing, royalties, leasing and outright product sales; there was some early evidence of service-based models; we believe that outright sales to consumers will start to emerge as the market for low cost devices such as drones grows.

Automotive Engineering: The automotive market space is similar to aerospace with the important addition of outright sales of products to consumers.

Oil and Gas Engineering: The oil and gas firms deploy similar business models to aerospace with a few nascent examples of subscription-type business models.

Healthcare Products and Services: The firms in our data set showed a wide range of business models for business customers, consumers and affinity and knowledge-centric users, including licensing, transactions and subscriptions; for business customers, there was strong evidence of the use of NRE and royalty-based business models.

Biotechnology: The overall pattern of business models used in the biotechnology market space was the same as for aerospace and oil and gas with an exclusive focus on business customers; we did not see any early evidence of sales to consumers in this market space, although there were some signs of dialogues with knowledge-centric groups in academic institutions and R&D laboratories.

Energy and Lighting: The pattern of business model deployment was the same as aerospace for business customers; for consumers, we saw some evidence of subscription and transaction-based business models.

Financial Products and Services: This showed very similar behaviour to the software, systems and computational tools market space, not surprisingly because many of the products and services were based on implementing software and computational techniques. The target customers in this market space include businesses, knowledge-centric groups and to a lesser extent, consumers.

Education, Skills and Learning: Business models deployed here were the same as for financial services. The target customers in this market space include businesses, knowledge-centric groups and consumers.

Practical tools which help define the relationship between business models and market spaces are included in our Workbench, which is described in Chapter 21.

13.6 Business Model Metrics

The business model components described earlier in this chapter provide a comprehensive basis for defining the key metrics which firms need to track on a regular basis. In practice, all firms need to focus on a number of key metrics:

Sales revenue which is defined as the income from customer purchases of products and services. Typically, sales data may be correlated to advertising campaigns, price changes, seasonal forces, competitive actions, and other costs of sales.

Overhead costs are fixed costs that are not dependent on the level of products or services produced by the firm, such as salaries or rents being paid per month.

Variable costs are expenses that change in proportion to the activity of a firm. Fixed costs and variable costs make up the two components of the total cost. These include the 'cost of goods sold' and other items that increase with each sale, such as the cost of raw materials, labour, shipping and other expenses directly connected to producing and delivering products or services.

Customer loyalty is about attracting the right customer, getting them to buy, buy often, buy in higher quantities and bring in even more customers. There are three common methods for measuring customer loyalty and retention: customer surveys, direct feedback at the point of purchase, and purchase analysis. All of these require systematic processes, rather than *ad hoc* implementation.

Cost of customer acquisition which is a measure of the total cost associated with acquiring a new customer, including all aspects of marketing and sales. Customer acquisition cost is calculated by dividing total acquisition expenses by total new customers over a given period.

Gross margin which is calculated as total sales revenue minus the cost of goods sold, divided by the total sales revenue, expressed as a percentage. Tracking margins is critical for growing companies, since increased volumes should improve efficiency and lower the cost per unit.

Profit is not simply the difference between the costs of the product or service and the price being charged for it. The calculation must include the fixed and variable costs of operation that are paid regularly each month no matter what. These include such items as rent or mortgage payments, utilities, insurance, taxes, and people costs.

Cash flow, which tracks the actual cash in the firm on a regular basis; as we have observed earlier, this can differ from the profit or loss figure and impact the amount of capital required in a firm.

All technology firms need to ensure that they monitor these key metrics regularly, but the advent of *new service-based business models* has driven the need for firms to focus on some new metrics more relevant to managing the delivery of continuous services. These additional metrics are as follows:

Committed monthly recurring revenue (CMRR) is the combined value of the recurring subscription revenue on a monthly basis plus signed contracts currently committed and going into 'production', minus any "churn".

CMRR Pipeline (CPipe) is the sales pipeline for future subscription revenues not yet confirmed.

Churn is typically measured as the % of customers who cancel their subscriptions; customers who renew subscriptions at the end of the committed period determine the renewal rate.

Customer acquisition cost (CAC), usually measured in months, is the time required to recover the additional sales and marketing investment for new customer acquisition.

Customer life time value (CLTV) is the net present value of the recurring profit streams of a specific customer less the acquisition cost.

We have integrated these different elements into the business model tools which are incorporated in the Workbench summarised in Chapter 21.

Chapter 14

Intellectual Property Management

14.1 Generic IP Challenges

Historically, technology firms have not appreciated, recorded, protected and exploited their intellectual property (IP) portfolios adequately. This problem has arisen partly because funders and investors have traditionally focused only on registered rights.[146,147] In addition, the balance sheets of most technology firms do not typically quantify even these assets, although they can have a dramatic impact on the commercial success and sustainability of these firms.

We discuss our broader view of IP below, but irrespective of this, all firms face the same generic challenges when it comes to IP management: how to define, protect and actively exploit their IP.

Intellectual property rights (IPRs), due to their nature as property rights, can be bought, sold, or licensed. The owner of an IPR is the person entitled to commercially exploit it, hence it is important to establish ownership to avoid disputes. Provisions regarding ownership of IPRs can be quite complex and vary depending on the type of right. This means that a creation can give rise to a number of different rights and the owners of each may not be the same person or entity.

Exploitation typically depends on **incorporating the IP** into the firm's products or services, **assigning the IP**, or **licensing the IP**, to another entity for incorporation into their products and services. Inventors and entrepreneurs, in particular, sometimes misunderstand the concepts of assigning or licensing of IPRs, but the differences are important:

An **Assignment** of IPR means the transfer of those rights absolutely to a third party in exchange for some commercial consideration. On the assignment of the rights to an assignee, the assignee becomes the owner of those rights and the ownership of the IPR is formally transferred to the assignee as beneficial owner. The assignee will usually require an assignment with full title guarantee, which means no encumbrances on the IPR such as a commercial charge. The assignee derives rights from the transfer of the IPR and can perform all acts in relation to the IPR, including the right to initiate proceedings for infringement of the IPR.

Licensing IPR is different: as licensor, the owner may grant an exclusive or non-exclusive right to a licensee to use the IPR in a particular territory in return for royalties. However, the licensor continues to own all rights in the IPR. Granting an exclusive licence for a territory excludes all other parties from that territory. Unlike an assignment, a non-exclusive licensee has no right against the public, however, an exclusive licensee may initiate proceedings for infringement but must join the licensor in the action. When granting a licence for any IPR, it is important to expressly state the terms under which the license is granted: this includes the scope i.e., whether it is exclusive, sole or non-exclusive, duration, territory, royalty levels, restrictions on the IPR, including quality provisions and confidentiality, infringement of IPR, licensee's obligations, warranties and indemnities, and termination conditions.

The treatment of IP globally is mandated by the provisions of the World Intellectual Property Organisation (WIPO) to which virtually all countries involved in science and technology commercialisation are now signatories, so those who create, manage and exploit IP can be reasonably confident of the overall framework governing IP management. However, there can be significant variations in the actual practice of how these rules are applied, which creates both opportunities and challenges in the development of strategies and tactics for effective exploitation, and often requires expert advice from IP specialists. This is a broad subject beyond the scope of this book and we refer readers to the excellent summaries provided by WIPO on the subject.[148] We should also observe at this point that the valuation of IP can be subject to 'local' legal and regulatory conditions reflecting the nature of the transacting parties, compliance, enforcement and tax treatment of investment and IP generation.

Science and technology firms are affected by all these issues but need to be particularly aware of the following specific issues: **defining IP precisely** can be a big challenge, especially given the wide range of base and application technologies coupled with different models of technology deployment; **differentiating between** generalised knowledge, often referred to as **background IP** and specific new advances, referred to as **foreground IP** can be problematic; and defining the **ownership of IP** can be difficult, especially where the ideas are developed by teams of developers, where the activity operates at the interface between academic and commercial activities, or where those funding the research and development activity have claimed specific ownership rights. Addressing these issues requires detailed understanding of the specific circumstances surrounding each innovation.

14.2 IP Typology for Science and Technology-enabled Innovation

IP is critical for building sustainable business models for technology companies. Although most financial balance sheets do not currently quantify the value of IP explicitly (a situation which needs to change in our view), it is critical to the generation of sustainable revenues.

IP is often seen as being synonymous with patents, but in reality, patents constitute only a part of the overall picture. Our wider definition of IP covers registered rights (including patents), unregistered rights and 'open' rights. This broad view of IP can underpin the development of robust business models: for example, strong copyright protection or design rights can sustain higher pricing of licenses or the pricing of products and services. This can also constitute a key element of competitive differentiation.

Figure 32 shows all these elements of IP which represent potential sources of commercial value for technology firms. The *y*-axis here represents the different types of IP; the *x*-axis covers the different types of product and service components.

	IP Component	Customers	Services	Products	Meta-Content	Content	Apps, Tools and Processes	Platforms and Infra	Application Tech	Base Tech
Registered rights	Patents			Product patent			Process patent		Application-based patent	Base tech patent
	Trademarks		Service trademark	Product trademark			Process trademark			
	Design rights		Registered service design	Registered product design	Format rights	Format rights	App and process design	Registered platform design	Application design	
	Copyright			Product copyright	Meta-content copyright	Content copyright	App copyright			
Unregistered rights	Trade secrets						Knowledge of apps and tools take-up			
	Know-how (technology and process)						Process Know-how			
	Algorithms and software		Service algorithms	Product algorithms			Process algorithms	Infrastructure code eg workflow tools	Software applications	
	Specialised customer knowledge	Detailed Insight into customer behaviour								
	Value of brands		Service brand	Product brand				Infrastructure brand	Powered by e.g. LinkedIn	Powered by e.g. Dolby
Open rights	Open source						Software tools and apps	Software tools and apps		
	Creative commons licensing			Rights to use and limitations	Rights to use and limitations	Rights to use and limitations	Rights to use and limitations	Rights to use and limitations		
	Fair use rights				Content use and limitations	Content use and limitations				

Figure 32:   IP Potential Sources of Commercial Value.

There are four types of **registered** rights:

Patents protect technical features and processes, i.e. inventions. They reserve to the patent owner the right to make, use, or sell the invention. Typically, they last up to 20 years subject to payment of an annual renewal fee.

Trade marks protect any sign that distinguishes goods and services from competitors. They can be maintained indefinitely subject to renewal every 10 years.

Design rights protect the physical appearance and visual appeal of products. Registered designs can be maintained up to 25 years subject to the payment of a renewal fee every five years. Unregistered designs are automatic and only protect three dimensional aspects of a design, excluding surface ornamentation. They last for up to 15 years.

Copyright gives automatic protection to original written, dramatic, musical and artistic works, published editions of works, sound recordings, films and broadcasts. Creator's copyright generally lasts until 70 years after death.

There are five types of **unregistered** rights:

Trade secrets encompass manufacturing or industrial secrets and commercial secrets. They can include sales methods, distribution methods, consumer profiles, marketing tactics, lists of suppliers and clients, and manufacturing processes.

Technology and process know-how typically covers practical knowledge on how to accomplish something. It can sometimes be tacit knowledge, but capturing this formally as explicit knowledge can be commercially valuable for a firm.

Software and algorithms include operations which enable calculation, data processing, and 'automated reasoning' based on software; they can be critical to the function of many products, services, platforms and applications across a wide range of market spaces; software cannot be patented and so these unregistered rights need to be protected in more subtle ways.

Specialised customer knowledge can include detailed insights into customer behaviour, information about how customers interact with specific products and services, and their purchasing behaviour.

Brand value: Brands can represent a significant source of commercial value, not just for products and services but where a brand can be associated with a key enabling base or application technology; technology platforms can also be branded to generate sustainable commercial value. Unfortunately, most firm valuation techniques tend to ignore the commercial value of brands.

The promotion of 'open innovation' as a key construct in commercialisation market spaces has unfortunately obscured the commercial implications of 'open rights'. In practice, there are three types of 'open' rights, which although 'open' in theory, may have practical limitations on how they can be used or exploited:

Open source: Generically, open source refers to a program in which the source code is available to the general public for use and/or modification from its original design free of charge. Open source code is typically created as a collaborative effort in which programmers improve upon the code and share the changes within the community. Open source emerged in the technology community as a response to proprietary software owned and managed by firms which was seen as an impediment to innovation.

Creative commons licenses are public copyright licenses that enable the free distribution of an otherwise copyrighted work. A creative commons license is used when an author wants to give people the right to share, use, and build upon content, not software, that they have created. Work licensed under a creative commons license is governed by applicable copyright law.

Fair use rights is a legal doctrine that permits limited use of copyrighted material without acquiring permission from the rights holders. Examples of fair use in copyright law include commentary, search engines, research, and scholarship. Technology firms need to note the implications of this when commercialising research and development.

Figure 32 also illustrates how the different types of rights can be used to protect and exploit the ways in which technology is packaged to take it to market. Examples based on our research include: detailed insights into customer behaviour can have significant value and need to be protected; services can be protected by using trademarks, registered designs and brands, while keeping service algorithms secret; patents, trademarks, registered designs and copyright can be used to protect products; content and meta-content can be protected using copyright and format rights; applications, tools and platforms can be protected the same as products with additional protection based on process and domain knowledge; base and application technologies are best protected by patents or sometimes more effectively by secrecy.

14.3 Changing IP Priorities along Commercialisation Journey

This wider definition of IP leads directly to the need to appreciate the relative importance of the different types of IP at different stages of the commercialisation journey and the related maturity of the firm. For example, an early emphasis on the generation and protection of patents may give way to the need to protect design rights, copyright protection of algorithms and software, or metadata which enables the functioning of new devices or processes.

Figure 33 shows the relative importance of the different types of IP along the commercialisation journey: this is an aggregate view based on data from all 12 market spaces discussed previously. The key points which emerge from this analysis are: at the early stages of commercialisation, around Chasm I, there are only 3–4 key IP variables of importance, led by patents, copyright and algorithms; as the commercialisation journey develops, around Chasm II, a wider number of IP variables become relevant with this number falling slightly once Chasm III has been crossed.

What this illustrates very clearly is the need to understand the broader IP issues at stake as commercialisation proceeds: an approach focused solely around the core technology patents and algorithms is unlikely to harness the full commercial value of the innovation, which is a key message management teams need to take on board.

There are several other observations worth making here: unregistered rights in the form of technology and process know-how can be a critical component of differentiation which improves the likelihood of successfully crossing Chasm II; enforcing content copyright and using specialised

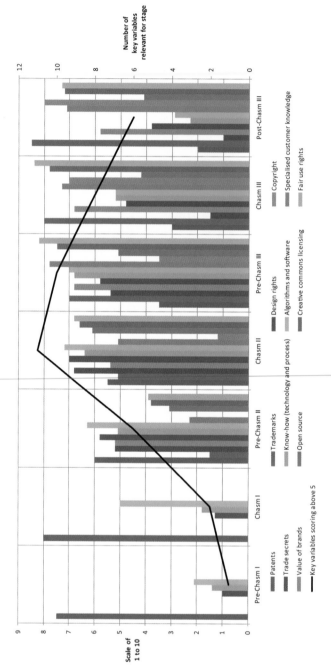

Figure 33:   Relative Importance of IP Components Along the Commercialisation Journey.

customer knowledge in a 'protected' way can significantly improve customer scaling around Chasm III.

14.4 Market Spaces and IP Priorities

Our analysis of IP management across the 12 market spaces discussed in Chapter 5 showed some systematic variations in behaviour, based on the number of potential sources of new value, as discussed earlier in this chapter.

Broadly speaking, we can group the 12 market spaces into three groups, based on the number of IP variables which are important.

Digital-intensive market spaces showed the most complex behaviour based on the largest number of potential sources of commercial value, as shown in Figure 34. This covered the following market spaces: media and

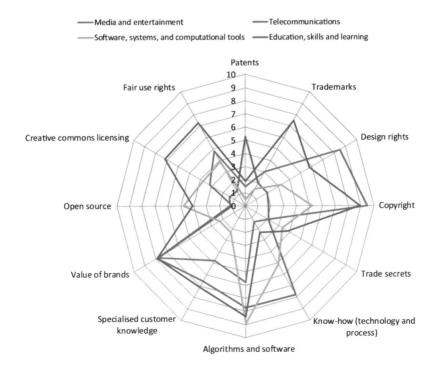

Figure 34:   IP Priorities for Digital-intensive Market Spaces.

entertainment; telecommunications; software, systems and computational tools; and education, skills and learning. The results illustrate the need for quite sophisticated IP management strategies and tactics for these market spaces given the multiple opportunities to exploit IP.

In contrast, for **engineering-intensive market spaces** shown in Figure 35, a smaller number of IP sources are important, focused mainly around registered rights: this enables more focused IP management strategies covering the following market spaces: biotechnology, aerospace engineering, automotive engineering, and oil and gas engineering.

The third **hybrid** group showed intermediate behaviour between the digital-intensive and engineering-intensive market spaces, with an intermediate number of sources of IP-based value. This covered the following market spaces: electronics and computing hardware, energy and lighting, financial services, and healthcare services.

It is worth noting that this hybrid group constitutes those market spaces where a traditional emphasis on engineering-based IP is being augmented by new digital technologies and their associated IP. The

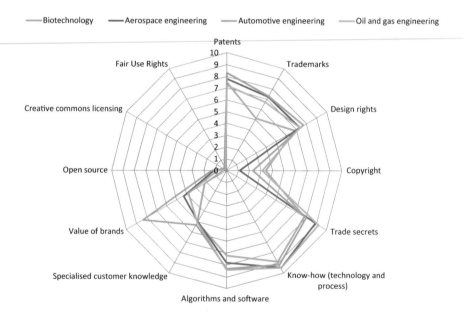

Figure 35:   IP Priorities for Engineering-intensive Market Spaces.

emerging field around the 'Internet of Things' is a good example of this change. This transition creates important challenges around IP protection and exploitation for firms which have historically been less concerned about the value of data, metadata, and product and service architectures.

Overall, these results illustrate the critical importance of developing and applying the most appropriate IP management strategies and tactics. More detailed treatment of these results is included in the commercialisation Workbench.

Chapter 15

Funding and Investment

15.1 Sources of Funding

Commercialising science and technology-enabled innovation depends critically on the Funding and investment vector as discussed in Chapter 4, given the need to deploy significant resources along the commercialisation journey.

At a macro level, as we discussed in Chapter 2, the key distinction is between public and private finance with the balance between them usually driven by the ideological complexion of the governing political environment. In practice, most funding and investment over the last three decades has been driven by a mix of public and private sources. One of the key objectives of our research was to understand this investment mix: the sources of funding, the differences in funding across market spaces, the changing nature of investment based on the maturity of the commercialisation process, and what this means for science and technology firms looking for funding.

The overall backdrop for our research was framed by general perceptions about the increasing concentration of wealth in private hands, ideological biases against state funding and by the apparent preference for corporate investment to be judged by short-term criteria. This has tended to highlight the importance of private funding, but our research has exposed some interesting differences between the rhetoric and reality.

We first need to distinguish between different *types* of funding, which can apply to all the different funding sources, to varying degrees:

Grants, where the funds are provided outright, with no financial returns expected, although there may be other targets set, such as generation of intellectual property (IP), the level of technology readiness, or the number of new jobs created as a result of the funding.

Loans, where the funds provided need to be returned at some point; the cost of servicing these loans and the security required can vary with interest rates for borrowing the money ranging from zero to rates linked to the cost of borrowing in commercial markets.

Payments contingent on the provision of specific products and services, for example, some firms raise funds by providing specific services linked to their offerings.

Equity funding, where the investment is provided in return for ownership of part of the firm; this ownership can be structured using a number of financial instruments, usually shares in the firm, with attached conditions spelt out in the term sheet; see for example Smith and Kiholme[149] and Bhide.[150]

Table 16 provides a summary of the different sources of funding accessed by the firms in our research data set. Personal savings and support from families and friends of entrepreneurs need little explanation. Crowd funding, however, is less well defined: this refers to a large group of investors, the crowd, each providing relatively small amounts of money, usually as equity funding, although there have been a number of examples of crowd-based loan funding.[151]

State agencies, at local, national and international levels, play a significant role in funding the commercialisation of science and technology, usually in the form of grants and loans, and sometimes equity. State funding can be critical for technologies which require the creation of new infrastructure, for example, in nanomaterials or quantum computing. It can also be important in supporting the development of new applications and tools with broad applicability, for example, new healthcare products and services enabled by digital technology.

Table 16:   Overview of Funding Sources.

Funding Sources	Description
Personal savings	Personal savings and borrowing by founder or founding team.
Friends and family	Usually small amounts of funding from close friends and family on generous terms; generally for equity or loans on soft terms.
Crowd funding	Funding based on relatively small sums from a large body of individual investors, usually for equity.
State agencies	Funding provided by civic, regional and national institutions and bodies, as grants or loans, less commonly as equity.
Angels	Investment from individuals, usual high net-worth, where the angel commonly has knowledge of the market space or is in local ecosystem.
Seed funds	Formally constituted investment funds, usually for small, early stage investment, as equity (sometimes as convertible loans).
Incubators	Formally constituted investment and advisory companies, who provide funding for equity stakes, usually at early stages of growth.
Accelerators	Formally constituted investment and advisory companies, who provide funding for equity stakes, usually when firm has been established.
Venture capital	Formally constituted and regulated investment vehicle with money from venture partners, managed by professional investment managers; usually equity, sometimes convertible loans.
Private equity	Funds with more fire-power than VC, usually greater financial structuring expertise; usually invest for equity, but may combine with debt finance for larger amounts required for rapid expansion.
Public markets	Open to firms once they have listed on appropriate stock exchange; equity bought and sold under well-defined rules; investors can be individuals, organisations or firms who trade in listed stocks and shares.
Corporates	Larger firms, who may want access to new products and services, new markets or financial returns on their investment, usually invest for equity but may pay for joint development of new things.
Banks	Typically lending institutions, who provide structured loan funding against 'secured' assets; may sometimes make investments for equity.
Customers	Customers who use and pay for the firm's products and services, thereby providing funding to run and grow the firm; usually the cheapest form of finance.

The availability of state funding as grants, soft loans and equity investment, however, is strongly influenced by the ideological influences in the meso-economic environment, as we discussed earlier in Chapter 2. At a practical level, this can be manifested by different financing structures, including state and private public funding partnerships, which can be different in different countries and market spaces at different times.

Angels[152] are typically high net-worth individuals who provide equity funding and commercial expertise to firms; seed funds operate in the same space and often consist of a group of angels, constituted as an investment vehicle.

Incubators and Accelerators are 'intervention' agencies who provide a range of services to early-stage firms, usually investment of money and resources in return for equity. We discuss incubators and accelerators in more detail in Chapter 19.

Venture Capital (VC) and Private Equity[153] consists of formally constituted and structured investment vehicles, run by professional managers who handle equity investment of funds provided by wealthy individuals, firms and other organisations; VC may also sometimes provide loan finance in addition to equity investment. We discuss VC in more detail in Section 15.3.

Public markets are usually only used by firms to raise expansion capital, where they typically sell a part of the firm to public investors to generate cash to fund growth plans. Larger firms participate routinely in public markets, but they may also invest directly into smaller higher-growth firms where they have a strategic interest. Banks, of course, are familiar as sources of loan finance.

Customer funding, where 'early' customers support the development of new products and services, is a critical source of funding that is often overlooked: we discuss this in Section 15.4.

15.2 Investment in Science and Technology-enabled Innovation

Most published work on the commercialisation of science and technology-enabled innovation has tended to focus on early concept generation or the challenges of 'scaling' with different ways of defining what scaling actually means: the crucial 'middle' phase is not well understood and therefore sometimes described in meta-physical terms such as the 'valley of death', with the implication that it is hard to control or manage this process.

Our analysis of the funding profile for firms was based on segmenting the commercialisation journey into 15 segments: the pre-Chasm I phase was divided into three segments; following Chasm I, the phase between Chasms I and II was again divided into three segments; and the same approach was adopted for the phase between Chasms II and III and for the post-Chasm III phase. Our approach provided consistency with the 3-segment approach adopted by venture capitalists to describe their interventions post Chasm II, as Series A, B, and C. This level of granularity enabled us to understand the role played by different types of funding along the commercialisation pathway. It also enabled us to explicitly explore the different types of funding used when crossing the chasms.

Our analysis, summarised in Figure 36, showed some interesting divergences from popular perceptions about how funding works. There is a wide range of funding options available to support initial concept development and the crossing of Chasm I, where concepts are turned into prototypes. Friends and family, Angels and public sector institutions play a critical role in funding the crossing of Chasm I. VC hardly plays any role in crossing Chasm I.

There is a serious gap in funding for firms trying to cross Chasm II. In spite of popular perceptions to the contrary, VC is largely conspicuous by its absence in crossing Chasm II. Most 'high risk' VC comes into the picture *once a firm has crossed Chasm II*, as examination of a typical VC term sheet confirms, with its need to have clarity on customers and a proven, sustainable business model *before* investment. Customer funding can play a critical role at all stages of the commercialisation journey.

Our research data allowed us to quantify the relative contributions from the different types of investments at the different stages of growth. This is shown in Figure 37.

The results show the importance of state funding at pre-Chasm I, Chasm I, pre-Chasm II, and Chasm II; the importance of funding from state agencies only declined significantly once Chasm II has been crossed.

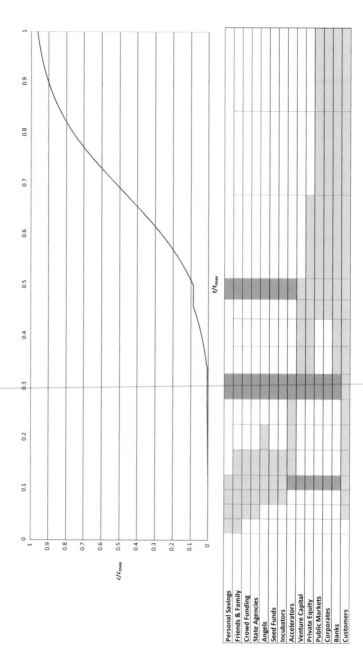

Figure 36:   Funding Sources vs the Triple Chasm Model.

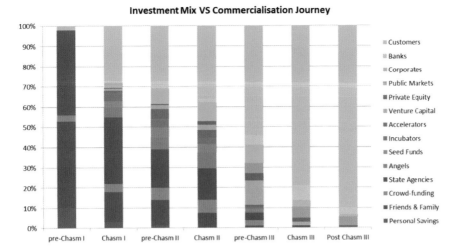

Figure 37: Detailed View of Funding Sources Across the Chasms.

They also show that customer funding plays a crucial role at all stages, even at the earlier stages of the commercialisation journey. Overall, the data confirms that the later stages of commercialisation could not happen without the intervention of public capital *earlier* in the journey.

Given the importance of Chasm II identified and discussed in Chapters 3 and 4, we looked in detail at the typical funding profile at Chasm II for the firms in our data set.

This highlights the critical role played by customer funding, state agencies, and corporates (large firms), in decreasing order of importance, in crossing Chasm II. Critically, it confirms the relatively small role played by VC in crossing the chasm critical for commercial success.

We discuss below the implications of this and how it is actually consistent with the reality, rather than the rhetoric, of the VC model.

15.3 Private Equity and Venture Capital in Perspective

Over the last 30 years, VC has become a highly visible form of financing for innovative technology companies, mainly in the US; this approach has gradually spread into other parts of the connected global financial system, starting with Europe, then spreading into Asia, Latin America and lately into Africa. In the US, it is estimated that a fifth of current publicly listed firms received VC funding at some point in their growth trajectory.[154]

While a small number of firms were funded by the first generation of venture capitalists in the 1960s, the VC industry only emerged in the US after a regulatory change in 1979 that allowed pension funds to invest in VC. The rule change, known as the Prudent Man Rule, led to a significant increase in the amount of money entrusted to VC funds. To put this in context, however, over the last 50 years, the US VC industry has invested over $0.6 trillion, mainly in US firms; over that same period, the private equity industry raised four times as much, about $2.4 trillion. In 2014, the private equity industry raised $218 billion, almost 10 times the $31 billion raised by VC. In fact, venture capitalists typically invest in less than 0.2% of new US firms, although this figure is estimated to rise to nearly 2% when we only consider technology firms.

So what creates the popular narrative where VC is synonymous with the creation of new technology firms?

Firms backed by VC include some of the most innovative companies in the world. In 2013, VC-backed US public firms spent $115 billion on research and development compared to practically zero in 1979.[155] These firms which were backed by VC *in their earlier growth phases* now account for over 40% of the R&D funding by US public firms. VC-backed firms also constitute a consistently high fraction of those companies undergoing initial public offerings. Between 1979 and 2013, over 2600 VC-backed US firms had their initial public offerings, equivalent to 28% of the total number of US IPOs during that period, although this number fluctuated year by year.

The prevailing narrative is that VC is a form of financing that is usually targeted at young, innovative, and highly risky firms; these investments are typically highly speculative so that most of the firms that receive VC funding will fail, even as a very small number of firms become extremely successful. From the investors' perspective, these odds should be attractive because the small number of huge winners should more than compensate for the losses of the others. This theory has been challenged in the last few years by detailed analysis showing that the average return on capital across the industry is relatively poor. For example, an aggregate analysis of all European VC from inception to 2013 showed an IRR of 1.68%; the equivalent figure for the US was an IRR of 5.86%. This compares poorly with the figures for European and US buyouts, which were 9.63% and 13.52%, respectively. The figures for VC, however, showed a very strong bias where much better returns, with IRRs exceeding 15%, were restricted to a small number of larger VC funds focused on high-growth market spaces in media and entertainment, software and computing systems and financial technologies.

Typically, VC funds look to invest in firms where small investments can generate huge returns in the process usually avoiding market spaces with high capital needs. What this means in practice is that despite the popular rhetoric, most firms are unlikely to attract VC investment to fund their growth.

As Zider[156] has noted, contrary to popular perception, VC plays only a minor role in funding basic innovation; most of the money invested by venture capitalists goes into building the infrastructure required to grow the business. What is even more important, from the perspective of a firm looking for investment, is that most VC investment is actually focussed on firms which have demonstrably crossed Chasm II and therefore have a lower risk profile than before they have established a sustainable business model. Figure 38 demonstrates this starkly, where our research data highlights the gap between the rhetoric and the reality: the rhetoric is that VC is designed to support firms in the risky transition from concept to sustainable business. As our data shows, the reality is that very little VC investment is available until firms have crossed Chasm II; investments billed as Series A, B, and C actually support firms in the growth phase post Chasm II leading to tackling Chasm III.

There are some key points about VC which all growing firms need to recognise, so that they can make the right funding decisions:

Venture funding is *not long-term money*; the objective of VCs is to invest in a firm's balance sheet until it reaches a sufficient size and credibility so that it can be sold to a larger firm or that the firm can be listed on the stock market, so that institutional public equity markets can step in and provide liquidity. This exit, with the associated gain in value, is the primary motivation for the VC, irrespective of any long-term objectives the firm may have harboured prior to the VC investment.

The VC *niche is underpinned by the structure and rules of capital* markets, which are usually driven by macro-economic policy, so firms need to understand how this environment operates and when it may change and affect the prospects of the firm.

Venture capitalists typically invest in market spaces with the potential for dramatic changes in reality or sentiment: the idea that they invest in great teams and great ideas may only be true if the primary criterion is satisfied. This explains why the majority of VC is deployed largely in a few market spaces: media and entertainment, software, systems and tools, and financial technologies, which all meet the short-term nature of the bets placed by VCs. Occasionally, VCs may have a burst of investment in market spaces such as renewable energy or biotechnology when there is a perception that there are short-term opportunities, in the form of exits for the VCs, based on market rationalisation.

Venture funding comes with significant strings attached, not just in terms of the conditions of investment but also new constraints on the firm's declared commercial strategy based on the interests of the VC concerned.

Given these factors, it is not surprising that a very small number of firms actually get venture funding; in our research data set, less than 2% of firms received VC funding, which is consistent with the data from the other studies discussed above.

Given the Chasm II-crossing challenges discussed in Chapter 4, what this means is that *most firms cannot rely on venture funding for their commercialisation journey* and need to find credible alternatives. This has major implications not just for the firms, but for policy makers and intervention agencies, which we discuss in Chapters 17–19. One important potential solution to this problem is funding based on customer revenues, which we discuss in Section 15.4.

15.4 Customer Revenues as a Source of Funding

Customer revenues represent the cheapest form of funding for a firm,[157] because the firm does not have to give up equity in return for the money.

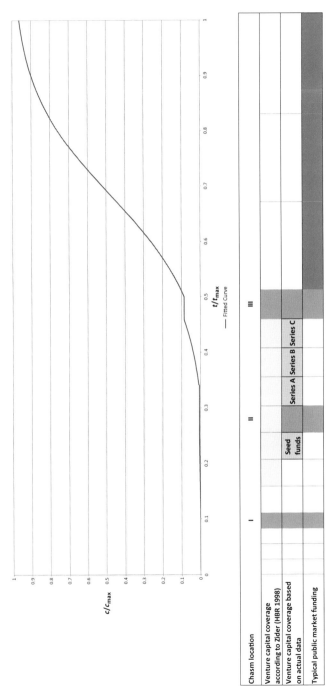

Figure 38:   Venture Funding Rhetoric vs Reality.

There are also no borrowing costs associated with the funding, as there would be if loans were involved.

Customer funding can play a critical role in the funding of early stage technology firms. At the earliest stages of growth, bootstrapping can be used to fund start-ups.

Bootstrap is a situation in which an entrepreneur starts a firm with little or no capital but uses operating revenues to fund growth, although this strategy on its own is unlikely to succeed in most situations.

Post start-up, customer funding can play a critical role: in our data set, about 30% of the funding to cross Chasm II came from customers. This type of funding has added benefits: it also provides deeper dialogues with customers which can help shape new products and services which are then more likely to succeed in the market.

There are several different types of customer funding which are best understood in the context of the different types of revenues and business models discussed previously in Chapter 13.

Pay-in-advance models: These typically cover the costs of customising a product or service or non-recurrent engineering (NRE) costs, or sometimes asking for payment for products or services before they are actually delivered; often, the commercial justification for this is to give the 'charter customer' early or privileged access to new or enhanced functionality.

License revenues can be a significant source of customer revenues, where the firm can charge upfront, as a commitment or enabling fee, for a percentage of the total license fee payable for products and services; license fees are often charged in conjunction with NRE fees, along with coverage of some or all of the costs of the firm supplying the technology or product to the customer.

Matchmaker models: These typically consist of payments made to facilitate dialogues or interactions between the charter customer, partners, suppliers, and customers.

Subscription models: Most customers are comfortable with the idea of paying monthly or annual subscriptions in advance for services yet to be rendered; the rationale for this is the need for the firm to build out infrastructure or capability in order to provide the service.

Upfront subscription revenues typically include access fees, payment for provision of different types of functionality, or the delivery of content or related services. They can also include access to other types of capability, such as manufacturing know-how or market intelligence. Product to service models also depend on generating revenues using a mix of 'packaged' products and services associated with making these products available as services, for example, some software-based products.

Scarcity models: These include upfront payments to secure access to scarce resources or discounted access in return for upfront payments. This can be particularly helpful where firms can trade off lower margins versus earlier access to scarce capital.

Sponsorship can be used by firms as a way of generating early revenues, which can help with the costs of developing new products and services; this type of funding can also be used to support marketing costs.

15.5 Equity Funding and Valuation

The valuation of technology firms plays a critical role in equity-based funding: a higher valuation means that the firm has to give up a smaller percentage of the firm's equity in return for an investment. This can have a significant bearing on the management and control of the firm, not to mention the value accruing to the other shareholders on 'exit' when the firm lists on the public markets or is acquired by another firm. However, the valuation of early stage firms is far from an exact science. When firms list on public markets, there are generally accepted criteria based on experience which can be used to value firms on the basis of revenues, profits and market-specific growth metrics. However, for earlier stage companies which may have little or no revenues, or where the growth trajectory is still subject to uncertainty, valuation of the firm can be a challenge.

For these firms, valuation, like beauty, can be in the 'eyes of the beholder', with the valuation based on whether the person doing the valuation is buying or selling! Not surprisingly, there is an entire industry devoted to justifying the valuation of technology firms: for example, some of the approaches used include sophisticated financial models based on the idea of net present value (NPV) and discounted cash flows.[158] However, when it comes down to it, valuing a firm is more of an art than a science: ultimately, any valuation can be reduced to an aggregation of many different components, and the relative importance of these different components can vary with the maturity of the firm, as shown in Table 17.

The key components of valuation are: the value of underlying IP, including key technologies, processes and brands, the overall packaging and positioning of IP in the marketplace, the usual commercial metrics, including size of market, market structure, and market share, the usual metrics of financial performance, in particular, revenues, profitability, and cash flow, the maturity of the firm in terms of how far has it travelled

Table 17: Valuation Components.

Main Contribution to Valuation	Stage of Maturity			
	Pre-Chasm 1	Pre-Chasm 2	Pre-Chasm 3	Post-Chasm 3
The value of underlying intellectual property				
Technology				
Process				
Brand				
The overall packaging and positioning of this IP in the marketplace				
The underlying business model and its resilience				
General metrics				
Size of market				
Market structure				
Market share				
Usual metrics of financial performance (revenues, profitability)				
Revenues				
Profit (EBIT, EBITDA, etc.)				
Perceptions of future prospects				

along the commercialisation pathway, and perceptions of the future prospects for the firm.

Business models can have a very big impact on the valuation of a firm. For example, software firms based on licensing or subscription models can attract higher valuations than firms based on product sales because their business models are perceived as being more sustainable. By way of contrast, some electronic hardware firms, including semiconductor-based manufacturers, which have business models based on royalty payments and licensing, can be valued more highly than firms with pure licensing models. In the media and entertainment market space, content firms with multiple time-based distribution models are typically valued more highly than those with a single distribution outlet. In biotechnology market spaces, firms with license models can be valued more highly than those involved in integrated 'full-service' models. In all cases, the positioning, reach and span of the business model can dramatically affect investment, risk, and valuation.

Chapter 16

Human Capital: Talent, Leadership, and Culture

16.1 The Challenge for Technology Firms

There is a significant body of literature covering the general human capital challenges facing firms, especially around the areas of organisational dynamics, teams, and leadership. Much of this insight is based on analysing the behaviour of stable, mature, larger firms. More recently, there have been attempts to understand the challenges facing fast-growing technology firms,[159] where some of the learnings from more static environments may be less relevant.

When we embarked on our research programme to understand the challenges of commercialising science and technology-enabled innovation, we realised that we would need to frame the overall human capital changes more explicitly than we had observed in most of the prevailing literature. Our detailed survey and subsequent discussions led us to formulate the key variables relevant to the inception and growth of science and technology-enabled firms, which in aggregate constitute the talent, leadership, and culture vector described in Chapter 4. The 15 variables we identified, clustered into five groups, are shown in Table 18.

The general issues around **talent** recognition, development, and management have been discussed by many authors already. For science and technology-enabled innovation, our research showed three specific areas of interest: core competences, entrepreneurial orientation, and the hybrid

Table 18:   Human Capital Management — The Key Variables.

Talent	Core competences
	Entrepreneurial orientation
	Hybrid techno-commercial skills, including 'T-shaped' expertise
Teams	Use of psychometric profiling tools and techniques
	Team roles and processes
	Team performance management
Organisational structure and management	Size vs structure trade-offs
	Control systems
	Communications
Leadership	Conventional leader-follower-shared goals paradigm
	Hybrid approaches to leadership
	'Flat' structures based on the DAC paradigm
Culture	The narrative: Stories and myths
	Power structures
	Remuneration and rewards

skills required to synthesize new products and services, as discussed in Chapter 9. These are discussed in more detail below.

Teams in technology firms can draw on the general tools developed over the last few decades for profiling team members and combining them into effective teams. Our research highlighted the need for more relevant behavioural and psychographic measures, better understanding of how processes are mapped against roles, and how teams are managed.

We address three key aspects associated with **organisational structure and management**: the trade-offs between the size of the firm and the structure which underpins how teams are organised, control systems used by firms, and how the firm manages communication inside teams and between teams.

Much of the literature, and associated tools and techniques concerned with **leadership**, have historically followed the leaders–followers–shared goals paradigm. Some of the firms in our research sample have applied a more radical outcome-oriented paradigm emphasising the need for direction, alignment and commitment, based on very flat organisational structures. Many of the firms in our data set have adopted a hybrid leadership approach, often based on switching from flat to more 'directed' structures, as the firms have grown. We discuss this in Section 16.5.

The *culture*, behaviour and rewards in science and technology firms have been explored by several researchers, but recent research has been heavily biased by detailed studies on a small number of highly successful digital firms funded by venture capital (VC); these 'outlier' firms do not constitute the norm, as we discuss in Section 16.6. We look in particular at the overall narrative of the firm, the power structures, and remuneration and rewards schema.

Figure 39 summarises the results of our research, based on surveying the firms in our data set. This shows how the human capital mix, based on the 15 variables grouped into five areas, changes as the commercialisation journey proceeds. These results highlight the human capital challenges for fast growing technology firms. The most important point to note is that the number of variables affecting this journey rises rapidly around Chasm II before starting to drop off; this illustrates once again why the crossing of Chasm II is the hardest part of the journey.

16.2 Talent

There has been much discussion over the last decade, in particular, about how the success of technology firms is highly dependent on their ability to attract the right talent.[160] This has included general observations about the importance of entrepreneurial orientation in the talent pool[161] without examining what this means in practice. There has also been some recognition about the need for cross-functional skills,[162] sometimes referred to as T-shaped profiles, where broad expertise across a number of disciplines, the top of the T, is combined with in-depth knowledge of a specific area, the bottom part of the T. Underpinning all this of course is the need to have the right core competences, as defined by Prahalad and Hamel,[163] in place for the commercialisation journey.

The importance of *entrepreneurial orientation* for commercialising science and technology is well recognised. The strands of this debate include discussions about whether entrepreneurs are born or made, how

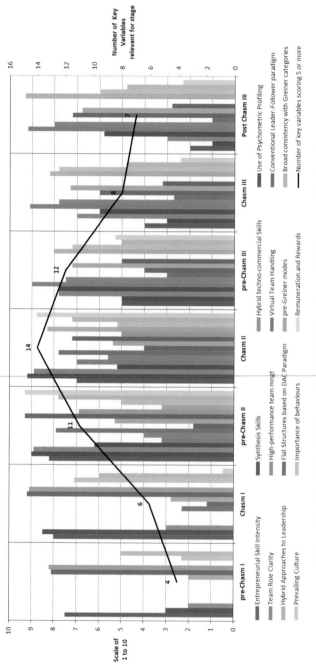

Figure 39:   Variation in Human Capital Metrics Across the Commercialisation Journey.

scientists and technologists can become more entrepreneurial, whether entrepreneurship can be taught or learned, and creating networks which can support and mentor entrepreneurs. In our experience, however, the critical issues, which are hard to quantify, are the motivation, self-awareness, social skills and relationship management capabilities of entrepreneurs which often hold the key to success.

Critical for science and technology-enabled innovation is the ability to synthesise new ideas, concepts, products and services: typically synthesis skills require the ability to understand and integrate a range of technologies and to couple technology capability with potential users and customers. These *hybrid techno-commercial synthesis skills* are critical for crossing Chasm II as Figure 39 shows. Synthesis skills can be taught systematically, using a variety of tools and techniques. The challenge is that this often requires a mental paradigm shift because so much of the scientific tradition concentrates on analysis, often at the expense of synthesis. Our research data showed that the availability of these hybrid skills, even in small numbers, was critical for their success. Unfortunately, little attention has been paid to the systematic development of this skill so far. Practical approaches to the synthesis of new products and services are discussed in Chapter 9.

16.3 Teams

When it comes to assembling effective teams, two key things matter: functional, subject matter expertise; and behaviour types, as defined by one of the common behavioural metrics, such as the Belbin method. Functional subject matter expertise, as defined by core competences, clearly depends on the technologies under consideration and the target market species, but we discuss the common behavioural metrics here. Despite some criticisms and reservations, the Belbin approach[164,165] to team role inventory and analysis is still the most widely used tool; provided it is not used as a psychometric instrument, the 9-role tool with 360° feedback is a helpful approach to defining roles in technology firms. These nine roles are: plant, resource investigator, co-ordinator, shaper, monitor evaluator, team-worker, implementer, completer/finisher, and specialist.

Typically, teams in science and technology firms need to use role models in conjunction with psychometric indicators. The Myers–Briggs Type Indicator (MBTI)[166] is the most commonly used psychometric indicator, based on Jung's typology theories which postulated a sequence of four cognitive functions (thinking, feeling, sensation, and intuition), each having one of two polar orientations (extraversion or introversion), giving a total of eight dominant functions. The MBTI based on these eight hypothetical functions continues to be used, despite many reservations, because it is a simple tool which can provide useful behavioural insights.

The performance of entrepreneurial teams has been the subject of much qualitative research over the last two decades,[167] and some of this can be applied to science and technology-enabled firms, at the early stages of their commercialisation journey, but as with the research and tools developed for behavioural profiling, this remains a difficult area to confidently provide guidance to firms growing rapidly. The general research and our data does point to the importance of the following factors: prior experience of members of the team in relevant market spaces, previous relationships with other members of the team, team tenure implied by these relationships, and finally the actual size of the team; we discuss the relationship between firm size and structure below.

Our research data also showed significant interest in how to create and manage *high-performance teams*, particularly for more mature technology firms where there was a need to retain high levels of technology expertise in the delivery of the products and services.

A critical issue for technology firms is the challenge posed by *virtual teams*: the key question emerging is how these teams can operate effectively and reliably when team members need to interact over different geographies and time zones with no physical interaction. There is little credible research in this space, however, and our research highlighted the importance of this without providing any specific and useful insights.

16.4 Organisational Structure and Management

Greiner's work[168] provided some of the early basis for understanding the structure and dynamics of technology firms as they grow, but our research revealed several limitations of this approach in the current context:

The insights were based on analysing the growth of relatively well-established firms, typically with more than 50 employees, although there are several observations about the general applicability of the results to early stage firms.

Much of the discussion about organisational structures effectively assumes that all firms, as they grow, develop M-form divisional structures based on distinct product groups, and that integrated U-form structures based on functional lines gradually atrophy as the firm grows. We suspect that these conclusions reflect the fact that Greiner's data came from US Corporations overwhelmingly operating M-form models in the 1990's, and so does not include more recent preferences for U-form structures, where even larger firms have highly unified organisational structures arranged along functional categories, such as design or manufacture, not by types of products or product groups; we discuss this further in Chapter 20.

While Greiner's model illustrates that the pace of change between the different stages of growth can be affected by the pace of change in the external market space, the transition between the different stages themselves, based on periods of evolution interspersed by periods of revolution, seems rather idealised, based on the aggregate impact of internal metrics, such as how decisions are made.

In order to understand the link between size and organisational structure, we analysed our data and compared how five key metrics, also referred to by Greiner, changed with the effective size of the firm. The five metrics we used were: the Management Focus, in terms of the commercial objective of the firm; the general nature of the Organisation Structure, based processes, roles and relationships; the Management Style, based on Greiner's categories; Control Systems, which reflect the need to manage resources and outputs; the Management Reward emphasis, which looks at how non-salary-based rewards are prioritised.

We use 10 categories, which reflect the size of the firm as it grows, as follows: the single entrepreneur category, which reflects the effective starting point for some firms; the initial founding group, which is much more common for firms focused on science and technology innovation, where the idea of the lone entrepreneur is less common; *ad hoc* teams, which are typically teams with full-time and part-time inputs which may form and morph rapidly; early teams, which are the first formal teams to emerge from *ad hoc* structures; launch teams, which are strongly focused on getting the first product or service into the hands of a charter customer: high-performance teams focused on the effective delivery of new products and services; integrated teams, who are optimally organised to deliver the firm's overall commercial objectives; U-form teams, which reflect unitary organisation of the firm, functionally organised, as it delivers a range of products and services; M-form teams, which are organised into distinct divisions each responsible for a particular product or service, or product and service families; H-form teams, which reflect a hybrid of U-form and M-form organisation.

We should emphasise that not all firms traverse all stages of this pathway always; indeed, some of the data in our research came from firms which started life as fully formed early teams, and some of the firms skipped the stage when they built high-performance teams because speed to market was more important. These results can, however, provide useful insights for firms about their relative maturity.

Table 19 shows the results of our analysis, which illustrate how the team focus changes over time.

Combining our analysis with customer growth data from the Triple Chasm Model discussed in Chapter 3 enabled us to map these organisational phases against customer acquisition, as shown in Figure 40.

What these results reveal is that firms need to change the way in which they are organised, as they grow and acquire new customers; this may sometimes conflict with the cultural preferences of the founders or managers of the firm. We discuss the practical implications of this further in Chapter 19.

16.5 Leadership

The success of firms based on science and technology-enabled innovation depends critically on the leadership philosophy and management structures deployed, especially given the diverse talent mix in these firms. The conventional approach to leadership of all firms, which has been well documented over the last three decades, is based on the *tripod of leaders, followers and their shared goals.*[169] As the context for leadership in

Table 19: Organisation and Management vs Teams.

	Single Entrepreneur	Founding Group	Ad hoc Team	Early Team	Launch Team	High performance Team	Integrated Team	U-form Team	M-form Team	H-form Team
Management focus	The idea	First prototype	Developing prototype	First charter customer	Commercially viable product	Develop commercial product	Prepare for full launch	Major commercial launch	Develop markets	Maximise revenue
Organisational structure		Informal relationships	Formal responsibilities	Process vs role mapping	Formal organisational map	Streamlined organisation	Functional responsibilities	Functional structure	Divisional structure	Matrix structure
Management style	Highly personal	Collaborative combative	Collaborative	Focused on results	Focused on results	Performance focus	Firm focus	Directive	Delegative	Delegative
Control system				Resource allocation	Cost management	Performance management	Market results	Market result	Reporting and profit centres	Goal setting and monitoring
Management reward emphasis	Ownership	Shared ownership	Shares + early options	Structured options	Structured options	Performance incentives	Group bonuses	Personal bonuses	Profit Sharing + stock options	Profit Sharing + stock options

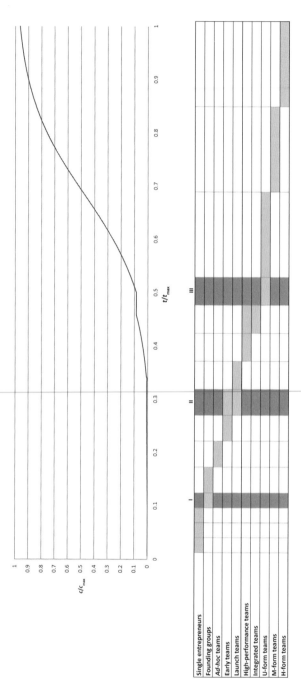

Figure 40:   Teams and Organisational Structures *vs* Commercialisation Journey.

technology firms has become more peer-based and collaborative there is recognition that the tripod ontology with its strong emphasis on leaders and followers has become increasingly strained, as it imposes limitations on leadership theory and practice.[170,171]

In the last decade, Drath *et al.*[172] have proposed a new leadership ontology, commonly referred to as DAC, in which the essential entities are three leadership *outcomes*: direction, alignment, and commitment. They define these three entities as follows:

Direction: Widespread agreement in a 'collective' or group sense on the overall goals, aims, and mission of the firm.

Alignment: The organisation and coordination of knowledge and work in the team working collectively.

Commitment: The willingness of members of this collective to subsume their own interests and benefit within the direction and alignment agreed by the collective.

The DAC approach to leadership in inherently collaborative and some of the published research on this leadership ontology has commented on the challenges of creating a culture which supports this leadership model,[173] especially in well-established and mature firms. This is discussed below in the context of culture, motivations and rewards.

Although many firms in our research data were enthusiastic about the DAC philosophy, very few had committed to it: what we observed was a significant number of *hybrid approaches*, where the DAC approach was implemented in some parts of the business while the top leadership still subscribed to the conventional leader–follower paradigm. Others have also commented on this hybrid behaviour.[174–176] Some of the firms in our data set also showed a tendency to be more collaborative when they first started, but gradually moved to a more explicit leader–follower model as they expanded. This is also reflected in organisational structures which we discussed earlier, but as we noted, some of these decisions were also affected by the impact of new investors, which we discussed in Chapter 15.

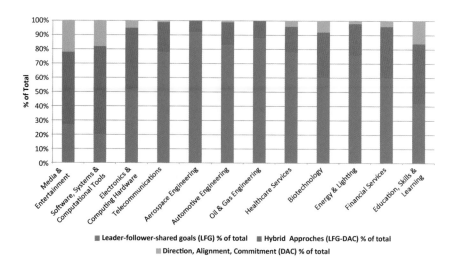

Figure 41:   **Approaches to Leadership in Different Market Spaces.**

We explored how the 12 market spaces in our data set broadly adopted these three different approaches to leadership: leader–follower–shared goals, DAC-inspired, and hybrid approaches. The results are summarised in Figure 41.

They show that in many technology-intensive market spaces, for example, in engineering and telecommunications, the conventional leader–follower–shared goals leadership paradigm is still dominant, although hybrid approaches were more common in the less mature firms in our data set. The 'flatter' DAC-based leadership paradigm is strong in media and entertainment, software and computational tools and educational markets, where hybrid approaches are widespread. Hybrid approaches are also more prevalent in newer market spaces based on biotechnology, and in energy and lighting and financial services, compared to the heavier engineering-based markets. Although the overall data did not show this explicitly, anecdotal evidence suggests that DAC-based approaches are slowly gaining ground, especially in firms active in high-growth market spaces such as media and entertainment and telecommunications.

16.6 Culture in Technology Firms

Our research data provided a number of useful insights into the culture, behaviour and rewards in science and technology-enabled firms but revealed little that would enable a rigorous approach to this challenge. The main insights were as follows:

There was a general understanding of the importance of culture in technology firms, but the precise relationship between culture and the performance of the firm is not clear.

There was widespread agreement that the culture in a firm impacts strongly on the behaviour of members of the firm, but less consensus on the relationship between rewards and behaviour; in some firms, there were strong views about how reward structures can influence behaviours both positively and negatively.

The links between performance and rewards generally appeared to be weak in the firms in our research data.

So why does this matter?

Given the critical importance of human talent in the commercialisation process, better understanding of the links between culture, behaviours and rewards has the potential to improve the chances of success for a firm.

Organisational researchers have long debated the meaning and consequences of organisational culture,[177] but the relationship between culture and organisational performance is still not well understood. Conventional wisdom suggests that a strong culture that aligns members' behaviour with organisational objectives should boost performance; because strong cultures are associated with greater adherence to routines and behavioural uniformity, they can be less effective than firms with weaker cultures in dynamic environments.

Chatman *et al.*[178] argue that these views fail to recognise that culture is actually a three-dimensional construct: the content of *norms*, for example, teamwork and integrity; how forcefully these are held by organisational members, the *intensity*; and how widely members agree about the norms within the organisation, the *consensus*. They argue that strong cultures will boost performance in dynamic environments if a norm of adaptability is intensely held and cultural norms are widely shared among members.

It has also been argued that technology firms need a more egalitarian approach with rewards for technology talent who may not rank very highly in the firm's hierarchy.[179] The principle of wider firm ownership, which challenges the traditional primacy of the role of capital over labour has also been proposed as a way of linking behaviour and rewards; indeed, some writers have gone so far as to talk about how this heralds a new industrial revolution, with the rebirth of the craftsman, albeit in a different guise.

These approaches are clearly linked to questions about funding and ownership discussed in Chapter 15. Many of the firms in our data set used both outcome and behaviour-based performance criteria to reward key talent with cash and shares in the firm.

In the absence of well-structured responses to tackling this overall challenge, we use culture webs to explore the key issues which can shape the performance of technology firms, as shown in Figure 42.

Our construct of the culture web is based on understanding the impact of the following key variables on the evolving culture of the firm, recognising that the impact of these variables changes with the maturity of the firm:

Stories and myths: these constitute the 'internal narrative' of the firm, based on the stories of how the firm was created and developed, based on the values and motivations of the founders, how these changed over time based on experience and what the unchanging 'essence' of the firm, either in actual reality or in the 'manufactured' reality represented by the 'official' myth. These stories and myths can have a very powerful impact on the culture of the firm.

Power structures in the firm which determine who makes decisions and how these decisions are actually made; these power structures may actually be in conflict with the stories and myths and the level of dissonance can have a significant bearing on the motivation of individuals and the performance of the firm overall.

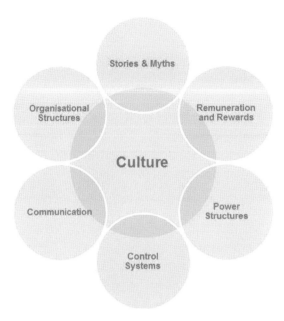

Figure 42:   The Culture Web Framework.

Remuneration and rewards: The way in which individuals are rewarded for their contribution in terms of financial rewards and overall recognition can have a dramatic impact on the overall culture. In a sense, this is where the stories and myths can come into conflict with power structures, as the overall narrative and myth is tested against the practical implications for individuals in the team.

The control systems which are used to manage the firm are another practical manifestation of the balance between the stories of the firm, power structures and the system of rewards. These control systems can depend heavily on the form of the organisation structure, which we discuss in Chapter 20.

How communication actually happens in the firm provides a clear test of the robustness of the stories and myths which underpin the firm: in this context, one sign of a problem is where there is a disconnect between communications inside and outside the firm; the rapid growth of social media means that any such dissonance is likely to be exposed more easily than before. Communication can contribute both positively and negatively to the overall culture of the firm.

The organisational structure of the firm can determine the formal and informal relationships between employees of the firm and hence impact the culture strongly. The form of this organisational structure, which we discuss further in Chapter 20 can set the tone for the culture, and indeed lead to single or multiple cultures in larger firms.

We discuss the importance of these key variables on the overall pace and trajectory of commercialisation in Chapter 17.

Our research also highlighted the changes in culture as firms grow, particularly across the chasms, but the volume and quality of our data did not enable us to quantify this explicitly: this is clearly an area where further research would be valuable.

Part IV

The Commercialisation Canvas, Actors, and Interventions

Chapter 17

The Commercialisation Canvas
for Single-product Firms

17.1 The Commercialisation Canvas

About 80% of the firms in our data set were focused on a *single* product or service rather than working on a family of products targeted at different customers. This is not surprising given the relative maturity of these firms, which enabled us to apply the Triple Chasm Model with confidence and integrate the impact of the 12 vectors into a unified framework for evaluating the overall commercialisation process. Most early stage companies are focused on creating a single product, so this approach has very broad applicability.

The larger, more mature and well-established firms in our data set typically had a portfolio of products and services, often aimed at different groups of customers. Typically, the challenge for corporate innovation is how firms handle the development of *multiple* new products, often for different types of customers: we discuss how our approach can be applied to these corporates in Chapter 20.

The Triple Chasm Model based on customer adoption of a *single* product, the key vectors discussed previously, and the modified Technology Readiness Levels (mTRLs) led us to construct on overall framework to characterise science and technology-enabled commercialisation. This overall commercialisation canvas shown in Figure 43 enables us to systematically

The journey		Research	Idea to Concept	I	Prototype To product	II	Viable Product	III	Scaling
Overall commercial summary									
	Commercial proposition overview								
	Maturity assessment								
	Multiple propositions								
Market spaces									
	Defining market spaces								
	Market space-centric value chains								
	Chasms vs market spaces								
	Characteristic times vs market spaces								
Proposition framing and the competitive environment									
	Proposition framing								
	Competition								
	Partners andsuppliers								
	Regulation								
Customer definition									
	Customer typologies								
	Governments								
	Consumers								
	Affinity and knowledge-centric users								
	Businesses								
Distribution, marketing, and sales									
	Go-to-market key issues								
	Channels to market								
	Positioning, branding, promotion								
	Service-centric delivery								
Commercialisation strategy									
	Strategic ecology								
	Weighting-based priorities								
	Priorities vs maturity								
	Managing disruptive changes								
Business model development									
	Architecture								
	Components								
	Revenue models								
	Business model metrics								
Ip management									
	General ip issues								
	Ip typology for S&T firms								
	Ip maturity management								
	Ip mngt for market spaces								
Manufacturing and assembly									
	Manufacturing unpacked								
	Scaling for manufacture								
	Process innovation								
	Integrated manufacturing delivery								
Product and service definition and synthesis									
	Synthesis unpacked								
	Voice-of-the-customer approaches								
	Technology-mapping approaches								
	New approaches to synthesis								
	Proposition deconstruction								
	Service definition								
Technology development and deployment									
	Commercialisation options								
	Base vs application technologies								
	Technology platforms								
	Application and tools								
	Products and services								
	Managing technology deployment								
Talent, leadership and culture									
	Talent and entrepreneurial intensity								
	Teams and roles								
	Org structure and management								
	Leadership								
	Culture, behaviours, and rewards								
Funding and investment									
	Sources of funding								
	Funding vs maturity								
	Early stage funding								
	Venture capital								
	Customer funding								
	Firm valuation								
Generalised support infrastructure									
	Mentors								
	Shared prototyping tools and platforms								
	Legal and financial services								
	Premises and general facilities								
mTRL	*Mtechnology readiness levels*	0	1 2 3		4 5 6		7 8 9		

Figure 43:   The Commercialisation Canvas.

explore and calibrate the key drivers affecting the commercialisation journey.

The *x*-axis of this canvas shows three key factors which change over time:

The three chasms along the commercialisation journey, defined in Chapter 3, are shown at the top of the canvas.

The transitions from concept to prototype, from prototype to working product with a commercially viable business model, and then to scalable product, which depend on successfully crossing the three chasms, as discussed in Chapters 3 and 4; this transition is shown at the top of the canvas.

The change in the mTRL as the commercialisation journey proceeds, as discussed in Chapter 1. The increase in mTRL values from 0 to 9, with discontinuities at the three chasms, is shown at the bottom of canvas.

This systematic framework provides a powerful way of analysing the 'maturity' of any product or service: the precise level of maturity can be positioned on this grid. As we will see later, this approach enables an assessment to be made of the 'interventions' required to progress from the left to the right of the framework, along the commercialisation journey.

The *y*-axis of this framework covers the overall proposition, the 12 vectors, and general support for the commercialisation journey, as discussed below.

At the top of the canvas, we have a parameter summarising the overall commercial proposition of the firm, which includes the commercial priorities and the management of multiple propositions by the firm.

We then have the key vectors and sub-vectors, which affect the aggregate behaviour of a firm, as follows:

Market Spaces: This includes the definition and characterisation of market spaces and market space-centric value chains, which we discussed in Chapter 5. This enables a detailed understanding of the environment that new products and services are delivered into.

Proposition Framing and the Competitive Environment: This vector focuses on framing the overall value proposition, in the context of the competitive and regulatory landscape, using market space-centric value chains.

Customer Definition: This includes an understanding of customer typologies as discussed in Chapter 7, and the characteristics of the four types of customers: consumers, affinity and knowledge-centric groups, governments, and business customers.

Distribution, Marketing, and Sales: This covers all the key issues associated with taking the product or service to market, as discussed in Chapter 11, including channels to market, positioning, branding and promotion of the product, and the delivery of integrated services.

Commercialisation Strategy: This covers the overall strategic ecology, a new approach to dynamic strategy development, the key strategic challenges around Chasm II and the issues associated with ongoing strategy refinement and strategic pivots in response to rapid changes in the overall ecology.

Business Models: This key vector, sometimes neglected by science and technology firms, covers the business model architecture, definition of the key components of the business model, an assessment of potential revenues, and an understanding of key business model metrics, as discussed in Chapter 13.

IP Management: This vector covers generic IP issues of relevance to all firms, IP typologies for science and technology firms, managing IP maturity and identifying key IP issues for different market spaces.

Manufacturing and Assembly: This vector covers the generic manufacturing challenges, scaling technologies for manufacture and the challenges of manufacturing process innovation, as discussed in Chapter 10.

Product and Service Definition and Synthesis: This covers the critical question of product synthesis, as discussed in Chapter 9. It includes three types of synthesis: approaches based on voice of the customer, technology-mapping approaches, and hybrid synthesis approaches which focus on viable business models; it also includes product and service definition and deconstruction based on the Proposition Framework.

Technology Deployment: This vector covers the potential ways of 'packaging' technology to take it to market, as discussed in Chapter 8, as base technologies, application technologies, technology platforms, tools and applications, or integrated products or services.

Talent, Leadership, and Culture: This vector, discussed in detail in Chapter 16, focuses on talent, teams, types of organisational and management structures, leadership models, and culture, behaviour, and reward structures in firms.

Funding and Investment: The final vector addresses the different sources of funding, their merits and demerits at different stages of firm maturity; it also looks at gaps between rhetoric and reality, as discussed in Chapter 15, enabling firms to make the best decisions appropriate to their specific circumstances.

At the bottom of the commercialisation canvas, we show the overall support infrastructure required by all growing firms, which includes the availability of mentors, premises and facilities, and access to legal and financial services.

The relative importance of these 12 vectors and their sub-components varies with the 'distance travelled' along the x-axis, which broadly describes maturity of the firm. We use this canvas below in order to explore and map typical commercialisation trajectories for science and technology-enabled firms.

17.2 Commercialisation Trajectories

Many aspects of commercialisation have been discussed over the last three decades,[180–184] but there has been little systematic work on the precise commercialisation trajectories of firms, and very little research based on a large enough sample size which enables reliable empirical insights. In Chapter 4, we discussed the relative importance of the 12 vectors, when crossing the three chasms based on our research data. We now look in more detail at the relative importance of each sub-vector, at a greater level of granularity, for firms at different levels of maturity. This enables us to understand the typical trajectory of a science and technology firm and to understand when the firm needs to address specific challenges and issues. This detailed view can provide a powerful guide for leadership teams in confronting critical issues at appropriate times.

Figure 44 shows the typical trajectory for commercialising science and technology-enabled innovation based on our research data.

We will use this trajectory, and the underlying canvas, later, in Chapter 19, to understand where the key 'actors' involved in the commercialisation journey play critical roles which can impact the trajectory of typical science and technology firm.

There are a number of insights which emerge from this commercialisation trajectory.

The technology deployment vector is strategically important early on at Chasms I and II. Strategic missteps at these early stages can have serious consequences later in the commercialisation journey, which typically should be concerned with technology execution and deployment.

At the early stages around Chasm I, broad awareness of the market space is important, but detailed insights into customer behaviour and targeting are much more important at Chasm II.

The biggest challenges for all firms are around Chasm II, where the key vectors concern the synthesis and precise definition of the product or service and the associated business model which will enable sustainable business operation by the firm; this includes a detailed understanding of the key business model metrics.

Given this, it is not surprising that the commercialisation trajectory leading up to Chasm II also highlights the critical importance of having the right funding and talent to increase the likelihood of crossing Chasm II successfully.

Distribution, marketing and sales also become important around Chasm II and beyond because this ultimately controls the growth trajectory of the firm.

The trajectory also shows the importance of mentors and general support at the earlier stages; we discuss this in Chapter 19.

Overall, the key observation to make about this commercialisation trajectory is the 'patchy' nature of the coverage of the canvas, which

The journey		Research	Idea to Concept	I	Prototype To product	II	Viable Product	III	Scaling
Overall commercial summary									
	Commercial proposition overview								
	Maturity assessment								
	Multiple propositions								
Market spaces									
	Defining market spaces								
	Market space-centric value chains								
	Chasms vs market spaces								
	Characteristic times vs market spaces								
Proposition framing and the competitive environment									
	Proposition framing								
	Competition								
	Partners and suppliers								
	Regulation								
Customer definition									
	Customer typologies								
	Governments								
	Consumers								
	Affinity and knowledge-centric users								
	Businesses								
Distribution, marketing and sales									
	Go-to-market key issues								
	Channels to market								
	Positioning, branding, promotion								
	Service-centric delivery								
Commercialisation strategy									
	Strategic ecology								
	Weighting-based priorities								
	Priorities vs maturity								
	Managing disruptive changes								
Business model development									
	Architecture								
	Components								
	Revenue models								
	Business model metrics								
Ip management									
	General ip issues								
	Ip typology for S&T firms								
	Ip maturity management								
	Ip mngt for market spaces								
Manufacturing and assembly									
	Manufacturing unpacked								
	Scaling for manufacture								
	Process innovation								
	Integrated manufacturing delivery								
Product and service definition and synthesis									
	Synthesis unpacked								
	Voice-of-the-customer approaches								
	Technology-mapping approaches								
	New approaches to synthesis								
	Proposition deconstruction								
	Service definition								
Technology development and deployment									
	Commercialisation options								
	Base vs application technologies								
	Technology platforms								
	Application and tools								
	Products and services								
	Managing technology deployment								
Talent, leadership, and culture									
	Talent and entrepreneurial intensity								
	Teams and roles								
	Org structure and management								
	Leadership								
	Culture, behaviours, and rewards								
Funding and investment									
	Sources of funding								
	Funding vs maturity								
	Early stage funding								
	Venture capital								
	Customer funding								
	Firm valuation								
Generalised support infrastructure									
	Mentors								
	Shared prototyping tools and platforms								
	Legal and financial services								
	Premises and general facilities								
mTRL	*Mtechnology readiness levels*	0	1 2 3		4 5 6		7 8 9		

Figure 44: **Typical Trajectory for Science and Technology Commercialisation.**

suggests that firms can focus and apply resources more effectively rather than assuming that all things matter all the time.

17.3 Maturity Assessment based on the Triple Chasm Framework

The overall framework based on the Triple Chasm Model allows us to map the position of each firm in our data set in terms of how far the firm had travelled already along the 'maturity curve': we can locate the current position of any single firm along the x-axis of our commercialisation canvas. This can provide powerful insights for the firm in terms of future trajectory and the resources required, disaggregated into the 12 vectors and associated sub-vectors: this level of granularity can provide practical guidance to the leadership of a firm in tackling the challenges it faces.

Figure 45 illustrates the relative maturity of several firms, in terms of the number of chasms crossed, starting from the centre of the circle and

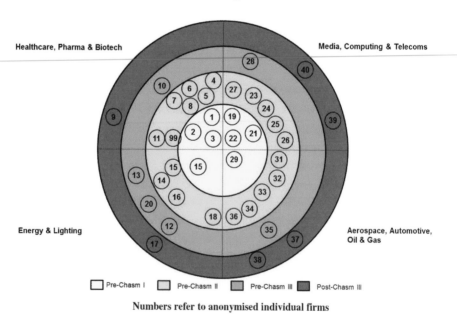

Figure 45: Chasm-based Assessment of Maturity in an Ecosystem.

travelling outwards radially. It provides a powerful demonstration of the value of this type of analysis, which summarises results from our research data, based on looking at a number of different market spaces in a single geographic innovation ecosystem. This type of snapshot can help not just the firm, but can provide useful insights for stakeholders in the ecosystem, including investors and policy makers. For example, these results show many firms 'stuck' in the zone between Chasms I and II in this particular ecosystem. These results could be used to design better policy interventions to improve the trajectory and pace of commercialisation. We discuss the potential implications of this in Chapter 19.

17.4 Camels, Tigers, and Unicorns

At the start of this book, we set out a simple narrative to describe firms based on animal metaphors as follows:

Camels are internally resourced firms which take little or no external investment, who constitute about 98% of firms.

Tigers are firms which take money from angels and venture capital (VC), who constitute less than 2% of firms, where the investment follows conventional business logic.

Unicorns are firms which take huge investments, effectively large high risk bets based on the hope that some kind of sustainable business model will emerge, who unsurprisingly constitute a tiny fraction of firms, but they attract a lot of press attention!

The popular narratives around science and technology innovation-enabled companies have changed over the last two decades, especially with the advent of the social and economic revolutions enabled by digital technologies. The metaphors used to describe these firms have also undergone a transformation, with many different kinds of analogies deployed to convey the sense of how different things are, without the need for semantic clarity and detailed definition.[185,186] These narratives have taken on additional significance within the radical neo-liberal paradigm, which we discussed in Chapter 2, as the opportunity for the general public to invest capital in these new firms has grown, the so-called retail investors. Some of these narratives have also embraced animal metaphors: it is in this same spirit that we have adopted our tale of camels, tigers and unicorns in order to capture this popular zeitgeist!

In the context of the Triple Chasm Model, 'camels' describes firms which adopt an organised and patient approach to commercialisation. This reflects an understanding that this is a long and difficult journey which needs to be broken down into discrete steps based on access to internal resources with a clear focus on the key challenges involved in crossing each of the three chasms. The analogy with how camels cross the desert, based on patient progress from one oasis to another, is what we wish to convey, as well as the adaptations enjoyed by camels to cope in the harsh environments they occupy. When we refer to camels, we mean, for example, engineering firms which ensure they are suitably equipped at each stage of the journey and make patient planned progress, unlike the popular perception, rarely borne out in reality, of a firm which can develop a new software product in days and reach market maturity in months!

The term 'tigers' has a number of antecedents and we use the metaphor here to describe those firms which are very agile and able to adapt quickly to change. Tigers inhabit volatile market spaces where conditions can change very quickly, such as, for example, in the media and entertainment market space. We are also referring to firms which adapt themselves well to a number of difficult environments where the competition is less predictable and agility is therefore an important attribute. What this means is that the challenges of crossing chasms may be qualitatively different than for camels: the key feature of tigers is that they typically need significant external funding to navigate these environments, which is why they turn to investment from angels and VC.

Unicorns are mythical creatures and we use the term to describe those firms which do not adhere to conventional commercial logic but use 'magical' notions to address the challenge of crossing chasms, especially Chasm II. For example, unicorns typically address the Chasm II challenge by denying the need to have a sustainable business model at this point: instead, their approach assumes that with sufficient capital available, they can acquire a large number of 'customers', who are not paying for services but can be claimed as customers because they are users. In this mindset, the approach is to create sufficient momentum and market dominance so that some kind of sustainable business model will appear in the future. This rarely happens of course, which is why so much is written about the failure rates of unicorns. This kind of betting strategy may of course suit some types of investors where there is a surplus of capital. One way of dealing with these failures is to move the goal posts, which is why the media definition of unicorns has morphed recently, mainly at the instigation of investors, based on some arbitrary threshold of the firm's value, where this valuation is also based on the dynamics of an investment bubble.

We want to emphasise here that when we describe firms as camels, tigers, and unicorns, we are not doing this in any precise taxonomical sense, but more as a short-hand method to convey some of the narratives around the commercialisation of science and technology-enabled innovation. We summarise some of these broad features in Table 20.

17.5 Using the Commercialisation Canvas

The commercialisation canvas provides a powerful tool to assess the relative progress of a firm to assess the challenges ahead and to provide guidance on actions likely to increase the chances of success.

The approach to doing this starts with detailed assessment of the relative importance of the 12 vectors for the firm's growth: this includes clarity on the market space and the relevance of the science or technology innovation which drives the firm.

The next step is to map the current status of the firm, in terms of progress with the relevant vectors and sub-vectors, relative to the locations of the three chasms, so that the position of the firm can be visualised on the canvas.

This mapping can then be used to understand the relative maturity of the firm relative to where it needs to get to; this includes an appreciation of the eventual commercial objective for the firm, also visualised on the canvas.

Finally, this approach can be used to construct an executional plan which reflects the different activities associated with each vector and sub-vector; assessing this in the broader context of the canvas can also provide useful insights into setting priorities in the execution plan.

Table 20: Comparing Camels, Tigers, and Unicorns.

	Growth Profile	Speed to Market	Defining Characteristic	Investment Profile	Valuation	Primary Offering	Exit
Camels	Firm trajectory consistent with norm	Realtively slow (par for industry sector?)	The endurance game	Limited or no external investment-predominantly funded by customer revenues	Valuation consistent with industry norms based on well defined business metrics	Science and tech intensive	Trade sale/M&A
Tigers	Accelerated trajectory	Faster than camels	The trend-setter	External investment to enable accelerated growth at key points-usually requires demonstration of business model	Valuation uplift based on accelerated growth potential	Tech-enabled, Strong product focus	Mix of trade sale/M&A and public markets
Unicorns	Early hyper-acceleration	Can be very fast because effectively buying customers	The mythical creature defying normal business logicc	Large external investment in advance of demonstrable business model	Elevated Valuations not consistent with normal business parameter	Tech-enabled, Service focus	Targeting public markets

For some of the firms in our research data set, it enabled a reappraisal of how far the firm had actually travelled along the commercialisation trajectory, the opportunity to reassess the challenges ahead and to make corrections to strategy. For example, several firms made radical changes to business models as a result of this insight; others changed their execution priorities and funding tactics based on a better understanding of the challenges ahead.

Chapter 18

Commercialising Across Borders

18.1 Why Does This Matter?

The trade in technology products across borders has changed significantly over the last decade. Three decades ago, this trade largely consisted of the distribution and sale of products created, developed, and manufactured in Europe and North America, which meant that the expertise and experience of technology commercialisation was largely concentrated in the larger firms in these economies.

With the advent of globalisation, this picture started to change, with the outsourcing of manufacturing, particularly to Asia, driven initially by the economics of lower cost supply chains, manufacturing and assembly; this was further strengthened by the need to reduce distribution costs as markets in Asia and Latin America for technology products started to grow rapidly.

This wave of outsourcing of manufacturing then gave way to the creation of outsourced research and development in 'captive' centres outside Europe and North America, again driven by the cost of doing research and development. Throughout this period, 'indigenous' research and development in these fast growing markets started to grow but was constrained by some of the meso-economic factors discussed in Chapter 2. In particular, the growth of new product and service innovation in these territories was constrained by the weakness of the innovation market spaces, access to capital and connections to the right market spaces.

Over the last decade the picture has changed as governments across Asia, Latin America, and Africa have recognised the importance of developing expertise across all aspects of the process of commercialising science and technology, from fundamental research to crossing all three chasms, although this has not always been articulated with precision, with most policy statements framed around the general importance of entrepreneurship and innovation.

More recently, as the global balance of economic power has shifted, there has been a heightened awareness of the need to generate and exploit intellectual capital based on science and technology in a broader way. Examples of this interest include heavy investment in science and technology research, the creation of incubators, accelerators and other 'interventions', which we discuss in the next chapter, and targeted acquisition activity to buy access to intellectual property. In addition, there have been a number of initiatives focused on cross-border research and development.

The research for this book revealed some evidence that commercialisation journeys in market spaces with limited or reduced access to resources could exhibit special characteristics. There have been several studies suggesting that *ad hoc* approaches for taking technologies to market can be important. For example, in India, it has been suggested that *ad hoc* approaches based on local improvisation can be important: these approaches, labelled *jugaad*[187] in order to emphasize the 'can-do' mentality of local entrepreneurs, have been held out as examples of the power of this approach. Our research programme did not corroborate this; on the contrary, we found that the findings embodied in the Triple Chasm Model applied to all science and technology commercialisation and transcended geographic and cultural boundaries, albeit within the constraints of local market spaces reflecting the meso-economic parameters discussed in Chapter 2.

Our research showed that most cross-border initiatives have produced mixed results so far for two important reasons:

Firstly, most of the cross-border activity is still dominated by larger firms, who, as we noted in Chapter 2, are strongly driven by short-term economic considerations: as a result, their primary motivations are access to large markets, cost reduction, and control of intellectual property;

for these firms, cross-border innovation and commercialisation structures are secondary goals.

The other key problem has been poor understanding of the entire commercialisation process: once there is a clear view of the overall value creation process, it is easier to decide where this activity can and should be carried out, and how and where the overall activity is actively funded and managed.

We discuss this in Section 18.2.

18.2 Characterising the Different Types of Interaction

Our research on cross-border commercialisation activity has revealed a number of issues which can significantly impact the scope, scale and pace of technology commercialisation in a global context. Some of these challenges have been studied over the last decade,[188,189] but our research has provided a wider perspective based on the Triple Chasm Model. The key areas we have identified are as follows:

Differences in *IP creation capacity* across borders lead to challenges in successfully managing cross-border research and development programmes.

Differences in *IP management and exploitation* policies, regimes and styles across borders can create significant barriers.

Gaps in the available *talent pool* to drive commercialisation and barriers which impede the movement of talent across borders hinder cross-border development.

The availability of appropriate *investment* coupled with the challenges of cross-border investment can be a serious constraint.

Understanding *market asymmetries* across borders is critical. In particular, the differences between highly 'stratified' markets in the less industrialised nations and more 'homogeneous' markets in more industrially mature economies: this is clearly an area where more research is required — the world is *definitely not flat*, despite many popular assertions to the contrary.

The need to *reshape products and services* consistent with differences in customer and user behaviour across borders: the degree of reshaping required can vary across market spaces, products, and service types.

Differences in *pricing, business models and distribution* across borders, based on affordability, cost structures and different perceptions of value: this is a critical area and the reason why many cross-border commercialisation initiatives have faltered.

These areas cover a wide range of vectors at different stages of maturity along the commercialisation trajectory, which makes any integrated analysis of the critical issues quite difficult. However, analysis of our research data revealed three specific types of challenges firms need to tackle if they are to successfully commercialise science and technology-enabled products across borders. Which of these areas is relevant, of course, relates to the maturity of the firm at the point at which it tackles the cross-border challenge, but all three can be important at different points in the journey. The three key areas are as follows:

Cross-border Research and Development or Technology Translation: This relates to situations where the cross-border activity is based on developing and translating technologies well before crossing Chasm II. This can include situations where technology packaging and scaling for manufacture require collaboration across borders; for example, the development of application technologies and platforms in healthcare services or bioprocessing. Some of these challenges may reflect the desire of investment partners to build local market space capability to enable future competitiveness, which can give rise to interesting discussions about IP ownership.

Cross-border Chasm II Translation: This covers situations where firms may have successfully crossed Chasm II in their 'home' market but now need to make significant changes to the product and business model, effectively crossing Chasm II again, for a different market. Examples of this include situations where consumer products in electronics or healthcare need to be re-engineered in order to support lower pricing and very different business models. This can be a complex challenge to tackle but one which is increasingly common.

Cross-border Chasm III Translation: This relates to situations where firms have crossed Chasm II but now want to, or need to, address cross-border markets as they cross Chasm III, where they can achieve significant increases in customer numbers. Typically, this requires a focus on a different set of vectors, concerned primarily with go-to-market issues, including packaging, manufacturing, and distribution. Examples of this include taking automotive or oil and gas products across borders where there is little or no change to the product, pricing or business model but where the emphasis is on distribution reach.

Figure 46 maps these three areas against the commercialisation canvas described in Chapter 17: it situates them on the commercialisation journey and highlights the key vectors of relevance for cross-border commercialisation based on our research data. What this illustrates is how clarity on the nature of the cross-border challenge can be invaluable in setting priorities and allocating resources.

18.3 Managing IP Across Borders

The management of intellectual property (IP) was identified as a key issue for cross-border commercialisation: the larger firms in our data set dominated this debate with most of the discussion focused around compliance management. Our research however highlighted the importance of a much broader set of issues, raised by research and development institutions and smaller firms interested in exploiting cross-border opportunities.

The first area concerns a better understanding of the different types of IP and how business practice and regulatory regimes can treat these types differently in different markets. We have already discussed the different types of intellectual property in Chapter 14. In the cross-border context, it is worth noting the differences between registered, unregistered, and 'open' rights.

Registered rights are generally treated consistently across most territories, although as noted above, there are concerns around compliance management. However, the boundaries between registered and

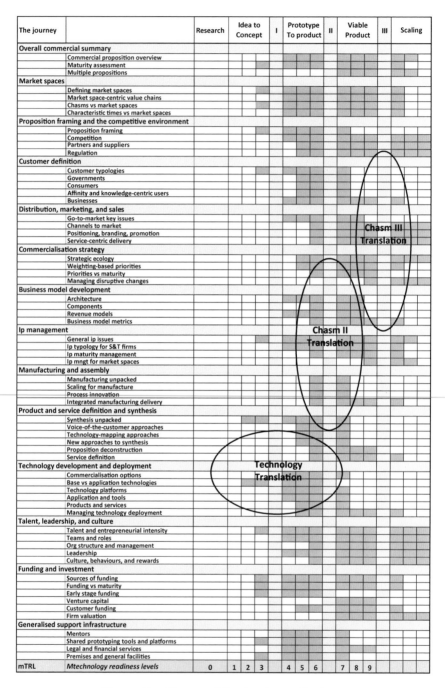

Figure 46:   Commercialisation Across Borders.

unregistered rights can vary significantly across territories; for example, the treatment of metadata can be significantly different across different jurisdictions. Unregistered rights can be problematic in most territories because they can depend on business practices, which can vary significantly across borders. Open rights present the biggest cross-border challenge: attitudes to the development and exploitation of open innovation reflect not just the prevailing ideology but the relative scarcity of resources in some territories which can lead to more robust forms of exploitation.

The second key issue concerns where and how new IP is actually generated. This includes an understanding of the institutions and firms which create the IP and the role of scientific, technical, and commercial talent involved in the innovation. It also covers the roles of the public and private sectors in funding research and development and any rules on IP ownership and exploitation. Where IP is jointly developed across borders, rules around ownership and exploitation need to be explicitly articulated. For cross-border state-funded research and development, in particular, clarity on exploitation rules is critical.

The third key issue covers how IP is actually exploited across borders. As shown in Figure 46, there are a number of generic ways in which IP can be commercialised. Some of the issues discussed above are particularly important around Chasm I, but the IP challenges around Chasm II can be more complicated, especially where cross-border commercialisation results in the generation of 'secondary' IP. For example, medical devices developed and deployed in one territory may have the same form factor and functionality but may deploy different metadata and different suggested therapies in other territories; in this situation, the management of new registered rights will need careful treatment.

We address these issues in more detail in our commercialisation Workbench summarised in Chapter 21; Most of these challenges need to be addressed at a more granular and specific level, but we want to emphasise here that the cross-border IP management challenges are much wider than just the issues of compliance.

18.4 Managing Business Model Discontinuities

Our research confirmed the critical importance of the business model vector for cross-border commercialisation, especially where the product or service has to be re-engineered to cross Chasm II again. Most European and North American markets are relatively homogeneous in character, where the same product or service can be sold to different customers. In contrast, many Asian, Latin American, and African markets are much more heterogeneous, with *stratified* layers of customers, who buy different products tailored to their needs and their ability to pay: what this means is that products and services may need to be re-engineered in order to provide a different value proposition to the end-customer. There has been surprisingly little research on this market stratification, with the tacit assumption that the same products can be sold across borders with changes in pricing, positioning and packaging, without significant re-engineering of form, functionality, and usability.

We can illustrate this by examining several products: for example, the same automotive vehicles can be sold to customers across borders, provided the 'right' layer is targeted in a stratified market. For smartphone devices, however, heterogeneous markets require a wide range of models, with different form, functionality and price points to address the different layers in the stratified market. While there will be a class of users who buy the same product as in homogeneous markets, there will be other classes of users who want to buy a range of different products. Producers of smartphone products may therefore need to re-engineer their products to cross Chasm II again in multiple ways.

These challenges have the potential to drive a race to the bottom in terms of pricing, which is why many firms engaged in heterogeneous markets and cross-border commercialisation focus their resources on value-based pricing strategies. These responses include the development of more innovative business models incorporating, for example, additional paid-for services or surrogate revenues based on advertising. We have already discussed the wide range of possible business models in Chapter 13: what our research shows is that firms involved in cross-border commercialisation need to think creatively about how new business models can be deployed to build sustainable propositions. We include tools for doing this in our commercialisation Workbench which is summarised in Chapter 21.

There is one other issue we need to discuss here. Our research confirmed the challenge of sustaining differential pricing across borders for products with the same functionality, as some firms have attempted to do, for example, by having different licensing rates in Europe vs Asia. These kinds of strategies are unsustainable unless there is a genuine difference in the value propositions. This is a problem all firms face now given the ubiquity of electronic communication and distribution networks: the challenge is to develop defensible and sustainable business models across territories with different cost structures where pricing and features can be very easily compared.

Chapter 19

Actors, Roles, and Interventions

19.1 Interventions in Context

The central actors in the technology commercialisation journey are the innovators and entrepreneurs and their core teams, but success depends on the active involvement of other actors. Our analysis of the three chasms and 12 vectors in Chapter 4 has already highlighted the potential for structured interventions in improving the probabilities of success for any venture.

These interventions depend on a variety of actors, whose behaviour may be shaped by different motivations, including financial, strategic, political, academic, personal, corporate, technological, and social considerations. There is rarely a simple correlation between actors and motivations, but our research showed that it is possible to characterise the key interventions by grouping types of actors together.

Figure 47 summarises the main types of actors and where their impact is typically experienced during the commercialisation journey. Popular descriptions and perceptions of the different forms of intervention can sometimes deviate from the reality,[190] so we characterise these actors as follows.

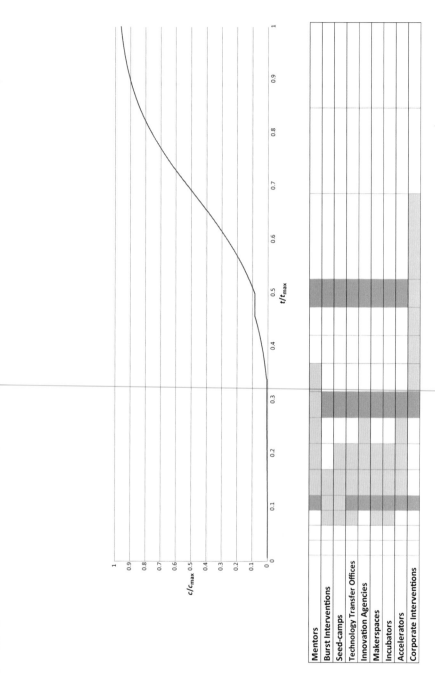

Figure 47:   Actors, Roles, and Interventions vs Triple Chasm Model.

Mentors: A mentor is usually an experienced 'performer' who takes a personal interest in helping to guide and develop an entrepreneur or innovator. A mentor can facilitate personal and professional growth in an individual by sharing the knowledge and insights that have been learned over time; mentors can bring experience, perspective and distance, challenging the mentee, and using candour to encourage re-examination and re-prioritisation. Mentors may operate independently or as part of a structured intervention such as an incubator or accelerator.

Burst Interventions: 'Burst' interventions come in a number of shapes and sizes, ranging from day-long 'boot-camps' to 'hackathons' run over a few days. The usual premise behind these types of intense, short-duration interventions is to provide an environment in which entrepreneurs can share enthusiasm, ideas and resources in a focused way, with active curation and guidance provided by more experienced players who may also bring market challenges to the table. These kinds of approaches are more appropriate for some market spaces than for others. Our research showed that these kinds of interventions produced more useful outputs in market spaces with shorter characteristic timescales as discussed in Chapter 5.

Seed-Camps: Seed-camps differ from burst interventions by providing more structured environments, with defined programmes lasting for periods of time ranging from a week to several months. Typically, seed-camps are focused on a single market space, for example, media and entertainment, or a technology-based thematic area such as the Internet of Things, or a convergence of both these things, such as FinTech. Many seed-camps try to organise their programmes to provide instruction in key areas combined with access to mentors, potential customers, and investors.

Technology Transfer Offices (TTOs): The technology transfer industry has grown dramatically over the last two decades, as universities (and similar educational institutions) and research and development laboratories and institutes have focused on trying to extract commercial value from intellectual property (IP) generated inside these institutions.[191,192] Their approach to doing this is typically based on setting up TTOs who are tasked with generating this commercial value.

Innovation Agencies: These are typically state-instigated agencies which can operate at various levels in a geographical hierarchy, including cities, regions, states, and at a federal level.[193] The funding for these agencies is usually provided by public funds, but there are some examples of public–private hybrid funding. Innovation agencies can play important roles in building the market spaces required to support technology commercialisation, as discussed in Chapter 2.

Makerspaces: Makerspaces and hackerspaces have become more popular in the last decade, especially in environments where access to resources can be limited[194]: they are community-operated workspaces where people with common interests, for example, in computers, machining, technology, science, digital art or electronic art, can meet, socialize and collaborate. One of the key aspects of most makerspaces is the provision of shared equipment and tools to support the building of prototypes.

Incubators: Incubators are typically physical spaces which provide early stage support to entrepreneurs, usually around Chasm I, when they are trying to turn concepts into prototypes.[195,196] They share some characteristics with makerspaces but tend to be less open, with entry 'gating' criteria based on the potential of an idea. They also typically provide mentorship and education on the commercialisation journey, and sometimes, small amounts of financial support. Unlike the burst interventions discussed above, entrepreneurs may typically be 'resident' in an incubator for periods of many months or even longer.

Accelerators: The entry criteria for accelerators are usually more stringent since they are typically interested in working with entrepreneurial *teams* with a *proven concept*, which means that in practice they want to work with fledgling products which have already crossed Chasm I.[197] Access to accelerators can be highly competitive because the managers of these resources want the best returns from their financial, commercial and managerial investments. Some accelerators have programmes based on fixed dwell times (the time that the start-up is 'resident' in the accelerator), usually measured in months, where the fledgling firms are supported for a period and then actively 'graduated' out, while others may provide support over extended periods of time. The emphasis on shorter dwell times tends to bias their focus towards market spaces and technology areas with short characteristic timescales or the prevalent venture capital 'fashion', as discussed in Chapter 15.

Corporate Interventions: Corporate interventions are motivated by the desire to inject innovation and create radically new products and services, which large firms frequently find difficult doing on their own. These interventions can include the provision of customer insights, resources to fast-track product development or simply financial investment. Given the typical risk profile of corporates, most financial investment is made post Chasm II, as discussed in Chapter 15, but customer and product insights can help early-stage firms to accelerate their commercialisation. We discuss these challenges from a corporate perspective in Chapter 20.

19.2 Mentors, 'Burst' Interventions and Seed-camps

Our research explored the relationship between entrepreneurs and mentors and how this could affect the pace and trajectory of the commercialisation process, especially early in the journey.

The role of the mentor can be critical quite early on, especially when crossing Chasm I. At this early Chasm I-crossing phase, clarity on potential customers and the outline product service proposition can have an important bearing on the ability to cross Chasm II successfully later. Mentors can provide useful guidance or advice on developing the right approach to funding and early connections to potential investors.

Figure 48 shows the typical areas in which 'burst' interventions and seed-camps operate. The most obvious thing to note from this research is the limited number of areas where their impact is actually realised, which is somewhat at odds with the popular perception of the significant role played by these kinds of interventions, certainly in the context of the overall commercialisation journey.

The impact of the interventions provided by seed-camps is usually restricted to crossing of Chasm I, which involves turning conceptual ideas into prototypes. The primary focus of this intervention is around the creation of the initial product or service and possibly providing funding support. Very little of this activity addresses broader commercial issues around market spaces, customer definition, the commercial logic and business models. The typical hackathon provides a good exemplar of both the power and limitations of this kind of intervention. Figure 48

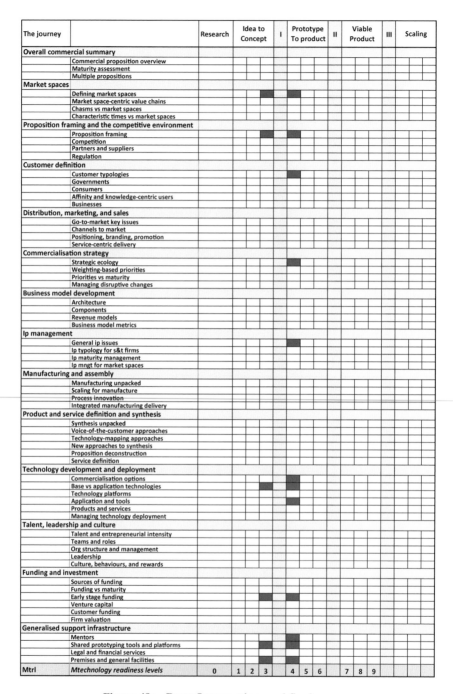

Figure 48: Burst Interventions and Seed-camps.

confirms the relatively narrow impact of burst interventions on the overall commercialisation journey.

19.3 Tech Transfer Offices and Innovation Agencies

Universities and research and development laboratories have invested significant resources over the last two decades to set up systematic commercialisation initiatives. As a consequence, there is now a major 'technology transfer industry' complete with specialist journals dedicated to analysing this subject. Our motivation here is to look at the practical implications of this from the perspective of the innovators and entrepreneurs trying to create new commercial value based on this technology.

Our research revealed that, TTOs come in several different guises, based on the objectives, motivations and constraints of the key stakeholders. Detailed analysis of these findings is beyond the scope of the current book, but we need to make the following observations here:

The dominant characteristics of TTOs are not shaped by the geographic locations of the institutions, so that, for example, universities in Europe and North America do not generally display different behaviours by reason of location. The attitude of the TTOs can be shaped by the size and strength of their IP portfolios, but this is a second-order effect.

TTO behaviour and performance are typically driven by their underlying commercial models. The key issues are: the desired balance between short-term cash generation and medium to long-term value generation, and the allocation of value between the institution and those working within the institution on IP generation.

However, our research showed a lack of consistency in terms of business models, both over time for the same institutions, and across similar institutions operating in the same market spaces. Our results also revealed poor understanding of the *overall* commercialisation journey, leading to sub-optimal decision-making by TTOs in terms of the value generated.

Figure 49 shows the typical areas of operation of TTOs and related players and highlights the relatively narrow focus of their operations around Chasm I. Even those TTOs which have set up 'captive funds' largely operate in this constrained way, in spite of access to larger financial resources, partly because their strategies are based on venture capital mindsets, as discussed in Chapter 15.

The journey		Research	Idea to Concept	I	Prototype To product	II	Viable Product	III	Scaling
Overall commercial summary									
	Commercial proposition overview								
	Maturity assessment								
	Multiple propositions								
Market spaces									
	Defining market spaces								
	Market space-centric value chains								
	Chasms vs market spaces								
	Characteristic times vs market spaces								
Proposition framing and the competitive environment									
	Proposition framing								
	Competition								
	Partners and suppliers								
	Regulation								
Customer definition									
	Customer typologies								
	Governments								
	Consumers								
	Affinity and knowledge-centric users								
	Businesses								
Distribution, marketing, and sales									
	Go-to-market key issues								
	Channels to market								
	Positioning, branding, promotion								
	Service-centric delivery								
Commercialisation strategy									
	Strategic ecology								
	Weighting-based priorities								
	Priorities vs maturity								
	Managing disruptive changes								
Business model development									
	Architecture								
	Components								
	Revenue models								
	Business model metrics								
Ip management									
	General ip issues								
	Ip typology for S&T firms								
	Ip maturity management								
	Ip mngt for market spaces								
Manufacturing and assembly									
	Manufacturing unpacked								
	Scaling for manufacture								
	Process innovation								
	Integrated manufacturing delivery								
Product and service definition and synthesis									
	Synthesis unpacked								
	Voice-of-the-customer approaches								
	Technology-mapping approaches								
	New approaches to synthesis								
	Proposition deconstruction								
	Service definition								
Technology development and deployment									
	Commercialisation options								
	Base vs application technologies								
	Technology platforms								
	Application and tools								
	Products and services								
	Managing technology deployment								
Talent, leadership and culture									
	Talent and entrepreneurial intensity								
	Teams and roles								
	Org structure and management								
	Leadership								
	Culture, behaviours, and rewards								
Funding and investment									
	Sources of funding								
	Funding vs maturity								
	Early stage funding								
	Venture capital								
	Customer funding								
	Firm valuation								
Generalised support infrastructure									
	Mentors								
	Shared prototyping tools and platforms								
	Legal and financial services								
	Premises and general facilities								
Mtrl	*Mtechnology readiness levels*	0	1　2　3		4　5　6		7　8　9		

Figure 49:　TTOs and Innovation Agencies.

Our research on the operation of innovation agencies showed that the typical coverage of these agencies mirrored the activities of TTOs, perhaps not that surprising given the common origins of both types of interventions as publicly funded players. The innovation agencies, however, displayed a number of subtle differences based on their span of geographic coverage (city, region, national, federal), market focus, and technology specialisation. Our research showed that the most important differences between the behaviour of different innovation agencies arose from the prevailing ideological bias in the relevant market spaces, as discussed in Chapter 2.

Most innovation agencies are heavily focused on activities around Chasm I and a little beyond but stop short of tackling the important challenges around Chasm II. This is the critical area which needs to be addressed if the returns on science and technology investment are to be improved significantly.

There has been some recent recognition of this challenge: however, the problems need to be addressed with new thinking at the meso-economic level, which requires better understanding of the economic issues and the willingness to challenge conventional political ideologies. It also needs to reflect the relative balance of the public and private sectors, the effectiveness of key actors in this space, consideration of business models and value distribution between the stakeholders.

This is clearly a much broader issue which we signpost in our commercialisation manifesto towards the end of this book.

19.4 Makerspaces, Incubators, and Accelerators

Active interventions to support entrepreneurs and early-stage firms can be usefully segmented into three types of players, based on the resources, facilities, and support they offer for the commercialisation journey. We divide them into three types of players, makerspaces, incubators and accelerators, as summarised earlier.

In general, **makerspaces** provide environments to support peer learning and knowledge sharing in the form of workshops, presentations, and lectures. They can be viewed as open 'community' spaces incorporating elements of machine shops, workshops, and studios where entrepreneurs can share resources and knowledge to design, build and make new products. They typically provide physical infrastructure, computing and networking resources, and shared access to prototyping and small scale manufacturing facilities, such as 3D printers and laser cutters.

Makerspaces only address a small and limited part of the overall journey with a strong focus on crossing Chasm I. The key focus of makerspaces is in supporting entrepreneurs to synthesize new products and to build prototypes using access to shared tools and resources.

Makerspaces have a strong ideological bias towards sharing of resources and therefore can be perceived as pre-commercial environments. As a consequence, they can have a focus on products where there is a stronger emphasis on design and 'intelligent' construction rather than deep IP. Makerspaces form an important component of commercialisation environments in market spaces with significant resource limitations.

Incubators, in contrast, have a strong focus on providing commercial and financial support in addition to those facilities provided by makerspaces. Incubators usually extract value for their services from entrepreneurs and start-up firms in a number of ways:

They may charge fees for the services they provide, including general and specialised resources. Mentors deployed in the incubators may also want to charge for their services in addition to charges levied by the incubator. Incubators and mentors may accept payment for their services in cash or equity in the start-up firms in the form of options, warrants, and shares. Where incubators invest directly in start-ups, they can take significant equity positions in start-up firms in return for the money, which entrepreneurs need to assess carefully.

Where incubators facilitate investment from third parties, they may well charge fees for enabling this, which typically need to be paid by start-up firms from the money actually raised. Generally, incubators are commercial operations with their own business models based on taking a share of the commercial value generated by the firms inhabiting the incubator.

Figure 50 shows the typical contributions from incubators to the commercial journey. The key inputs provided are: support in synthesising new products and services, identifying key resource requirements and facilitating access to appropriate complementary talent, access to experienced mentors with relevant expertise in markets, technologies, and commercial

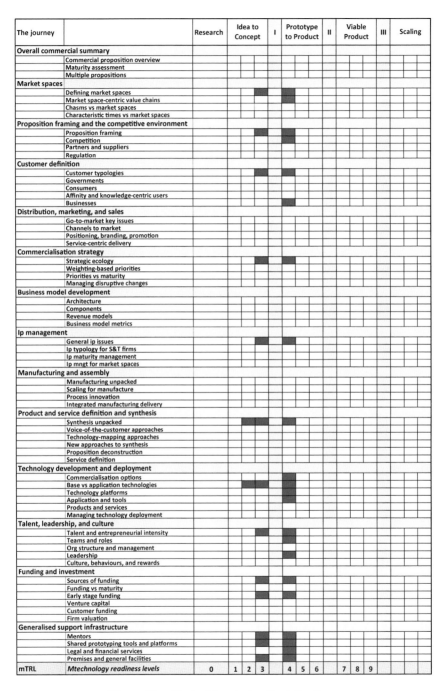

The journey		Research	Idea to Concept	I	Prototype to Product	II	Viable Product	III	Scaling
Overall commercial summary									
	Commercial proposition overview								
	Maturity assessment								
	Multiple propositions								
Market spaces									
	Defining market spaces		■		■				
	Market space-centric value chains								
	Chasms vs market spaces								
	Characteristic times vs market spaces								
Proposition framing and the competitive environment									
	Proposition framing		■		■				
	Competition				■				
	Partners and suppliers								
	Regulation								
Customer definition									
	Customer typologies		■		■				
	Governments								
	Consumers								
	Affinity and knowledge-centric users								
	Businesses				■				
Distribution, marketing, and sales									
	Go-to-market key issues								
	Channels to market								
	Positioning, branding, promotion								
	Service-centric delivery								
Commercialisation strategy									
	Strategic ecology		■		■				
	Weighting-based priorities								
	Priorities vs maturity								
	Managing disruptive changes								
Business model development									
	Architecture								
	Components								
	Revenue models								
	Business model metrics								
Ip management									
	General ip issues		■		■				
	Ip typology for S&T firms								
	Ip maturity management								
	Ip mngt for market spaces								
Manufacturing and assembly									
	Manufacturing unpacked								
	Scaling for manufacture								
	Process innovation								
	Integrated manufacturing delivery								
Product and service definition and synthesis									
	Synthesis unpacked		■		■				
	Voice-of-the-customer approaches								
	Technology-mapping approaches								
	New approaches to synthesis								
	Proposition deconstruction								
	Service definition								
Technology development and deployment									
	Commercialisation options								
	Base vs application technologies		■		■				
	Technology platforms								
	Application and tools								
	Products and services								
	Managing technology deployment								
Talent, leadership, and culture									
	Talent and entrepreneurial intensity		■		■				
	Teams and roles								
	Org structure and management								
	Leadership				■				
	Culture, behaviours, and rewards								
Funding and investment									
	Sources of funding		■						
	Funding vs maturity								
	Early stage funding		■		■				
	Venture capital								
	Customer funding								
	Firm valuation								
Generalised support infrastructure									
	Mentors		■		■				
	Shared prototyping tools and platforms		■						
	Legal and financial services		■						
	Premises and general facilities		■						
mTRL	*Mtechnology readiness levels*	0	1 2 3		4 5 6		7 8 9		

Figure 50: Typical Incubator Contributions.

issues, generalised support services and access to legal and accounting expertise, and shared access to prototyping tools and technologies.

Incubators are typically focused on providing support to cross Chasm I and do not provide any support for crossing Chasm II.

Accelerators typically pick up the support challenge from incubators, although in practice, there can often be significant overlap between the activities of incubators and accelerators. Accelerators usually play a much broader role in supporting the commercialisation journey but critically provide *little support in crossing Chasm II*, which is a major challenge for most start-up firms.

Accelerators can support the transition from modified Technology Readiness Levels of mTRL = 3 to mTRL = 6, as illustrated in Figure 51.

Accelerators typically provide support in defining market spaces and market space-centric value chains based on harnessing networks and expertise in relevant markets; this reinforces the importance of selecting an accelerator which can provide this kind of expertise. They can also support the development of the overall value proposition in the context of the competitive environment by providing senior staff and mentors in the accelerator who understand the relevant market space.

Accelerators usually provide limited inputs in understanding and pro-filing customers to enable better framing of propositions, although they may be able to provide access to early charter customers. They do not usually provide much support in developing distribution, marketing and sales support to resident firms. Business model development is a key issue for firms, but most of the accelerators in our research data set provided very little support in this critical area. None of the accelerators in our data set provided any significant support for firms looking at manufacturing issues. However, most accelerators provided significant support in the development of products and services, especially based on the provision of technology expertise and resources. In general, accelerators were very good at providing access to funding sources, experienced mentors and generalised support covering premises, legal and accounting services.

Most accelerators tend to specialise in specific market spaces or in defined technology areas, but critically their support usually falls short of helping firms to cross Chasm II, where as we have discussed already, firms face the biggest challenge.

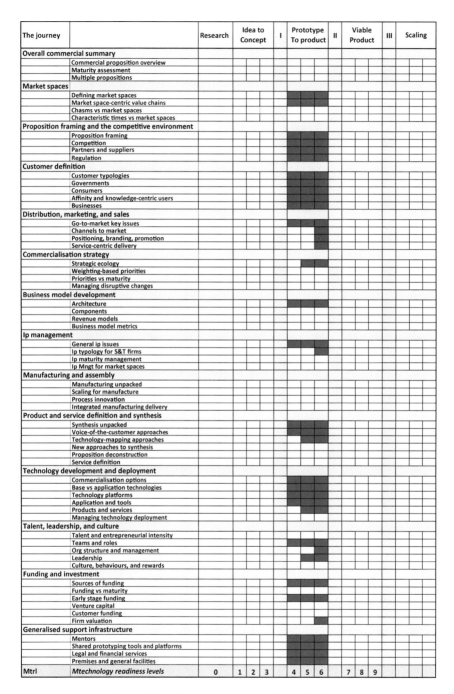

The journey		Research	Idea to Concept		I	Prototype To product		II	Viable Product		III	Scaling
Overall commercial summary													
	Commercial proposition overview												
	Maturity assessment												
	Multiple propositions												
Market spaces													
	Defining market spaces												
	Market space-centric value chains												
	Chasms vs market spaces												
	Characteristic times vs market spaces												
Proposition framing and the competitive environment													
	Proposition framing												
	Competition												
	Partners and suppliers												
	Regulation												
Customer definition													
	Customer typologies												
	Governments												
	Consumers												
	Affinity and knowledge-centric users												
	Businesses												
Distribution, marketing, and sales													
	Go-to-market key issues												
	Channels to market												
	Positioning, branding, promotion												
	Service-centric delivery												
Commercialisation strategy													
	Strategic ecology												
	Weighting-based priorities												
	Priorities vs maturity												
	Managing disruptive changes												
Business model development													
	Architecture												
	Components												
	Revenue models												
	Business model metrics												
Ip management													
	General ip issues												
	Ip typology for S&T firms												
	Ip maturity management												
	Ip Mngt for market spaces												
Manufacturing and assembly													
	Manufacturing unpacked												
	Scaling for manufacture												
	Process innovation												
	Integrated manufacturing delivery												
Product and service definition and synthesis													
	Synthesis unpacked												
	Voice-of-the-customer approaches												
	Technology-mapping approaches												
	New approaches to synthesis												
	Proposition deconstruction												
	Service definition												
Technology development and deployment													
	Commercialisation options												
	Base vs application technologies												
	Technology platforms												
	Application and tools												
	Products and services												
	Managing technology deployment												
Talent, leadership, and culture													
	Talent and entrepreneurial intensity												
	Teams and roles												
	Org structure and management												
	Leadership												
	Culture, behaviours, and rewards												
Funding and investment													
	Sources of funding												
	Funding vs maturity												
	Early stage funding												
	Venture capital												
	Customer funding												
	Firm valuation												
Generalised support infrastructure													
	Mentors												
	Shared prototyping tools and platforms												
	Legal and financial services												
	Premises and general facilities												
Mtrl	*Mtechnology readiness levels*	0	1	2	3	4	5	6		7	8	9	

Figure 51:   Typical Accelerator Contributions.

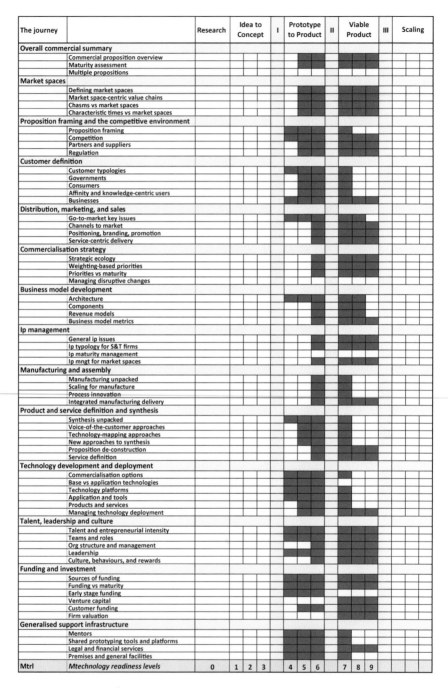

Figure 52:   Profile of a New Intervention — The Reactor.

19.5 Addressing the Chasm II Challenge: The Reactor

The results presented above make a very strong case for the need to design new types of interventions which help technology firms to cross Chasm II.

While designing this kind of intervention is difficult, we believe it is essential if we are to increase the number of successful firms enabled by science and technology-enabled innovation. We need to design and implement new structured interventions, not resign ourselves to accepting vague metaphors based on the 'valley of death' or believing that the problem can be solved by the application of more capital in an untargeted way.

Figure 52 shows the typical components of the ideal new intervention, using the map of the commercialisation journey. This new type of intervention, which we designate a **Reactor**, to distinguish it from incubators and accelerators, should focus on improving the likelihood of crossing Chasm II.

The reactors should have the following characteristics:

Provide tools and experience to map the maturity of the firm and clarify the overall commercial priorities.

Enable detailed understanding of the changing or new market spaces and associated market space-centric value chains, including the roles of key players.

Support the development of competitive value propositions enabled by innovative technologies.

Enable detailed mapping and profiling of the target customers and market sizing.

Support business model development and testing coupled with the implementation of appropriate business model metrics.

Provide detailed assessment of manufacturing and assembly options, including scaling for manufacture.

Enable creative approaches to new product and service synthesis.

Provide expertise in developing the right technology packaging and deployment strategy and tactics.

Support critical interventions in the development of appropriate talent, organisational structure and culture, including access to appropriate mentors.

Provide the right mix of funding and investment, in particular customer funding.

This new kind of intervention focused on crossing Chasm II could have a significant impact on the overall success rate for new science and technology innovation-enabled firms.

Chapter 20

Innovation in Mature Firms: The Corporate Challenge

20.1 The Corporate Challenge

Discussion over the last three decades about how larger established firms (usually referred to as Corporates) can exploit science and technology-based innovation has tacitly assumed that the formulation of the firm, the perceived potential for technology-based disruption and the prevailing market space form a relatively stable backdrop for any analysis.

Perez[198] has argued that step-changes in technology over the last three centuries have driven technology-based disruption on a cyclic basis: she has identified five techno-economic cycles with the industrial revolution and the current digital revolution as manifestations of two of these cycles. In her view, the impact of technology adoption can be viewed as showing four different phases which she refers to as irruption, frenzy, synergy, and maturity. This long-run view of technology-based disruption echoes Kondratieff's views on economic cycles. While the ideas expressed by Perez have been cited in many discussions about corporate innovation,[199] we believe that our research and analysis need to be grounded in the current reality, as discussed in Chapter 2, with a strong emphasis on *causality and drivers* rather than observations of long-term patterns.

In particular, we take our cue on understanding industry structures, firms and the disruptive impact of technologies from the work of Dosi *et al.*[200,201] because we are primarily interested in how science and technology-based commercialisation in Corporates is shaped by the practical forces at play. These inevitably reflect four key factors: current *ideology*, which defines the relative importance of the role of capital vs labour; prevailing *narratives*, or the current 'story' of how ideas are commercialised; the *shape* of the commercialisation journey, as discussed in Chapter 17, which encapsulates the role of the key actors and, especially in this context, the role of the firm; and *organisational paradigms*, discussed in Chapter 16, which describe how human talent and labour is organised, managed and rewarded.

Against the backdrop of sluggish economic growth over the last two decades, leaders of technology-intensive firms face a major challenge in how they grow top-line revenues. The wider picture is one of flat revenues, share buy-backs and expensive mergers and acquisitions to assuage pressures from investors eyeing the cash piles many of these firms have built up. Overall, many 'incumbent' firms are struggling with how they can generate significant revenue growth, based on new products and services or through business model innovations, as they pursue the elusive 'holy grail' of 'corporate innovation'.

The response to this challenge requires strategic clarity, better understanding of the alternatives, and the courage to seize the initiative rather than merely reacting to approaches from financial investors, who are not always driven by medium-term or long-term industrial logic, but by the desire to engineer short-term financial exits.

So how can firms respond to this innovation and value-creation challenge?

Strategic clarity is an essential first step in this process, but this requires a deep understanding of the current and future market spaces that the firm operates in. This is not an easy task as market spaces are shape-shifting in unexpected and radical ways based on developments in technology, demographics, customer behaviour, and business models. It also requires the ability to accept the uncertainty associated with these changes and to compare and 'calibrate' different opportunities based on a realistic assessment of the available resources, as measured by the 12 vectors defined in Chapter 4.

We discuss the impact of firm size, organisational structure and culture on corporate innovation later in this chapter, but we need to first set out the three broad strategic responses available to Corporates when innovating to create new products and services, to grow revenues and profits, and to increase the value of the firm.

Build, Buy, or Partner?

The **Build** option is based on developing new products and services internally within the firm.

The **Buy** option depends on acquiring a (usually smaller) more innovative firm which has developed new products and services.

The **Partner** option comes in many shades, all based on partnering with external resources and firms who provide complementary capabilities to create new products and services.

We discuss Build, Buy, and Partner options later in this chapter.

20.2 Multi-product Firms and the Commercialisation Framework

The Triple Chasm Model described in Chapter 3 is based on customer acquisition data for a *single* product, which is the reality for virtually all start-up firms. When looking at multi-product firms, we need to recognise that, strictly speaking, the insights from the Triple Chasm can only be applied to a single product within the firm's portfolio. However, these models can be applied to multi-product firms provided the *aggregate* behaviour is seen as the combination of several different products: this is consistent with the reality that different products in a multi-product firm will often be at different levels of maturity, have different customers, different business models and in some cases, deploy different technologies. When looking at Corporates, which typically have multiple products, we need to understand how to apply the insights of the Triple Chasm Model, the vectors, and the commercialisation canvas.

Firms where *multiple products* are targeted at the *same customers* in the *same market space*

Multi-product firms where all the products are targeted at the same customers in the same market space are the simplest to deal with: the vectors and the commercialisation trajectory for each product can be handled just as they would for a single-product firm; the key areas which need to be handled differently are as follows:

The overall commercial proposition of the firm needs to be treated as an aggregation of the individual product profiles.

Assessment of the maturity of the firm needs to reflect the aggregate maturity of the individual products; this can provide powerful insights into how firms can be rejuvenated by the launch of new products as older products become more mature.

Multi-product portfolio analysis can provide powerful insights into future strategy and priorities; framing a multi-product customer proposition for the firm can build on multi-product portfolio strategy.

The different products may be delivered using different business models, which may need careful positioning and management.

Distribution, marketing and sales tactics may need to be different for each product. One of the challenges here is in understanding and exploiting potential synergies across different products.

Firms exhibiting this behaviour can be found across all market spaces: consumer electronics firms provide a very good example, where firms can develop and sell a range of electronic hardware and software products and services, often providing different functionalities under a single brand, to the same group of consumers.

Firms where *multiple products* are targeted at the *same market space* but at *different customer groups*

Multi-product firms which target different types of customers, but still within the same market space, need to address all the factors described above, which relate to multiple products aimed at the same customers. Firms in this category, for example, include medical firms which provide products and services to consumers, patients and clinicians, all very different types of customers, but all in the same healthcare market space.

These multi-product firms also need to address three additional areas:

Understanding the different customers for the different products requires a clear understanding of the overall customer typologies and customer profiling for each product as discussed in Chapter 7, synergies between them, and the implications for the addressable market.

Dealing with different customers in the same market space often requires a clear understanding of the relative positioning of the different products and services across the value chain, as discussed in Chapters 5 and 6, and how they can impact different business models.

These firms also need to deal with the challenges of organisational structure, management and leadership resulting from the broader focus: this may require significant attention to how the firm is structured in order to address the market opportunity effectively; it also means that remuneration incentives need to reflect the overall commercial objectives. We discuss the organisational implications of this in Section 20.3.

Firms where *multiple products* are targeted at *different customers* and *different market spaces*

Multi-product firms which target their products at different customers across different market spaces need to address all the challenges discussed above and also two additional areas.

Firms need to understand the different market spaces in which they operate and the relevant value chains in these market spaces. As opposed to a single product firm which is typically dealing with a single value chain, these firms need to master different market spaces, which in turn may influence business models and go-to-market strategies.

The organisational, management and leadership challenges in these firms can be quite daunting because the cultures of the different market spaces may require very different ways of managing talent, teams and motivation. In particular, as we discuss below, firms need to address the trade-offs between 'unified' and 'distributed' organisational structures which reflect the reliability, pace and agility needed in different market spaces.

20.3 Organisational Structures and Commercialisation

Our research confirmed that the organisational structure of firms can have a significant impact on how they commercialise science and technology-enabled innovation in terms of both the overall trajectory and the pace of this activity.[202–204]

Single-product firms typically have an integrated organisational structure which supports the commercialisation process better than in multi-product firms, which have more complex structures. Multi-product firms typically deploy four types of organisational structures:

U-form, where firms have highly unified organisational structures arranged along functional categories, such as design or manufacture, not by types of products or product groups; these firms are similar to single-product firms which are integrated along functional lines.

M-form, where the firms are typically organised along product lines, so that each of the multiple divisions in the firm will have their own functional organisation within that group of products; what this means of course is that most commercialisation activity is constrained by the focus around existing product groups.

H-form, where firms are organised into groups under holding structures, which are typically managerial artefacts concerned with financial management rather than active commercial operations; usually, H-form structures provide an overarching management layer over several M-form firms.

Hybrid structures, where matrix organisational structures result in firms displaying both U-form and M-form behaviours in different parts of the firm.

So why does this matter?

Many corporates struggle with the innovation challenge and our research suggested that in most cases, the organisational structure and associated culture are seen as the major culprits for this failure. Kawasaki[205] and others have gone so far as to suggest that the only solution to this problem is to encourage insurrectional behaviour by 'intrapreneurs', who are effectively 'internal' entrepreneurs. They argue that 'intrapreneurs' can best succeed by subverting behavioural norms in the firm. Other research has suggested that corporates can be innovative to create radical new products by ring-fencing this activity while drawing on the larger resources of the firm.[206]

Our research shows that many M-form firms were focused on delivering shorter-term financial results consistent with the pressures from investors. These firms were typically poor at internal development of radical new products and much more likely to acquire smaller firms with innovative new products, using their superior financial resources, even where these acquisitions were perceived as expensive. Many of the corporates in our data set justified 'overpaying' for these acquisitions on the grounds that this was an essential part of their strategy, while continuing to search for 'cheaper' innovations.

In contrast, the smaller number of U-form corporates in our data set were able to take a longer-term perspective with a bigger emphasis on longer-term value, but they still worried about shareholder pressures to focus on more immediate financial performance. The most visible example of a U-form corporate of course is Apple, which has doggedly pursued a 'unitary' strategy where new products and services are created by

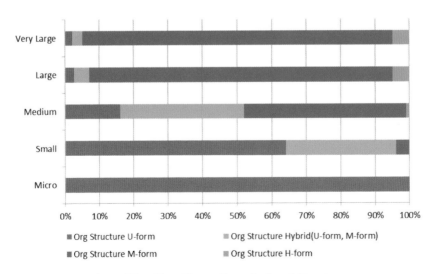

Figure 53:   Firm Size vs Organisational Structure.

functionally organised teams, without the need for divisions which focus on specific products[207]; indeed Apple has argued that this is the key to its success as a corporate innovator.

We analysed the firms in our research data to investigate the overall relationship between firm size, as measured by the number of employees, and the form of organisational structure used: the results are presented in Figure 53. The banding of employee numbers into five categories is based on the segmentation criteria widely used by national and international agencies when reporting on the effect of firm size.

The key findings from this analysis were as follows:

Micro-firms, with less than nine employees, overwhelmingly use highly integrated U-form structures.

The majority of small firms, with 10–49 employees are also strong users of U-form structures, but a significant number also exhibit hybrid forms, combining U-form and M-form structures.

Some medium size firms, with 50–249 employees, still deploy U-form structures but distinct M-form structures and hybrid structures are used by the majority of these larger firms.

Large firms, with 250–499 employees, predominantly deploy M-form structures with evidence of a few U-form and hybrid structures.

Very large firms, with more than 500 employees, strongly favour M-form structures for reasons we discussed above, but there are some interesting exceptions to this rule, for example, Apple, as we discussed above.

When we discuss corporates below, we are largely focused on firms in the Large and Very Large categories with more than 250 employees.

20.4 Corporate Research and Development

In most economies, corporate investment in research and development is seen as a critical component of the innovation market space to be encouraged and supported by a range of government policies and interventions. National and international bodies regularly publish Industrial R&D Scoreboards,[208] which aim to compare the relative performance of different industries and countries. These scoreboards highlight the wide variation in

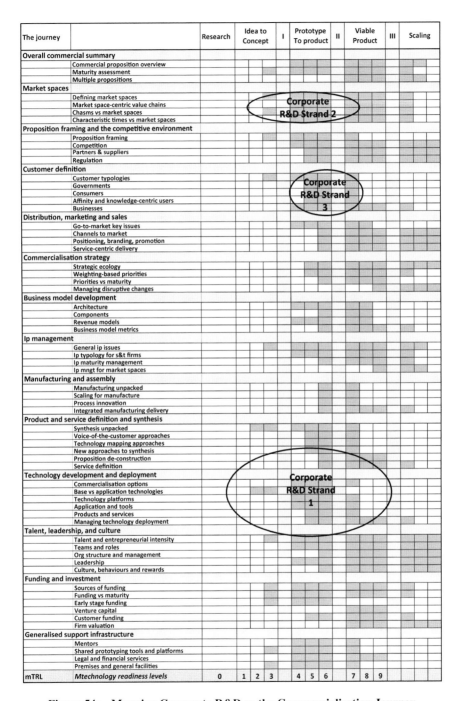

Figure 54: Mapping Corporate R&D vs the Commercialisation Journey.

corporate R&D by market sector, which reflects differences in corporate perceptions about the relative commercial value of different market spaces. On the positive side, this provides evidence for the value of market intervention in driving investment priorities; however, it also highlights the potential risks of low investment in 'strategically' important market spaces which do not meet shorter-term market criteria. The broader policy implications of this are beyond the scope of this book, but they do highlight the need to understand the precise make-up of R&D investment.

One of the less-discussed challenges of using data on corporate R&D investment is *how this research & development is defined and measured*, in particular how much of it covers basic research vs the development of new products and services and new market development. This difficulty is compounded by different perceptions of what constitutes R&D in the minds of policy makers, technology and product developers, not to mention tax authorities trying to decide whether an activity is entitled to special tax treatment!

Our approach to clarifying this and creating a practical operational view of corporate research and development activity is based on our definition of research and development activity in the context of modified technology readiness levels (mTRLs), as discussed in Chapter 1.

Figure 54 shows how typical corporate research and development activity maps onto the commercialisation canvas based on these definitions.

Strand 1 of Corporate R&D covers the development of technologies with mTRL levels from 1 to 6. The transition from 1 to 3 can mirror the activity of research institutions, often providing the basis for technology development partnerships; the development of mTRL from 3 to 6, however, is usually perceived as development activity not research. There is some evidence that, historically, larger firms were more active at TRL levels around 1, but we found virtually no evidence of this in our data set, even for those firms ranked very highly in the R&D expenditure comparison tables. This highlights the need for public funding of basic R&D.

Strand 2 of Corporate R&D is fundamentally concerned with understanding the nature of new market spaces, as discussed in Chapter 5. It typically focuses on the development of technologies with mTRL levels between 3 and 6, which reflect these changing market and application spaces. Much of the innovation here is concerned with application research which anticipates and responds to changes in market spaces and value chains.

Strand 3 of Corporate R&D is closest to commercial application with the focus on how technologies can be shaped to meet the needs of specific groups of customers. Typically, this strand is concerned with raising the mTRL from 4 to 6, and sometimes even 7, which implies that Chasm II has been crossed. Historically, this is the area of corporate R&D which has triggered discussion about the boundaries of publicly funded R&D and whether this later activity can be construed as intervening in the market from a competition law perspective.

What the data highlights is the underlying problem in trying to define an arbitrary boundary between pre-competitive R&D and development driven by the marketplace: in mature, stable markets, this kind of distinction may be possible, but in situations of dramatic change, which is where most firms hope to gain competitive advantage, this distinction is largely artificial with the risk that it merely enables political expediency when making decisions about the allocation of resources.

20.5 Product Portfolio Management

Irrespective of the organisational structure of the firm, multi-product firms need to have a coherent approach to the way they create, manage and retire products and services. The complexity of this task depends on whether the products are all targeted at the same customers, different customer groups or at different market spaces, as discussed earlier in this chapter.

In all cases, this coherent approach needs to be based on an understanding of the relative importance of the strategic, financial, and tactical objectives underpinning the product and service portfolio.

The strategic metrics are typically driven by a number of considerations, including market positioning and fit, portfolio fit, go-to-market complexity, and organisational impact. To do this, firms need to develop a coherent view of the structure and dynamics of the external market, integrating inputs from a wide range of sources. They also need to build a view of the relative scale, profitability, and competitive environment for the different business opportunities.

The financial metrics, which typically reflect the sustainability of the product portfolio, can be profiled using a number of criteria including potential revenues and profits, the business model, time-to-payback, net present value, the financial risk profile and sustainability. Firms need to use this perspective to drive both new internal projects and external dialogues, collaborations, partnerships, and investment.

Multi-product firms need to build product portfolio maps to define trade-offs between strategic, financial and tactical criteria as part of their decision-making process.

Figure 55 shows a typical product portfolio which maps 'strategic' value versus 'financial' value for a range of products for a multi-product firm organised on the basis of an M-form structure.

Firms need to understand the relative contribution to the firm's strategic and financial goals of any single new product or service; decisions

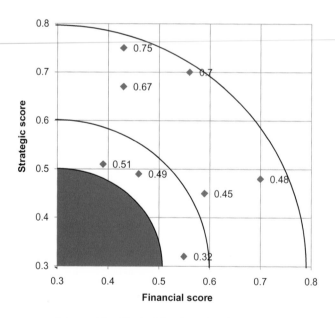

Figure 55:   Typical Product Portfolio Map.

about whether to develop and deploy a new product need to be viewed on an aggregate basis; for example, strategically valuable products may contribute to the positioning and the perceived value of a firm even where the metrics based on conventional financial metrics are less impressive.

Some potential products may inhabit a zone of the product portfolio map where they are deemed to be unviable; this involves setting some threshold boundaries. For example, Figure 55 illustrates a zone, marked in black, where the strategic value needs to exceed particular threshold values irrespective of the financial value; this kind of mapping clearly reflects decisions made by the leadership of a firm.

20.6 Build, Buy, or Partner?

Our research suggests that firms need to adopt a structured approach to harnessing innovation in order to grow revenues and improve profitability. Given market volatility and the complexity of the challenge, firms need to use the portfolio approach discussed above, based on an appropriate mix of Building, Buying, and Partnering initiatives within the overall strategic context.

Building new products and services within pre-existing firm structures and cultures presents a number of challenges:

Understanding new market spaces: As we discussed in Chapter 5, the problem for many firms is that internal knowledge about the market may be constrained by existing paradigms, awareness of existing players and critically, current ways of doing business and the associated business models. Some of the most significant innovations depend on changing current paradigms and doing things very differently.[210]

Synthesis of new products of services: It can often be difficult for teams inside well-established firms to think radically about the functionality, form and overall shape of products and services, especially when they are rooted in the experience of managing existing successful products. We have already discussed the overall challenge of synthesis in Chapter 9, but these problems are likely to be even more serious in mature well-established firms.

Developing new business models: Creating new business models can be
very difficult for 'incumbent' firms, especially when these new models may undermine existing models, and hence impact on shorter-term
profitability. The new business models may also undermine long-held
views on the nature of the market and challenge existing organisational structures.

The prevailing culture in established firms may not provide the right environment which supports the innovative creation of new products and services. Exhortations to create a more entrepreneurial culture are unlikely to
bear fruit if the organisational structure, decision-making and remuneration structures, and the criteria for judging success, continue to favour the
'old' way of doing things — innovation is not an extra that can be added
to an existing business culture and model. We have already discussed the
challenges around talent, leadership and culture in Chapter 16.

The build option is based on developing new products and services
internally within the firm. Our research identified two broad approaches
to doing this: *innovation silos*, where ring-fenced teams within the mature
firm take an integrated approach to defining new market spaces, new product and service concepts, and new business model, and *pervasive innovation*, which involves reshaping the entire firm and its strategic ecology.
Our evidence suggests that the former is more likely to succeed than the
latter.

Buying smaller firms with innovative products and services is often
seen as a way, especially by corporate leaders under pressure from investors, to deliver results quickly.[211–213] The general track record of firms successfully integrating acquisitions into their core businesses is mixed:
many larger firms manage these acquisitions under separate and distinct
management while paying lip-service to the strategic benefits of integration. This clearly acknowledges the impact of organisational structures on
innovation capacity, which we discussed above. What is clear, however, is
that for larger firms, in spite of these challenges, buying smaller firms
with innovative products and services is a key part of their overall commercial strategy.

This raises the fundamental point about acquisitions: the acquiring
firm needs to understand the trade-offs between financial valuation and

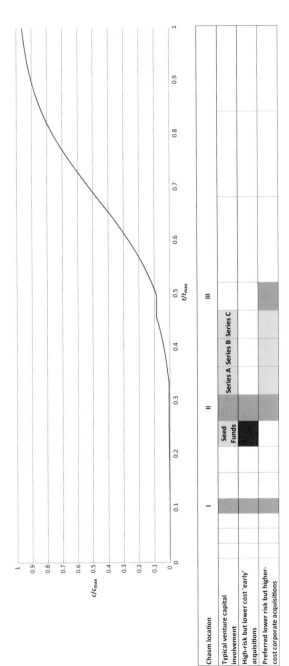

Figure 56: Corporate Innovation — The Buy Option.

risk which reflect the relative maturity of the firm being acquired, as measured by its progress along the commercialisation journey. The key issue in assessing the risk–reward equation is whether the firm has crossed Chasm II.

Our analysis shows that firms which have yet to cross Chasm II are likely to have low valuations but higher levels of risk and uncertainty associated with them, but they may be interesting for corporates who are able to provide access to potential customers and the resources to support business model innovation. Post Chasm II companies have the biggest potential for scaling, but are likely to be quite expensive — they are also likely to have existing financial investors who have a vested interest in high valuations. Firms that have crossed Chasm III will have the lowest relative risk but may also be prohibitively expensive to acquire. Figure 56 illustrates the valuation vs risk dilemma around Chasm II.

The buy option typically depends on acquiring a (usually) smaller more innovative firm which has developed new products and services. Our research showed that the success of these deals depended on pre-deal strategic clarity, good execution of the M&A transaction and post-deal implementation, but our evidence suggested that most failures resulted from poor post-deal implementation rather than the lack of strategic clarity.

Given the challenges with the build and buy options, **partnering** with smaller firms is a powerful way for larger firms to 'acquire' innovative new products and services. The right partnering strategy can often provide the appropriate balance between the overall risk and the level of investment required.

Technology Drivers: Working with the right technology partners can inject expertise and pace into corporate innovation, especially where the firms need to tap into new technologies outside the current core expertise of the larger firm; the technology partners can be academic and research institutions, technology firms, technology translation agencies (often publicly funded), or small agile early stage firms working on the commercialisation of leading-edge technologies.

Market Space Insight: As discussed before, larger firms can sometimes lack insight into significant potential changes in market spaces enabled by technology, regulation or customer behaviour. Partnering with players in emerging and new market spaces can provide the insights essential for developing new products and services.

Product Synthesis and Business Model Creation: Partnering with entrepreneurs and small agile firms can often enable larger firms to synthesise radically different products and services and to create new business models with the potential to transform the competitive marketplace.

There are a number of structural ways for larger firms to create and manage partnerships to harness these three key inputs, ranging from informal relationships and alliances to formally constituted partnerships. Detailed discussion of these approaches is beyond the scope of this book, but the key point to note is that the most successful partnerships rely on engaging with these partners *outside* the firm, thus avoiding the constraints imposed by structures within the firm discussed above.[214]

Innovation outposts can typically support three key activities: networking and partnering, investing, incubation and acquisition, and the actual design and building of new products. Our research identified three types of innovation partnerships: research partnerships, focused mainly on early stage IP creation; partnerships with intervention agencies, including national innovation agencies, incubators, and accelerators focused on specific products and services around Chasms I and II; and 'innovation outposts' which can provide broad access to new market spaces, new technologies and new business models with a much more open agenda. Our research showed limited success in the first two types of partnerships, but some optimism about the potential impact of innovation outposts.

Chapter 21

Orchestrating the Journey:
The Workbench

21.1 Our Approach

Our research and analysis created a robust framework for the provision of tools, data and insights to 'orchestrate' the commercialisation journey for firms enabled by science and technology-enabled innovation.

The Triple Chasm Model provided a strong basis for assessing the maturity of a firm. Coupling this with the 12 vectors driving growth enabled us to create the commercialisation canvas summarised in Chapter 17.

Building on this canvas, we developed a set of tools covering each of the 12 vectors and sub-vectors: we created around 50 such tools, most of which are completely new, although some were created by adapting existing tools and approaches. Our objective was to create a comprehensive set of tools covering all aspects of the commercialisation process and to provide them in an integrated toolkit which enables firms of all shapes and sizes to plan, monitor and execute their growth trajectories. It also enables stakeholders to monitor progress of the firms.

Our initial testing and validation of this toolkit also enabled us to develop additional data and metadata, which we bundled with the tools in order to increase their utility and relevance for different market spaces, technologies, and customers.

We then created a large number of case studies with firms from different market spaces, at different levels of maturity, to provide more detailed guidance on the use of the tools, combined with deep insights which can be used by firms engaged in similar areas of operation.

We integrated the tools, data, metadata, insights and case studies into a coherent Workbench, which can be used by firms, and their stakeholders, to understand their positions and intervene actively to improve the chances of success. We describe this Workbench in Section 21.2.

21.2 Overview of the Workbench

The commercialisation Workbench covers the entire journey for exploiting science and technology innovation from the outputs of research activity to full commercialisation.

Figure 57 shows a summary of the Workbench which can be used by firms in three ways: to appreciate where they are in the journey, to understand the key vectors which could shape their future trajectory, and finally to orchestrate interventions based on the tools in the Workbench which improve the likelihood of success.

The components of the Workbench are as follows:

Overall Commercial Overview: This covers the following tools: the *Commercialisation canvas*, the *triple chasm maturity model* and the *portfolio mapping tool.*

Market Spaces: The tools covering the definition of market spaces and market space-centric value chains are as follows: *Market space components, construction of new value chains, differences in chasm locations*, and *characteristic timescales for different market spaces.*

Proposition Framing and the Competitive Environment: These tools cover *framing tools and approaches, competitor mapping, partner and supplier mapping*, and *mapping regulatory constraints* against the value chains.

Customer Definition: The tools cover *customer typologies* and detailed ways of looking at *consumers, business customers, governments as* *customers, and affinity and knowledge-centric users*; also included is a tool for *market sizing.*

Distribution, Marketing and Sales: The tools cover *go-to-market challenges*, comparing *channels-to-market, the modified 7Ps model for positioning, branding, and promotion*, and a tool looking at *service-centric delivery.*

Commercialisation Strategy: The tools cover the *strategic ecology*, our *new approach to strategy development, changing strategic priorities across the chasms*, and managing *disruptive changes.*

Business Models: The tools cover *business model architecture and deconstruction, model types vs revenues, models vs market spaces*, and *business model metrics for different types of models.*

Intellectual Property (IP) Management: The tools cover *key IP issues, typology of IP for technology firms, managing IP Maturity*, and *IP differences across different market spaces.*

Manufacturing and Assembly: The tools cover *manufacturing deconstruction, scaling challenges, process innovation typology*, and *integrated manufacturing and service delivery models.*

Product and Service Definition and Synthesis: These cover *approaches to synthesis, voice-of-the-customer approaches, technology mapping, creative synthesis techniques, the Proposition Framework* for proposition deconstruction and defining the *wider service envelope.*

Technology Development and Deployment: These tools cover *technology commercialisation options, base vs application technology mapping, technology platform definition models, application tools vs value chains, product and service definition models*, and *technology deployment options.*

Talent, Leadership, and Culture: The tools cover *human capital management, talent and team profiling tools, measuring entrepreneurial intensity, organisational structure and management models, leadership models*, and *culture webs.*

Funding and Investment: The tools cover *comparison of funding sources, funding tactics, early stage funding options, understanding venture capital (VC), customer funding techniques* and *approaches to valuation.*

Vectors	Sub-vectors	Tools
Overall commercial management		
	Commercial proposition overview	Commercialisation canvas
	Maturity assessment	Triple chasm model
	Multiple propositions	Portfolio mapping tool
Market spaces		
	Defining market spaces	Market space components
	Market space-centric value chains	Constructing new value chains
	Chasms vs market spaces	Differences in chasm locations
	Characteristic times vs market spaces	Characteristic timescales
Proposition framing and competition		
	Proposition framing	Framing tools & approaches
	Competition	Competitor mapping
	Partners and suppliers	Partner and supplier mapping
	Regulation	Regulatory mapping
Customer definition		
	Customer typologies	B2b vs b2c vs b2k vs b2g
	Consumers	Consumer profiling
	Affinity and knowledge-centric users	Affinity user profiling
	Businesses	Business profiling
	Market sizing	Current, derivative & new markets
Distribution, marketing, and sales		
	Go-to-market key issues	Mapping challenges
	Channels to market	Channel comparison
	Positioning, branding, promotion	7 ps model
	Service-centric delivery	Service wrappers
Commercialisation strategy		
	Strategic ecology	Strategic ecology components
	Weighting-based priorities	Weighting-based priorities
	Priorities vs maturity	Priorities across chasms
	Managing disruptive changes	Refinement, pivots & disruption
Business model development		
	Architecture	Models deconstucted
	Components	Component analysis
	Revenue models	Revenue models
	Business model metrics	Conventional vs service metrics
Ip management		
	General ip issues	Mapping ip issues
	Ip typology for S&T firms	Types of rights
	Ip maturity management	Ip vs triple chasm model
	Ip mngt for market spaces	Ip vs market spaces
Manufacturing and assembly		
	Manufacturing unpacked	Manufacturing deconstructed
	Scaling for manufacture	Scaling challenges
	Process innovation	Process innovation typology
	Integrated manufacturing delivery	Integrated service models
Product definition and synthesis		
	Synthesis unpacked	Approaches to synthesis
	Voice-of-the-customer approaches	Voc techniques
	Technology-mapping approaches	Technology mapping
	New approaches to synthesis	Creative synthesis
	Proposition deconstruction	Product characterisation
	Service definition	Wider service envelope
Tech. Development and deployment		
	Commercialisation options	Comparing options
	Base vs application technologies	Base vs app tech mapper
	Technology platforms	Platform definition model
	Application and tools	App tech vs value chains
	Products and services	Products vs services
	Managing technology deployment	Tech deployment monitor
Talent, leadership, and culture		
	Talent and entrepreneurial intensity	Profiling tools
	Teams and roles	Team roles vs responsibilities
	Org structure and management	Organisational models
	Leadership	Leadership models
	Culture, behaviours, and rewards	Culture web
Funding and investment		
	Sources of funding	Funding comparator
	Funding vs maturity	Funding tactics
	Early stage funding	Funding options
	Venture capital	Understanding vc funding
	Customer funding	How to use customer funding
	Firm valuation	Approaches to valuation

Figure 57:   The Workbench.

The Workbench is designed to allow firms to use a sub-set of this full range of tools which is appropriate to the journey that the firm is embarked upon.

21.3 Core Data and Metadata Underpinning the Workbench

The tools summarised above are best used with 'core' data and metadata incorporated into the Workbench. This data provides both qualitative and quantitative insights into the following key areas:

Data on firms and portfolios from a number of market spaces: This includes typical maturity maps for several key science and technology clusters based on the application of the Triple Chasm Model.

Detailed definition for all 12 market spaces discussed in this book: This includes examples of typical market space-centric value chains for all the market spaces. These can be used to accelerate this type of analysis by firms in the same space.

Profiling of typical customer spaces for each of the market spaces based on the typography model: This also includes data and metadata for different types of customers.

Detailed data and metadata on the comparative behaviour of distribution channels and business models for the different market spaces.

Data on the manufacturing scaling challenges for different market spaces.

Data and insights on different technology deployment options and product and service synthesis for firms in different market spaces.

Comparative data on the relative importance of different issues around talent, leadership and culture across different market spaces with additional metadata.

Data on the ease of funding for firms in different market spaces and evidence of how the approaches to valuation vary across different market spaces.

21.4 Case Studies

During the development and testing of the Workbench, we applied the full set of tools, data and metadata to assess the performance of a large number

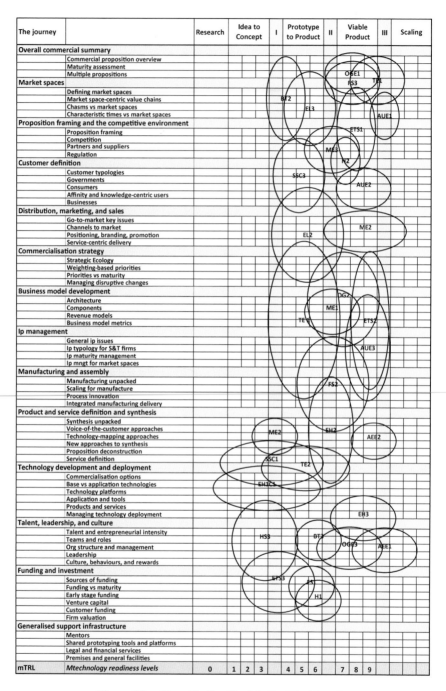

Figure 58:   Case Studies Used in the Workbench.

of firms of different size and maturity in order to build a library of examples of the use of the Workbench.

Some of these case studies have been integrated into the Workbench so they can be used to explain and guide the way in which the different tools can be deployed in practice. The case studies used were chosen to provide coverage of all 12 market spaces discussed earlier in Chapter 5, and also to show firms within each market space operating at different levels of maturity. Figure 58 shows this case study coverage mapped onto the commercialisation canvas, where each oval shape and legend on the canvas corresponds to the position of a single firm.

21.5 Using the Workbench

The Workbench can be used by the different actors in different ways to achieve their objectives. In overall terms, the Workbench provides tools which enable the actors, described in Chapter 19, to understand their current status and positions, to evaluate their options, and to make decisions which affect their future trajectories.

Early-stage firms can use the commercialisation Workbench in order to assess their current status, to understand relative importance of the vectors and sub-vectors for their objectives, and to systematically apply tools to improve their positions and chances of success.

High-growth firms can use the Workbench in the same way but can also focus on the creation of new products and services and drive accelerated growth.

Larger established firms can use the Workbench to adopt a more structured and robust approach to making the right build, buy, or partner decisions, and implementing the consequences of this more effectively.

Intervention agencies can use the Workbench in order to understand and improve the effectiveness of existing interventions and also to create new forms of intervention aligned with strategic and financial objectives and priorities.

Suppliers of services, for example, mentors and advisors can use the Workbench and tools to provide value-added services to their customers more effectively.

Investors can use the Workbench to better understand the investment opportunities and risks and make structured data-driven decisions.

And finally, **Policymakers** can use the Workbench to understand where and how to intervene in their broader objectives of new value creation; in particular, we believe that the data and insights in this book coupled with the Workbench provide a more robust basis for future policy development, including the creation of new national industrial strategies.

Chapter 22

The Commercialisation Manifesto

We believe that the sagacious commercialisation of science and technology-enabled innovation holds the key to balanced and sustainable growth across the world. To do this successfully, we need to understand and harness a wide range of factors based on an open debate with different stakeholders about the challenges and trade-offs.

We believe that we need a clear evidence-based understanding of the overall process of commercialisation, not just sentiments based on ideological considerations. In particular, we need to define the constituents of research and development more precisely and the role of innovation in this context. We also need to understand the vectors which can drive this process and the diffusion of new technologies, products and services into the marketplace.

Our research revealed a significant body of literature about innovation and entrepreneurship but very little systematic analysis of how technology-based innovation is commercialised. We found some excellent case studies mainly produced by academics in business schools, but virtually all these tended to look at either significant successes or failures: this emphasis on 'outliers' meant that there were few insights into the key influences and drivers affecting the majority of firms working on commercialising science and technology-enabled innovation; in particular, we observed that most research focused on empirical observations with little attention paid to causality. The research and analysis presented in this book should be viewed as an attempt to address this gap in our understanding.

We believe we need a serious debate about the economic backdrop and the key policy levers which can shape the process of turning ideas into valuable outputs. Taking our lead from Schumpeter, we need to embrace meso-economic thinking, which allows us to examine the dynamics which link macro-economic analysis to the micro-economic world inhabited by real firms. We then need to understand how to create and sustain better ecosystems and the balance between public and private actors in this space.

As we embarked on our research, we realised early on that much of what was written was based on what we would call 'secondary' measures of progress, such as amounts invested in technology firms and the valuation of these firms, all of which reflect specific perceptions of importance and value subject to general sentiment and of little value in trying to understand the key drivers and causality: in our view, this requires an approach based on 'primary' data not subject to these vagaries. Quite early in our research programme, we decided that the best primary measure of the progress of technology firms related to the *adoption* of technologies, and so we focused on collecting primary data on customers for new technologies, products and services. This approach enabled us to isolate the effects of market spaces, technologies and geographies in terms of driving adoption by customers.

We believe we need a clear intervention agenda, which enables us to increase the prospects of success rather than vague exhortations about market forces being the panacea for the difficulties in commercialisation. This means we need to design and execute better forms of intervention which actually address the real challenges.

Our diffusion theory-based analysis of the large volume of customer growth data led us to identify three specific chasms or discontinuities in the commercialisation journey from idea to products and services delivered to the maximum number of customers.

Our research enabled us to identify the 12 key vectors, which affect the progress of commercialisation: Market spaces, Proposition Framing and the Competitive Environment, Customer Definition, Distribution, Marketing and Sales, Commercialisation Strategy, Business Models, IP

Management, Synthesis of new Products and Services, Manufacturing and Assembly, Technology Deployment, Funding and Investment, and Talent, Teams and Leadership.

Mapping the vectors and sub-vectors against the Triple Chasm Model enabled us to define the commercialisation canvas on which we could map the typical trajectories of technology firms, and to understand the relative importance of each of the vectors at different points in the maturity curve.

We believe that we need to understand better how to support innovators, Entrepreneurs, and early stage firms based on firm evidence of where they face the biggest challenges and recognising the big contribution that these actors can make to overall economic growth.

Our research has produced two highly practical outputs: a commercialisation canvas and a Workbench which can be used by firms of all sizes to understand and support their commercialisation journeys and to increase the likelihood of success, and empirical data and insights into commercialisation across different technologies, market spaces and also across geographical boundaries.

Using these, we were able to understand the roles of different actors on this journey and to evaluate the potential impact of different types of interventions on the success of the commercialisation process: in particular, this allowed us to compare the roles of technology transfer offices, incubators and accelerators and the gaps in the support they provide.

We believe that the critical role capital plays in the overall commercialisation journey needs to be better understood by all the actors, so that they can all make better decisions about how this capital is provided and utilised. This means avoiding the simplistic rhetoric which currently confuses this debate.

Our research has major implications for all the actors concerned with the commercialisation journey: clearly, entrepreneurs and firms can draw on the Workbench and insights for practical support and guidance; those designing and implementing interventions can now better understand the relative value of their interventions; it also provides guidance of what is currently missing; investors now also have a more objective basis to judge investment rather than passing fads; and finally, policy makers now have a framework and data which allow them to evaluate policy options and design policy measures based on more rigorous criteria than the simple mantra currently promoted by stakeholders with vested interests.

We believe that corporates need to better understand the process of commercialisation and focus on the creation of sustainable value: This means an evidence-based approach to getting the balance right between build, buy and partner options. We recognise that some of these choices may be distorted by short-term pressures on corporates shaped by the exigencies of volatile financial markets, but this is where public policy could restore a degree of perspective.

Aggregating the results for multiple single-products enabled us to understand the behaviour of multi-product firms, and to explore the impact of different types of organisational structure on commercialising innovation. This in turn enabled us to explore the critical issues around corporate innovation.

Finally, we believe that the wider debate about the role of technology and innovation in the global economy needs rational evidence-based discussion. This is not a zero-sum game, but some of the valid questions about limits to growth and sustainable development need to be tackled head-on; we do not subscribe to the notion of a technological fix for most things, but do believe that the deployment of science and technology-based innovation plays a critical role in overall economic development.

We hope this book stimulates a new generation of researchers to analyse and understand the challenges of turning technology-based ideas into commercially valuable products and services, using an evidence-based approach.

Notes

1 Martin, Michael (1994), *Managing Innovation and Entrepreneurship in Technology-based Firms*, Wiley. This account looks at the application of conventional management techniques in larger technology firms.
2 Timmons (1995) *A. New Venture Creation*, 4th edition, Irwin/McGraw-Hill. Often credited with popularising the notion of intrapreneurship in corporations.
3 Bhide, Amar (2008), *The Venturesome Economy*, Princeton University Press. Based largely on data from venture-funded firms, this argues the merits of globalisation from a US perspective.
4 Snow, Charles Percy (1963), *The Two Cultures: A Second Look*, Cambridge University Press. Snow talks about two distinct cultures, arguing that this divide makes it harder to appreciate the true impact of technology, although others have disputed this strongly.
5 Schumpeter, J.A., Capitalism, Socialism and Democracy (1947), reprinted 2008, Harper. Schumpeter was probably the first economist to articulate a theory of entrepreneurship.
6 Roberts, E.B. (1991), *Entrepreneurs in High Technology: Lessons from MIT and Beyond*, Oxford University Press. A detailed but now rather dated account of computing firms on the US east coast in the 1980s.
7 Saxenian, Annalie (1996), *Regional Advantage: Culture and Competition in Silicon Valley and Route 128*, Harvard University Press. Detailed look at US tech firms in the main West Coast and East Coast clusters.
8 Garnsey, E., Longhi, C. (2004), "Complex processes and innovative places; The evolution of high tech Cambridge and Sophia-Antipolis", *International Journal of Technology Management*, 28(3–6), 336–355. Probably inspired

by the Saxenian work on US firm, this looks at the development of high tech clusters in two quite different European clusters.

9 Lubik, S., Garnsey, E., Minshall, T. and Platts, K., (2013), 'Value creation from the innovation environment; partnership strategies in university spin-outs', *R&D Management*, 43(2), 136–150. Looks at university spin-outs based largely on Cambridge spin-outs.

10 Chalmers, A.F. (1978), *What is This Thing Called Science?*, The Open University Press. In our view this is the best simple exposition of the difference between science and technology.

11 OECD (2007), *Frascati Manual: Proposed Standard Practice for Surveys on Research and Experimental Development*, 6th edition. The Frascati approach is under growing pressure as market and technology boundaries are eroded and the conventional boundaries become less relevant.

12 Freeman, C. (1987), "Changes in the national system of innovation", *Paper prepared for OECD Directorate for Science, Technology and Industry Ministerial meeting, Paris, OECD*. Freeman was a pioneer in characterising and measuring the economic impact of innovation, and defining a research agenda which still drives the work of SPRU at the University of Sussex, UK.

13 Morita, A. (1992), *"S" does not equal "T" and "T" does not eqaul "I"*, *The First United Kingdom Innovation Lecture, UK DTI Paper*, Morita's work had a strong influence on those working on new product development, especially in the high tech centres in Cambridge and Silicon Valley.

14 Nelson, R. (1981), "Research on productivity growth and productivity differences: Dead ends and new departures", *Journal of Economy Literature* (19). Nelson tried to build on Schumpeter's ideas on meso-economics, unfortunately with little impact on mainstream economists.

15 Pavitt, K. (1984), "Sectoral patterns of technical change: Towards a taxonomy and a theory", *Research Policy*, 13(6), 343–373. Pavitt's work was an attempt to build a systematic approach to technology commercialisation.

16 Saviotti, P.P. (1996), *Technological Evolution, Variety, and the Economy*

17 Coomb, R., Saviotti, P.P. and Walsh, V. (1987), *Economics and Technical Change*, Rowman and Littlefield, USA.

18 Dosi, G. (1993), "Technological paradigms and technological trajectories: A suggested interpretation of the determinants and directions of technical change," *Research Policy*, 22(2), 102–103.

19 Mankins, J.C. (1995), *Technology Readiness Levels*, NASA White Paper, Office of Space Access and Technology, NASA.

20 Friedman, T.L. (2005), *The World is Flat, Farrer, Straus & Giroux.* We do not share Friedman's simplistic notion about how globalisation is eroding differences across different geographic areas.

21 Kuhn, T.S. (1970), *The Structure of Scientific Revolutions*, University of Chicago Press, Chicago.

22 Needham, J. (1954), *Science and Civilisation in China: Introductory Orientations 1*, Cambridge University Press. Our work in China led us to question the supremacy of the Euro-centric view shaped by the Industrial revolution but our research did not reveal any alternative narratives.

23 Dharampal, Indian Science and Technology in the Eighteenth Century: Some Contemporary European Accounts, Impex India, Delhi, 1971; reprinted by Academy of Gandhian Studies, Hyderabad 1983. We found even less evidence of a unique Indian narrative to rival that of the Industrial Revolution.

24 Smith, A. (1779), *The Invisible Hand of Market Forces in 'An Inquiry into the Nature and Causes of the Wealth of Nations.*

25 Marx, K. (1847), *Wage Labour and Capital.*

26 Schumpeter, J. (1942), *Capitalism, Socialism and Democracy*, Routledge, London.

27 Porter, M. (1980), *Competitive Strategy*, Free Press, New York.

28 Christensen, C. (1997), *The Innovator's Dilemma*, Harvard Business University Press.

29 Chandler, A.D. (1977), *The Visible Hand: The Managerial Revolution in American Business*, Harvard University Press.

30 Lazonick, W. (2007), The US Stock Market and the Governance of Innovative Enterprise, *Industrial and Corporate Change*, 16(6), 1983–1035.

31 Stiglitz, J.E. (2004), *The Roaring Nineties: A New History of the World's Most Prosperous Decade*, Norton & Company.

32 Mazzucato, M. (2014), *The Entrepreneurial State*, Anthem Press.

33 Pavitt, K. (1999), *Technology, Management and Systems of Innovation*, Edward Elgar, Cheltenham, ISBN 1-85898-874-8

34 Edquist, C. (2001), *The Systems of Innovation Approach and Innovation Policy: An Account of the State of the Art.*

35 Nelson, R. and Winter, S. (1982), *An Evolutionary Theory of Economic Change*, Belknap Press Reprint 1985.

36 Dopfer, K. (2006), *The Origins of Meso-economics: Schumpeter's Legacy*, Papers on Economics and Evolution, No 0610, Max Planck Institute.

37 Dopfer, K., Foster, J., Potts, J. (2004), "Micro-meso-macro", *Journal of Evolutionary Economics.* 14(3), 263–279.

38 Klepper, S. (1996), "Entry, exit, growth, and innovation over the product life cycle", *American Economic Review*, 86(3), 562–583.

39 Klein, N. (2003), *The Shock Doctrine*, Knof Canada.

40 Hutton, W. (2010), *Them and Us*, Littlebrown.

41 Coase, R.H. (1993a) [1937], "The nature of the firm", In Williamson, Oliver E. and Winter, S.G. (Eds.), *The Nature of the Firm*, Oxford: Oxford University Press, pp. 18–33 (reprint).

42 Kirzner, I.M. (1997), "Entrepreneurial discovery and the competitive market process: An Austrian approach", *Journal of Economic Literature*, 35, 60–85.

43 Sautet, F.E. (2000), *An Entrepreneurial Theory Of The Firm*, Routledge, London.

44 Crepon, B., Duguet, E. and Mairesse, J. (1998), "Research, Innovation and Productivity: an Econometric Analysis at the firm level", *Economics of Innovation and New Technology*, 7, 115–158.

45 Coad, A and Hölzl (2010), *Firm Growth: Empirical Analysis.* Paper 1002, Papers on Economics and Evolution, Max Planck Institute of Economics, Jena, Germany.

46 Coad, A and Rao, R. (2008), "Innovation and firm growth in high-tech sectors: A quantile regression approach", *Research Policy*, 37(4), 633–648.

47 Davidsson, P. and Wiklund, J. (2006), "Conceptual and empirical challenges in the study of firm growth", In P. Davidsson, F. Delmar & J. Wiklund (Eds.), *Entrepreneurship and the Growth of Firms*, Cheltenham: Edward Elgar.

48 Rao, D. (2013), Why 99% of entrepreneurs should stop wasting time seeking venture capital, Forbes, http://www.forbes.com/sites/dileeprao/2013/07/22/

49 Gunter, F., Wuermseher, M. and Cattaneo, G. (2013), "Valuation of early stage high-tech start-up companies", *International Journal of Business*, 18(3), 2013.

50 Moore, G.A. (1991), *Crossing the Chasm.* New York: HarperBusiness. Moore provides some interesting discussion and insights around this Chasm but the absence of any hard data makes it harder to apply the results.

51 Libai, B., Mahajan, V. and Muller, E. (2008), "Can you see the chasm? Innovation diffusion according to Rogers, Bass and Moore", In N. Malhorta (Ed.), *Review of Marketing Research*, Armonk, NY: ME Sharpe Publications.

52 Chandrasekaran, D. and Tellis, G.J. (2006), "Getting a grip on the saddle: Cycles, chasms, or cascades?" *PDMA Research Forum*, Atlanta, 21–22 October.

53 Rogers, and Everett, M. (1962), *Diffusion of Innovations,* first edition, Glencoe: Free Press. One of the most cited publications on the subject: it is actually based on some simplified assumptions with little data but has influenced much thinking.

54 Bass, F.M. (1969), "A new product growth model for consumer durables", *Management Science*, 15(1), 215–227.

55 Mahajan, V., Muller, E. and Peres, R. (2010), "Innovation diffusion and new product growth models: A critical review and research directions", *International Journal of Research in Marketing* 27 (2010) 91–106. A very useful overview of the state of the art in thinking on this subject-the authors also comment on the absence of data from the early stages of customer growth for technology firms and suggest the potential for new insights based on such data.

56 Chandrasekaran, D. and Tellis, G.J. (2007), "A critical review of marketing research on diffusion of new products", In N. K. Malhorta (Ed.), *Review of Marketing Research*, Armonk, NY: M. E. Sharpe, pp. 39–80.

57 Bass, P. and Bass, F.M. (2001), "Diffusion of technology generations: A model of adoption and repeat sales", Working paper: University of Texas at Dallas.

58 Mahajan, V. and Muller, E. (1979), "Innovation diffusion and new product growth models in marketing", *Journal of Marketing*, 43(4), 55–68.

59 Bass, P. and Bass, F.M. (2004), "IT waves: two completed generational diffusion models", Working paper: University of Texas at Dallas.

60 Boswijk, P.H. and Franses, P.H. (2005), "On the econometrics of the Bass diffusion model", *Journal of Business & Economic Statistics*, 23(3), 255–288.

61 Chatterjee, R. and Eliashberg, J. (1990), "The innovation diffusion process in a heterogeneous population: A micro modeling approach", *Management Science*, 36(9), 1057–1079.

62 Mullins, J. and Komisar, R., (2009), *Getting to Plan B: Breaking Through to a Better Business Model*, Harvard Business School Press. Mullins in his most recent book has latched on to the importance of customer funding, which requires more business model iteration.

63 Kotler, Philip and Keller, Kevin Lane (2009), *Marketing Management*, 13th edition, Pearson Education International.

64 Wedel, M. and Kamakura (2002), "Introduction to the special issue on market segmentation", *International Journal of Research in Marketing*, 19, 181–183.

65 Victoria, K. Wells, Shing Wan Chang, Jorge Oliveira-Castro & John Pallister (2010), "Market segmentation from a behavioural perspective", *Journal of Organizational Behaviour Management*.

66 Foedermayr, E.K. and Diamantopoulos, A. (2008), "Market segmentation in practice: Review of empirical studies, methodological assessment and agenda for future research", *Journal of Strategic Marketing*, 16(3), 223–265.

67 Weinstein, A. (2006), "A strategic framework for defining and segmenting markets", *Journal of Strategic Marketing*, 14(2), 115–127.

68 Porter, Michael E. (1985), *Competitive Advantage: Creating and Sustaining Superior Performance*, New York.

69 Kaplinsky, R. and Morris, M. (2001), *A Handbook for Value Chain Research (Report)*, International Development Research Centre.

70 Christopher, Martin (2011), *Logistics and Supply Chain Management: Creating Value-Adding Networks*, 4th edition, Pearson.

71 Angel Gurría (2012), *The Emergence of Global Value Chains: What Do They Mean for Business.* G20 Trade and Investment Promotion Summit. Mexico City: OECD.

72 Dekimpe, M.G., Parker, P.M. and Sarvary, M. (1998), "Staged estimation of international diffusion models: An application to global cellular telephone adoption", *Technological Forecasting and Social Change*, 57(1–2), 105–132.

73 Dekimpe, M.G., Parker, P.M. and Sarvary, M. (2000), "Globalization: Modeling technology adoption timing across countries", *Technological Forecasting and Social Change*, 63(1), 25–42.

74 Desiraju, R., Nair, H. and Chintagunta, P. (2004), "Diffusion of new pharmaceutical drugs in developing and developed nations", *International Journal of Research in Marketing*, 21(4), 341–357.

75 Chatterjee, R., Eliashberg, J. and Rao, V.R. (2000), "Dynamic models incorporating competition", In V. Mahajan, E. Muller, and Y. Wind (Eds.), *New-product Diffusion Models,* New York: Kluwer Academic Publisher.

76 Mahajan, V., Muller, E. and Bass, F.M. (1990), "New product diffusion models in marketing: A review and directions for research", *Journal of Marketing*, 54(1), 1–26.

77 Iyengar, R., Koenigsberg, O. and Muller, E. (2009), "The effects of uncertainty on mobile phone package size and subscribers choice", Working paper: Columbia University.

78 Mahajan,V. and Muller, E. (1996), "Timing, diffusion, and substitution of successive generations of technological innovations: The IBM mainframe case", *Technological Forecasting and Social Change*, 51(2), 109–132.

79 Jain, D., Mahajan, V. and Muller, E. (1991), "Innovation diffusion in the presence of supply restrictions", *Marketing Science*, 10(1), 83–90.

80 Kauffman, R.J. and Techatassanasoontorn, A.A. (2005), "International diffusion of digital mobile technology: A coupled-hazard state-based approach", *Information Technology and Management*, 6(2–3), 253–292.

81 Russell, T. (1980), "Comments on the relationship between diffusion rates, experience curves, and demand elasticities for consumer durable technological innovations", *Journal of Business*, 53(3), 69–73.

82 Norton, J.A. and Bass, F.M. (1987), "A diffusion theory model of adoption and substitution for successive generations of high-technology products", *Management Science*, 33(9), 1069–1086.

83 Blackman and Srivastava (eds.) (2011), *Telecommunications Regulation Handbook*, 10th edition, IBRD, World Bank.

84 Stremersch, S. and Lemmens, A. (2009), "Sales growth of new pharmaceuticals across the globe: The role of regulatory regimes", *Marketing Science*, 28(4), 690–708. The Economist. (2009), "A special report on telecoms in emerging markets", September 26, 1–19.

85 Kotler, P. (1999), *Marketing Management: Analysis, Planning, Implementation and Control*. Prentice Hall Press.

86 Yankelovich, D. and Meer, D. (2006), "Rediscovering market segmentation", *Harvard Business Review*, 84(2), 122–131.

87 Kamakura, W.A. and Mazzon, J.A. (2013), *International Journal of Research in Marketing*, 30, 4–18.

88 Dutta-Bergman, M.J. (2002), *Beyond Demographic Variables: Using Psychographic Research to Narrate the Story of Internet Users*, University of Toronto Press.

89 Valentine, D.B. and Powers, T.L. (2013), "Generation Y values and lifestyle segments", *Journal of Consumer Marketing*, 30(7), 597–606.

90 Varela, P. and Ares, G. (2012), "Sensory profiling, the blurred line between sensory and consumer science: A review of novel methods for product characterization", *Food Research International*, 48, 893–908.

91 Ngai, E.W.T., Li Xiu, Chau, D.C.K. (2009), "Application of data mining techniques in customer relationship management: A literature review and classification", *Expert Systems with Applications,* 36, 2592–2602.

92 Ting, R. (2013), *The Customer Profile: Your Brand's Secret Weapon*, HBR, March 2013.

93 Mitchell, A., Logothetti, A., Thomas J.; Kantor, R.E. (1971), "An approach to measuring quality of life", SRI International Paper.

94 Anderson, J.C. and Narus, J.A. (1998), *Business Marketing: Understand What Customers Value*, HBR, Nov–Dec 1998 Issue.

95 Hickie, B. (2013), *The Science of B2B Market Sizing*. http://blog.openview-partners.com/b2b-market-sizing

96 Gallo, P.J. and Christensen, L.J. (2011), "Firm size matters: An empirical investigation of organizational size and ownership on sustainability-related behaviours", *Business Society*, 50(2), 315–349.

97 Smilor, R. and Matthews, J. (2004), "University venturing: technology transfer and commercialisation in higher education", *International Journal of Technology Transfer and Commercialisation*, 3(1).

98 Nilsson, H and Wene, C-O (2001), "Best practices in technology development policies", Workshop on Good Practices in Policies and Measures, 8–10 October 2001, Copenhagen.

99 Rosenberg, N. (1976), *Perspectives on Technology*, Cambridge University Press.

100 Christensen, C. (1997), *The Innovator's Dilemma*, Harvard Business University Press.

101 Bolles, G.A. (2003), Technology: Optimization, CIO Insight, 1 September.

102 Shupe, C and Behling, R. (2006), "Developing and implementing a strategy for technology deployment", *The Information Management Journal*.

103 Baškarada, S., McKay, T and McKenna,T. (2013), "Technology deployment process model", *Operations Management Research*, 6(3), 105–118.

104 Kuhn, T. (1970), *The Structure of Scientific Revolutions*, 2nd edition, University of Chicago Press.

105 Lakatos, I. (1969), "Criticism and the methodology of scientific research programmes", *Proceedings of the Aristotelian Society, New Series*, 69 (1968–1969), 149–186.

106 Tang, J., Kaemar, K.M. and Busenitz, L. (2012), "Entrepreneurial alertness in the pursuit of new opportunities", *Journal Of Business Venturing*, 27(1), 79–94.

107 Ulwick, A. (2005), *What Customers Want: Using Outcome-Driven Innovation to Create Breakthrough Products and Services*, McGraw-Hill Publications.

108 Kelley, D, (2002), TED 2002 Talk: David Kelley on Human-Centered Design, February 2002.

109 Cooper, R.G. and Edgett, S.J. (2008), "Ideation for product innovation: What are the best methods?", *PDMA Visions Magazine*.

110 von Hippel, Eric (1986), "Lead users: A source of novel product concepts", *Management Science*, 791–805.

111 Herstatt, C. and von Hippel, E. (1992), "From experience: Developing new product concepts via the lead user method: A case study in a "low-tech" field", *Journal of Product Innovation Management*, 9(3), 213–221.

112 Garcia, M.L. and Bray, O.H. (1997), "Fundamentals of technology road-mapping", Strategic Business Development Department Sandia National Laboratories.

113 Phaal, R., Farrukh, C. and Probert, D. (2001), "Technology roadmapping: Linking technology resources to business objectives", Centre for Technology Management, University of Cambridge.

114 Laube, T. and Abele, T. (2005), Technologie-roadmap: Strategisches und taktisches Technologiemanagement. Ein Leitfaden. Fraunhofer-Institut Produktionstechnik und Automatisierung (IPA), Stuttgart, Germany.

115 Chesbrough, H (2003) *Open Innovation: The New Imperative for Creating and Profiting from Technology*. Harvard Business School Press.

116 Lee, J., Bagheri, B. and Kao, H-A (2014), "Recent advances and trends of cyber-physical systems and big data analytics in industrial informatics", *IEEE International Conference on Industrial Informatics (INDIN)*.

117 Kotler, P. and Keller, K. (2006), *Marketing and Management*, Pearson Prentice Hall.

118 Ardichvili, A., Cardozo, R. and Ray, S. (2003), "A theory of entrepreneurial opportunity identification and development", *Journal of Business Venturing*, 18(1), 105–123.

119 Brown, T. (2008), *Design Thinking*.

120 Kolko, J. (2015), *Design Thinking Comes of Age*, HBR.

121 Friedman, L (2002), *Go To Market Strategy*, Butterworth-Heinemann, Elsevier Publications.

122 Kovac, M., Ledingham, D. and Weinger, L. (2012), *Creating an Adaptive Go-to-Market System*, Bain & Co Publications.

123 Lee, E. (1997), *The Handbook of Channel Marketing*, www.elew.com.

124 Dent, J. (2011), *Distribution Channels: Understanding and Managing Channels to Market*, Kogan Page.

125 Kerin, Hartley and Rudelius (2001), *Marketing, The Core*, 4th edition, McGraw Hill Publishing.

126 Sawney, M. (2011), "Branding in technology markets", In Tybout & Calkin (Eds.), Kellogg on Branding, John Wiley and Sons.

127 Porter M.E. (1980), *Competitive Strategy — Techniques for Analyzing Industries and Competitors*, Free Press, New York.

128 Prahalad, C.K. and Hamel, G. (1990), "The core competence of the corporation", *Harvard Business Review*, 68(3), 79–91.

129 Teece, D.J., Pisano, G. and Shuen, A (1997), "Dynamic capabilities and strategic management", *Strategic Management Journal*, 18(7), 509–533.

130 Burgelman, R. and Grove, A. (2012), *Strategic Dynamics: Three Key Themes*, Stanford University Research Paper No. 2096.

131 Johnson, P. (2007), Astute Competition, Elsevier.

132 Johnson, P., Foss, N.J. (2015), *Optimal Strategy and Business Models: A Control Theory Approach, Managerial and Decision Economics*, Wiley Online.

133 Ovans, A (2015), *What is a business model?, Harvard Business Review*. January 23, 2015.

134 Drucker, P.F. (1994), *The theory of the business, Harvard Business Review*. Sep-Oct 1994 Issue.

135 Teece, D.J. (2010), "Business models, business strategy and innovation", *Long Range Planning*, 43, 172–194.

136 Magretta, J. (2002), *Harvard Business Review*, May 2002 Issue.

137 Barrow, C., Barow, P. and Brown, R. (1992), *The Business Plan Workbook*, Kogan Page.

138 Johnson, M.W., Christensen, C, and Kagermann, H. (2008), *Re-inventing Your Business Model*, Harvard Business Review, Dec 2008.

139 Osterwalder, A and Pigneur, Y (2010), *Business Model Generation*, John Wiley & Sons.

140 Johnson, M.W. (2010), *Seizing the White Space: Business Model Innovation for Growth and Renewal*, Harvard Business Press.

141 Slywotzky, Morrison and Andelman (2002) *The Profit Zone: How Strategic Business Design Will Lead You to Tomorrow's Profits*, Three Rivers Press.

142 Mullins, J. and Komisar, R. (2009), *Getting to Plan B: Breaking Through to a Better Business Model*, Harvard Business Press.

143 Robbins-Roth, C. (2000), *From Alchemy to IPO: The Business of Biotechnology*, Barnes & Noble.

144 Kornberg, A. (2002), *The Golden Helix: Inside Biotech Ventures*, Barnes & Noble.

145 Michel, Coles, Golisano and Knutson (2003), *The Ultimate Competitive Advantage: Secrets of Continually Developing a More Profitable Business Model*, Berrett-Koehler Publishers.

146 UK HM Treasury (2006), *The Gowers Review of Intellectual Property.*

147 The UK IPO (2014), Banking on IP? The role of intellectual property and intangible assets in facilitating business finance.

148 World Intellectual Property Report (2015), *Breakthrough Innovation and Economic Growth*, WIPO Publications.

149 Smith, R and Kiholm, J. (2001), *Entreprenuerial Finance*, Barnes & Noble.

150 Bhide, A. (1992), Bootstrap Finance: The art of start-ups. *Harvard Business Review.*

151 The European Union (2015), *Understanding Crowdfunding and its Regulations*, Joint Research Centre, European Commission.

152 Osnabrugge, M.V. and Robinson, R.J. (2000), *Angel Investing*, Jossey-Bass.

153 OECD (2015), "Access to finance: Venture capital", In *Entrepreneurship at a Glance 2015*, OECD Publishing, Paris.

154 Gornall, W. and Strebulaev, I.A. (2015), "The economic impact of venture capital: Evidence from public companies", Stanford Faculty and Research Working Paper No 3362.

155 EVCA (2013), *Pan-European Private Equity Performance Benchmarks Study*, Thomson Reuters.

156 Zider, B. (1998), "How venture capital works", *Harvard Business Review*, Nov–Dec 1998 Issue.

157 Mullins, J. (2014), *The Customer-Funded Business*, John Wiley & Sons.

158 Westland, C. (2003), *Financial Dynamics: A System for Valuing Technology Companies*, John Wiley & Sons (Asia) Pte Ltd.

159 Collins, C and Smith, K.G. (2006), "Knowledge exchange and combination: The role of human resource practices in the performance of high-technology firms", 49(3), 544–560.

160 Michaels, E., Handfield-Jones, H. and Axelrod, B. (2001), The War for Talent, *Harvard Business Press.*

161 O'Shea, R., Allen, T.J., Chevalier, A. and Roche, F. (2005), "Entrepreneurial orientation, technology transfer and spinoff performance of U.S. universities", *Research Policy*, 34, 994–1009.

162 Denison, D.R., Hart, S.L. and Kahn, J.A. (2006), "From chimneys to cross-functional teams: Developing and validating a diagnostic model", *Academic Management Journal*, 39(4), 1005–1023.

163 Prahalad, C.K. and Hamel, G. (1990), "The core competence of the corpora-tion", *Harvard Business Review*, 68(3), 79–91.

164 Belbin, R.M. (1981), *Management Teams: Why They Succeed or Fail*, Elsevier-Butterworth-Heinemann.

165 Belbin, R.M. (2000), *Beyond the Team*, Elsevier-Butterworth-Heinmann.

166 Nowack, K. (1996), "Is the Myers Briggs type indicator the right tool to use? Performance in practice", *American Society of Training and Development*, Fall, 6.

167 Vyakarnam, S. and Handelberg, J. (2006), "Four themes of the impact of management teams on organisational performance: Implications for future research of entrepreneurial teams", *International Small Bus Journal*, 23(6), 236–256.

168 Greiner, L.E. (1998), *Evolution and Revolution as Organizations Grow*, Harvard Business Review.

169 Bennis, W. (2009), *On Becoming a Leader*, New Youk: Basic Books.

170 Miles, S.A. and Watkins, M.D. (2007), "The leadership team: Complementary strengths or conflicting agendas", *Harvard Business Review*.

171 Ospina, S. and Sorenson, G. (2006), "A constructionist view of leadership: Charting new territory", In Goethals, G. and Sorenson, G. (Eds), *The Quest for a General Theory of Leadership*, Edward Elgar.

172 Drath, W.H., McCauley, C.D., Palus, C.J, Van Velsor, E., O'Connor, P & McGuire, J.B (2008), "Direction, alignment, commitment: Towards a more integrative ontology of leadership", *The Leadership Quarterly*, 19, 635–653.

173 Ernst, C. and Chrobot-Mason, D. (2011), "Flat world, hard boundaries: How to lead across them", *MIT Sloan Management Review*, 52(3).

174 Hickman, G. and Sorenson, G (2014), *The Power of Invisible Leadership: How a Compelling Purpose Inspires Exceptional Leadership*, SAGE: Los Angeles.

175 Dosi, G., Levinthal, D.A. and Marengo, L. (2003), "Bridging contested ter-rain: linking incentive-based and learning perspectives on organizational evolution", In *Industrial and Corporate Change*, Vol. 12(2), Oxford University Press, pp. 413–436.

176 Dodge, H.R., Fullerton, S. and Robbins, J.E. (1994), "The stage of the organizational life cycle and competition as mediators of problem percep-tion for small businesses", *Strategic Management Journal*, 15(2), 121–134.

177 Schermerhorn, Hunt and Osborn (2003), *Organisation Behaviour*, John Wiley & Sons.

178 Chatman, J., Caldwell, D., O'Reilly, C. and Doerr, B. (2014), "Parsing organizational culture: The joint influence of culture content and strength on performance in high-technology firms", *Journal of Organizational Behaviour*, 35(6), 785–808.

179 Makri, M., Lane, P.J. and Gomez-Mejia, L.R. (2006), "CEO incentives, innovation, and performance in technology-intensive firms: A reconciliation of outcome and behaviour-based incentive schemes", *Strategic Management Journal*, 27(11), 1057–1080.

180 Scott, M. and Bruce, R. (1987), "Five stages of growth in small business", *Long Range Planning*, 20(3), 45.

181 Bhide, A. (2000), "Looking back to the next century, closing keynote address", *TIE Annual Conference*.

182 Chesbrough, Henry William (2003), "The era of open innovation", *MIT Sloan Management Review*, 44(3), 35–41.

183 Golder, P.N. and Tellis, G.J. (2004), "Growing, growing, gone: Cascades, diffusion, and turning points in the product life cycle", *Marketing Science*, 23(2), 207–218.

184 West, J. and Gallagher, S. (2006), "Challenges of open innovation: The paradox of firm investment in open-source software", *R and D Management* 36(3).

185 Talebinejad, M.R. and Dastjerdi, H.V. (2005), "A cross-cultural study of animal metaphors: When owls are not wise!" *Metaphor and Symbol*, 20(2), 133–150.

186 White, M. (2003), "Metaphor and economics: The case of growth", *English for Specific Purposes*, 22(2), 131–151.

187 Radjou, N., Prabhu, J. and Ahuja, S. (2012), *Jugaad Innovation: Think Frugal, Be Flexible, Generate Breakthrough Growth*, Wiley.

188 Calvino, F., Criscuolo, C. and C. Menon (2015), "Cross-country evidence on start-up dynamics", OECD Science, Technology and Industry Working Papers, No. 6, OECD Publishing, Paris.

189 The World Bank (2008), *The World Bank Report*, Global economic prospects: Technology diffusion in the developing world. Washington, DC: The International Bank for Reconstruction and Development/The World Bank.

190 U.S. Department of Commerce (2012), Accelerating technology transfer and commercialization of federal research in support of high-growth businesses.

191 Hockaday, T. (2014), *University Technology Transfer — Models, Components and Frameworks, Isis Innovation*, Oxford Report, October 2014.

192 Dowling, A. (2015), *The Dowling Review of Business-University Research Collaborations*, UK Govt Report, July 2015.
193 Ezell, S., Spring, F. and Bitka, K (2015), "The global flourishing of national innovation foundations", *The Information Technology and Innovation Foundation*.
194 Saunders, T and Kingsley, J. (2016), *Made in China: Makerspaces and the Search for Mass Innovation*, Nesta Publication.
195 Barrow, C. (2001), *Incubators*, John Wiley & Sons Ltd.
196 Hackett, S.M. and Dilts, D.M. (2004), "A systematic review of business incubation research", *The Journal of Technology Transfer*, 29(1), 55–82.
197 Miller, P. and Bound, K. (2011), The Startup Factories: The rise of accelerator programmes to support new technology ventures, NESTA Discussion paper.
198 Perez, C. (2002), *Technological Revolutions and Financial Capital: The Dynamics of Bubbles and Golden Ages*, Edward Elgar Publishing.
199 Dosi, G., Galambos, L., Gambardella, A. and Orsanigo, L. (Eds.) (2013), *The Third Industrial Revolution in Global Business*, Cambridge Books, Cambridge University Press.
200 Dosi, G., Gambardella, A., Grazzi, M. and Orsenigo, L. (2008), "Technological revolutions and the evolution of industrial structures: Assessing the impact of new technologies upon the size and boundaries of firms", *Capitalism and Society, De Gruyter*, vol. 3(1), 1–49.
201 Dosi, G. and Nelson, R.R. (2013), "The Evolution of Technologies: An assessment of the state-of-the-art", *Eurasian Business Review*, *Eurasia Business and Economics Society*, 3(1), 3–46.
202 Moss Kanter, R. (1990), "When giants learn to dance", *HBS*.
203 Tedlow, R. S. (2010), *Denial: Why Business Leaders Fail to Look Facts in the Face and What to Do About It*. Portfolio Publishing.
204 Christensen, C. (2011), *The Innovator's Dilemma: The Revolutionary Book That Will Change the Way You Do Business*, Harper Business.
205 Kawasaki, G. (2006), *The Art of Intrapreneurship*.
206 Pinchot, G. (1985), *Intrapreneuring: Why You Don't Have to Leave the Corporation to Become an Entrepreneur*, Harper & Row.
207 Thompson, B (2016), "Apple's organizational crossroads", *Stratechery Weekly Article*.
208 EU (2015), *The 2015 EU Industrial R&D Investment Scorecard*, Publications Office of the EU.
209 OECD (2015), *OECD Science, Technology and Industry Scoreboard 2015: Innovation for Growth and Society*, OECD Publishing, Paris.

210 Hansen, M.T. and Birkinshaw, J. (2007), "The innovation value chain", *Harvard Business Review.*

211 Granstrand, O. and Sjölander, S. (1990), "The acquisition of technology and small firms by large firms", *Journal of Economic Behaviour & Organization*, 13(3), 367–386.

212 Desyllas, P. Hughes, A. (2008), "Sourcing technological knowledge through corporate acquisition: Evidence from an international sample of high technology firms", *Journal of High Technology Management Research*,18, 157–172.

213 Dunlap-Hinkler, D., Marion, T.J. and Friar, J.H. (2011), "Educational acquisitions: The role they play in new product development in the global pharmaceutical industry", University of Warwick Papers, April 2011.

214 Blank, S. and Simoudis, E. (2015), "Re-imagining corporate innovation with a Silicon Valley perspective", https://corporate-innovation.co/.

Index

A

Affinity and Knowledge-Centric
Groups, 43, 86, 131, 204
Agent-Based Models, 30
Agricultural Sciences, 5
Angels, 169–171, 209–210
Apple, 247–248
Application Technologies, 7–8, 41,
44, 83, 90–92, 110, 132, 145, 160,
205, 261
Applications and Tools, 41, 44,
90–91, 95, 109, 168
Architecture of Revenues, Costs and
Profits, 142
Assignment of IPR, 156

B

Base Technologies, 8, 90–92, 98,
109–110, 145, 205
Bass, 30–31, 35, 37–39
Belbin, 187
Bhide, xxxi, 168
Bootstrap, 178
Broader Commercial Expertise, 98

Burgelman, 134, 136, 138
Burst Interventions and Seed-Camps,
229–230
Business Model Components,
143–144
Business Model Metrics, 152, 204,
206, 239, 261
Business Model Narratives, 147
Business Models, Definition of, 141
Business Models, Importance of, 141
Business Models Applications
aerospace engineering, 151
automotive engineering, 151
biotechnology, 151
education, skills and learning,
152
electronics and computing
hardware, 151
energy and lighting, 152
financial products and services,
152
healthcare products and services,
151
media and entertainment, 150

287

oil and gas engineering, 151
software, systems and
computational tools, 151
telecommunications, 151
Business Segmentation, 84
Business-to-Business (*see also* b2b)
Business Models, 31, 80
Business-to-Business-to-Consumer
(*see also* b2b2c) Relationships, 57,
80
Business-to-Consumer (*see also* b2c)
Business Models, 31, 80

C
Cambridge Experience, xxix
Camels
organised and patient approach
to commercialisation, xl
Case Studies, 66, 140, 260, 263–266
Challenge for Technology Firms, 183
Chandler, 15
Changes in Strategic Priorities,
138–139
Channels-To-Market, 122–123, 261
Characteristic Times for Market
Spaces, 65–66
Chasm Behaviour across Market
Spaces, 64
Chasm-Based Assessment of
Maturity in an Ecosystem, 208
Chasms Characteristics, 29
Chatman, 195
Christensen, 14, 19, 136
CMRR Pipeline (*see also* CPipe),
154
Coles, 150
Commercial Integration, 94
Commercialisation across Borders,
220

Commercialisation Canvas, xxxiv,
127, 201–202, 205, 208, 211, 243,
265, 268
Commercialisation Framework, 243
Commercialisation Journey, 19,
21–22, 25, 29, 35, 38, 46, 48, 50,
75, 77, 121, 135, 139, 161, 167,
173, 176, 185, 203, 219, 236, 252,
267
Commercialisation Manifesto, xxxv,
233, 266
Commercialisation of Science and
Technology-Enabled Innovation,
xxx, 17, 170, 211
Commercialisation Trajectories, 205
Commercialisation Vectors, xxxiv,
41, 46, 135, 139
Commercialisation Workbench,
xxxiv, 82, 135, 165, 221–222, 260,
262, 265
Committed Monthly Recurring
Revenue (*see also* CMRR), 153
Comparison of Camels, Tigers, and
Unicorns, 212
Competitive Landscape, 69, 71, 83
Complementary Technologies, 97–98
Consumerisation, 83, 129
Core Competences, 45, 67, 132, 134,
183, 187
Core Data and Metadata
Underpinning the Workbench, 263
Corporate Challenge, 241
Corporate Innovation, 201, 241–242,
269
Corporate Research and Development
Strand 1 of Corporate R&D, 250
Strand 2 of Corporate R&D, 250
Strand 3 of Corporate R&D, 251
Cost of Technology Deployment, 98

Counter-Hegelian Dichotomy, 14
Creative Synthesis, 104–105,
 107–108, 261
Creative–Destructive Forces, 14
Cross-Border Commercialisation,
 xxxix, 13, 217–219, 221–222
Cross-Border Initiatives, 216
Crossing the Chasm, 28
Culture in Technology Firms, 195
Culture Web Framework, 197
Customer Acquisition Cost
 (*see also* CAC), 154
Customer Acquisition, 129, 153–154,
 190, 243
Customer at the Centre of Analysis, 26
Customer Behaviour, 7, 38, 55, 87,
 159, 161, 206, 242, 257
Customer Growth for Media and
 Entertainment, 32, 34
Customer Funding Types
 license revenues, 178
 matchmaker models, 178
 pay-in-advance models, 178
 scarcity models, 179
 sponsorship, 179
 subscription models, 178
 upfront subscription, 179
Customer Retention, 129
Customer Revenues as a Source of
 Funding, 176
Customer Types
 business customers, 78
 consumers, 78
 governments, 78
 members of knowledge or
 affinity-based groups or
 communities,78
Customer Typology-Based Targeting,
 79

D
Data Modelling Approach, 31
Deconstruction, 109, 204, 261
Deconstructing Manufacturing
 Challenges, 114
Depth of Technology Expertise, 97
Dharampal, 13
Diffusion Modelling and Vectors, 48
Diffusion Theory, 29–30, 48, 267
Digital-Intensive Market Spaces, 163
Direction, Alignment, and
 Commitment (*see also* DAC), 184,
 193–194
Dominant Paradigms, 13, 21
Dosi, 7, 241
Drath, 193
Drucker, 141
Dynamic Vector-Based Approach to
 Commercialisation Strategy, 135

E
Economic Paradigms, Evolution of, 13
Economic Paradigms, Importance of,
 11
Economic Value Added (*see also*
 EVA), 25
Edquist, 16
Efficiency Technologies, 85
Empirical Data on Chasm
 Intervention, 47
Empirical Generalisations, 30
Engineering and Technology, 5
Engineering-Intensive Market Spaces,
 164
Entrepreneurial Orientation, 183–185,
 187
Equity Funding and Valuation, 179
Estimating Market Potential, 87
Evolutionary Economics, 16–17

F

Financialisation, 15
Firm Size vs Organisational Structure, 247
Firm-Centric Value Chain, 57–58, 136
Flexibility in Business Models, 99
Focal Technologies, 85
Franchise-Based Channels, 124
Frascati Classification, 4, 55
Freeman, 4
Friedman, 13
Functional Integration, 94
Funding Sources across the Chasms, 173
Funding Sources vs The Triple Chasm Model, 172

G

Generic Go-To-Market Challenges, 121
Generic IP Challenges, 155
Go-To-Market Challenges, 121–122, 261
Go-To-Market Vectors, 128
Greiner, 188–189
Gross Value Added (*see also* GVA), 25
Grove, 134, 136

H

Hamel, 134, 136, 185
Health-Related Applications and Tools, 95–96
High-Performance Teams, 188–190
Human Capital Management, 184, 261
Hybrid Techno-Commercial Synthesis Skills, 187

I

Ideation, 102
Ideological Narrative, 11
    market structure, 12
    funding and investment, 12
    capacity to innovate, 12
    boundaries, 12
Incubators and Accelerators, 170, 233, 236, 239, 257, 268
Industrial Revolution, 13, 118, 196, 241
Industry 4.0, 118
Industrial Evolution, design principles of, 118
    interoperability, 118
    information transparency, 118
    decentralised decision-making, 118
    technical assistance, 118
Innovation Outposts, 257
Innovative Development, 20
Integrated Approach to Customer Profiling, 81
Integrated Platforms, 94
Integrated Service Delivery, 129
Integration of Technology Functionality, 94
Interaction Characteristics, 217
Interventions in Context, 225
Investment in Science and Technology-Enabled Innovation, 170
Issues for Science and Technology-Enabled Firms, 127

J

Johnson, 134, 136

K
Kelley, 104
Kellogg, 125
Kerin, 125
Kiholme, 168
Kondratieff, 241
Kornberg, 150
Kotler, 77, 121
Kuhn, 13, 101

L
Lazonick, 15
Leaders–Followers–Shared Goals
  Paradigm, 184
Leadership Approach in Market
  Spaces, 194
Leasing of Technology Products, 148
Liberal or Free-Market Economics,
  14
Licensing IPR, 156
Limitations of Conventional Market
  Segmentation, 55
Linear-Linear Axes, 36
Log-Linear Axes, 37
Long-Term Industrial Strategies, xxx

M
m7P's model, 125
  product, 125
  positioning, 125
  price, 125
  place, 125
  promotion, 126
  process, 126
  partners, 126
12 Market Spaces
  aerospace engineering, 61, 65,
    140, 163, 193, 263, 265
  automotive engineering, 62, 140,
    163, 193, 263, 265
  biotechnology, 63, 65, 140, 163,
    193, 263, 265
    blue biotechnology, 63
    green biotechnology, 63
    red biotechnology, 63
    white biotechnology, 63
  education, skills, and learning,
    64–65, 140, 163
  electric vehicle propulsion
    technologies, 62, 140, 163,
    193, 263, 265
  electronics and computing
    hardware, 61, 65, 140, 163,
    193, 263
  energy and lighting, 63, 65, 140,
    163, 193, 263, 265
  financial services, 64, 65, 140,
    163, 193
  healthcare services, 62, 65, 140,
    163, 193
  media and entertainment, 31, 60,
    65, 140, 163, 193, 263, 265
  oil and gas engineering, 62, 65,
    163, 193, 263, 265
  software, systems and
    computational tools, 61, 65,
    140, 163, 193, 263, 265
  telecommunications, 60, 65, 140,
    163, 193, 263, 265
Macro-Economic Environment, 17
Macro-Economic Theory, 17
Macro–Meso–Micro Model, 17
Mahajan, 31
Managing Business Model
  Discontinuities, 221
Managing IP across Borders, 219

Manufacturing Process Innovation, 116, 204
Manufacturing Unpacked, 113
Market Drivers, 69–71
Market Segmentation, 56–58, 77
Market Space Insight, 256
Market Space-Centric Value Chains, xxxiv, 57–58, 60, 63, 67, 69, 73, 103, 203–204, 236, 239, 260, 263
Market, Technology and Regulatory Drivers, 70
Martin, xxxi
Marx, 14
Matchmaker Revenues, 148
Maturity Assessment based on the Triple Chasm Framework, 208
Mazzucato, 16
Medical and Health Sciences, 5
Meso-Economic Environment, 11, 17–19, 21, 170
Methods based on Design Thinking, 104
Micro-Economic Theory, 17
Mitchell, 82
Modified Technology Readiness Level (*see also* mTRLs), xxxiv, 8–10, 201, 203, 236, 250–251
Monte Carlo Methods, 30
Moore, 28, 31, 127
Multi-product Firms, 27, 243–246, 251–252, 269
Myers–Briggs Type Indicator (*see also* MBTI), 188

N
Nasa Technology Readiness Level (*see also* TRL) Model, 8, 250
Natural Sciences, 5

Needham, 13
Nelson, 7
Neo-Liberal Paradigm, 14–15, 209
Non-Equilibrium Behaviour, 17
Non-Recurring Engineering (*see also* NRE) Revenues, 147, 151
Normalised Customer Growth, 34

O
Organisation and Management vs Teams, 191
Organisational Researchers, 195
Organisational Structure and Management, 184, 188
Organisational Structures and Commercialisation
H-form, 190, 246
M-form, 189, 246–247, 252
U-form, 189–191, 246–248
Outcome Driven Innovation, 104, 107
Outright Sale of a Technology, 148
Overall Narrative, 142–143, 185, 197
Overview of Approaches to Synthesis, 104
Overview of Funding Sources, 169

P
3D Printing, 99, 114
Partnering Strategy, 256
Partners, Suppliers, and Collaboration, 73–74
Pavitt, 7
Perez, 241
Pervasive Technologies, 85
Platform for Multi-Channel Loyalty Programmes, 94
Platform Layer, 91, 110
Popular Folklore, xxxi

Porter, 14, 57
Positioning, Branding, and
  Promotion, 122, 125, 261
Practitioners
  business and strategy consultants,
    xxxiii
  entrepreneurs, xxxii
  investors, xxxiii
  leaders and managers in
    technology firms, xxxii
  leaders and managers, xxxiii
  policy makers, xxxiii
  researchers and students, xxxiii
  scientists and technologists
    engaged in innovation, xxxiii
Prahalad, 134, 136, 185
Principle Revenue Sources, 147
Private Equity, 15, 170
Product Layer, 91–92, 110
Product Portfolio Management, 251
Product Synthesis and Business
  Model Creation, 257
Profile of a New Intervention, 238
Proposition Framing, 22, 43, 46,
  48–49, 67, 69, 131, 204, 260, 267
Proxy Methods of Revenue
  Generation, 149, 151
Prudent Man Rule, 174
Pseudo-Neo-Liberal Agenda, 15–16,
  21
Public–Private Partnerships, 19

R
Regulatory Drivers, 69–71
Relative Importance of Vectors across
  Chasms, 46
Remuneration and Rewards,
  184–185, 197

Research Infrastructure, 19–20, 22
Revenue and Cost Allocation Logic,
  146
Revenue Sources of Business
  Models, 145
Robbins-Roth, 150
Rogers, 30, 37–39
Rosenberg, 89
Round Tables, xxxv, 28
Royalties, 145, 148–149, 151, 156

S
Saviotti, 7–8
Scaling for Manufacture, 115, 218,
  239
Schumpeter, 14, 30
Service Layer, 92, 110
Service Wrapper, 126, 130
Silicon Fen, xxix
Silicon Valley Experience, xxix
Smith, Adam, 13, 15
Snow, C. P, xxxi
Sources of Competitive
  Differentiation, 71
Sources of Funding, 167
  equity funding, 168
  grants, 168
  loans, 168
  payments, 168
Speed to Market, 46, 98–99, 190, 212
Stiglitz, 16
Strategic Clarity, 139, 242, 256
Strategic Ecology, 131–133, 204, 254
Strategic Responses to the
  Competitive Environment, 140
Strategy Formulation and
  Development Approach, 133,
  135–136

Subscription Revenues, 149, 154, 179

Supply-Chain-Centric Value Chains, 58

SWOT Model, 134, 136

Synthesis Challenge, 101

Systems of Innovation Approach, 16

T

Talent Recognition, 183

Technology Characteristics, 89

Technology Deployment Framework, xxxviii

Technology Deployment Model, 90–91

Technology Deployment Strategies, 97–100

Technology Drivers, 69–71, 256

Technology Mapping Approach, 103, 105

Technology Mapping on Media and Entertainment Market Space, 106

Technology Platforms, 41, 44, 92, 132, 145, 148–149, 160, 205

Technology Scaling Challenge, 115

Technology Scaling, 114–116

Teece, 134, 136, 142

The Invisible Hand, 13

The Proposition Framework, 109, 111, 204, 261

The Two Cultures and Scientific Revolutions, xxxi

Theories of the Firm and Growth Metrics, 25

Three Chasms, 27, 29, 34, 38, 45, 48, 65, 203, 205, 210–211, 225

Tigers
    agile, able to adapt, quickly to change, xl

Timmons, xxxi

Transaction Revenues, 148, 151

Translating Meso-Economic Components into Vectors, 22

Triple Chasm Model, 34, 52, 64, 190, 201, 208, 216, 226, 243, 268

Tripod of Leaders, 190

Types of Actors
    accelerators, 228
    burst interventions, 227
    corporate interventions, 229
    incubators, 228
    innovation agencies, 227
    makerspaces, 228
    mentors, 227
    seed-camps, 227
    technology transfer offices (*see also* TTOs), 227, 231

Types of Interventions, xxxiv, 233, 239, 268

Typical Accelerator Contributions, 237

Typical Commercialisation Strategy, 138

Typical Duration of Chasms, 35

Typical Incubator Contributions, 235

Typical Product Portfolio Map, 252

Typical Trajectory for Science and Technology Commercialisation, 207

Types of Registered Rights
    copyright, 159
    design rights, 159
    patents, 159
    trade marks, 159

Types of Unregistered Rights
    brand value, 160
    software and algorithms, 159

specialised customer knowledge, 159

technology and process know-how, 159

trade secrets, 159

Typology-Based Customer Targeting, 77

U

Ulwick, 104

Unicorns

magical notions to address the challenge of crossing chasms, xl

US Corporations, 14, 189

Usage of Technology by Businesses, 85

V

12 vectors

business model development, xxxvii, 22

commercialisation strategy, xxxvii, 22

customer definition, xxxvii, 22

distribution, marketing, and sales, xxxvii, 22

funding and investment, xxxvii, 22

intellectual property management, xxxvii, 22

manufacturing and assembly, xxxvii, 22

market spaces, xxxvii, 22

product and service definition and synthesis, xxxvii, 22

proposition framing and competition, xxxvii, 22

talent, leadership, and culture, xxxvii, 22

technology development and deployment, xxxvii, 22

VALS-Type Approach, 82

Valuation Components, 180

Value Chain for Media and Entertainment Market Space, 59

Variation in Diffusion Coefficients across Chasms, 36

Variation in Human Capital Metrics, 186

Vector-Based Commercialisation Strategy Formulation, 137

Vectors, Definition of, 41

Venture Capital (*see also* VC), 15, 26, 52, 169–171, 173–175, 185, 209, 231, 261

Venture Funding Rhetoric vs Reality, 177

Virtual Teams, 188

W

Winter, 17

Workbench components

business models, 261

commercialisation strategy, 261

customer definition, 260

distribution, marketing and sales, 261

funding and investment, 261

IP management, 261

manufacturing and assembly, 261

market spaces, 260

overall commercial overview, 260

product and service definition and synthesis, 261

proposition framing and the
competitive environment, 260
talent, leadership, and culture,
261
technology development and
deployment, 261
Workbench Tools, 265

World Intellectual Property
Organization (*see also* WIPO), 156

Z

Zero-Sum Approach, 15
Zider, 175

Printed in Great Britain
by Amazon